DEVELOPMENTAL ORTHOGRAPHY

DEVELOPMENTAL
ORTHOGRAPHY

by

PHILIP A. LUELSDORFF
Universität Regensburg

JOHN BENJAMINS PUBLISHING COMPANY
AMSTERDAM/PHILADELPHIA

1991

Library of Congress Cataloging-in-Publication Data

Luelsdorff, Philip.
   Developmental orthography / by Philip A. Luelsdorff.
   p.   cm.
Includes bibliographical references and indexes.
1. English language -- Study and teaching -- German speakers. 2. English language -- Orthography and spelling. 3. Second language acquisition. I. Title.
PE1129.G3L82   1991
428'.007 -- dc 20   91-7333
ISBN 90 272 2065 4 (alk. paper)   CIP

Acknowledgments

Acknowledgment is made to the publishers for permission to have the following articles reprinted: "A formal approach to error taxonomy" in *Text and protest: A Festschrift for Petr Sgall* (1986), John Benjamins B.V.; "Processing strategies in bilingual spellers", *Papers and studies in contrastive linguistics* XXI, 1986, Adam Mickiewicz University, Poznań; "Bilingual intralinguistic orthographic interference", *Papers and studies in contrastive linguistics* XXIII, 1988, Adam Mickiewicz University, Poznań; "A psycholinguistic model of the bilingual speller", in R.N. Malatesha and R. Valtin (Eds.), *Bilingualism and dyslexia*, 1990, Kluwer Academic Publishers.

The paper on error taxonomy was coauthored by Wojciech Busz-kowski of the Institute of Mathematics, Adam Mickiewicz University, Poznań, and the papers on developmental morphographemies, graphemic ambiguity, psycholinguistic determinants, and a psycholinguistic model were coauthored by E. Ann Eyland, Department of Statistics, Macquarie University, Sydney. Ann and Wojtek reconfirmed my conviction that two heads can be better than one and impressed me with just how interdisciplinary linguistics can be. I wish I had the talent to accept the skills they have to offer.

None of these studies would have been possible without the dedicated cooperation of several interested school teachers, who elicited and reelicited data in their classrooms over periods of many months. I am grateful for their patience and unfailing willingness to help and hope that the results reported live up to their expectations and eventually find their way home in the form of truly constructive teaching materials.

Then, the beginning of this work was facilitated by a grant from the Fritz Thyssen Stiftung, Cologne, affording me an extended leave-of-absence for the purpose of collating and analyzing a portion of the data.

Bertie Kaal, John Benjamins BV, voluntarily undertook the arduous task of post-editing an anything but easy manuscript. Thank you, Bertie, for your great patience and finely-honed editorial skills. In more ways than one you are an editor's editor.

No amount of gratitude would be enough to thank my wife, Marta, for her thousands of hours of conversation about developmental orthography, time which she would have doubtlessly better spent on her own pursuits. If these pages prove worth reading, it is in no small measure due to her incisive criticism and comment.

The work itself I dedicate in very loving memory to my father, Hans Ludwig Luelsdorff, 1906-1986, who would have been curious to see what absorbed the time due him during the final years of his life.

Contents

Preface

Collected here are eleven articles devoted to the subject of English orthography and its acquisition by German learners of English as a foreign language. The purpose of these papers is to describe the regularities evident in a large corpus of cross-sectional and longitudinal data in terms of error mechanisms and processing strategies within the framework of an explanatory developmental psycholinguistic model of the bilingual speller.

Obviously, developmental investigations demand an understanding of what it is that is developed. The essay on vowel spellings urges a hierarchical approach to the description of some of the English vowel spellings, incorporating both deep and surface dependencies and constituent structure. The complexity of English vowel spellings is seen to emerge from the fact that the number of vowel letters is far fewer than the number of vowel sounds.

There follows a formal approach to the taxonomy of errors of competence and performance, with special reference to spelling errors, but some attention paid to errors in syntax. It emerges that errors are relations between attempts and targets and that there is something to be gained by viewing errors as hierarchical, rather than linear. Further research in this area could profitably concern itself with the formalization of processing strategies, attempting to answer the question whether they are rules, conditions on representations, or something altogether different.

The study of processing strategies in bilingual spellers distinguishes between error mechanisms and processing strategies and explains most of the spelling errors in bilingual production as due to either interlinguistic or intralinguistic transfer. Such errors include either German or English letter-naming, either German or English phoneme-grapheme correspondences, and errors of either partial or total cognatization.

A supplementary study of bilingual intralinguistic interference offers a differentiated taxonomy of spelling errors based on whether the target and the attempt are primary, secondary, major, or minor patterns.

The resultant typology of 16 error types is exemplified, and it is observed with interest that it is the case that irregular patterns may be used productively. If this is correct, the dual-route-to-spelling hypothesis must be wrong.

In "The complexity hypothesis and graphemic ambiguity" it is shown that consonant singling is acquired before consonant doubling and that consonant doubling is acquired in the environment of suffixes such as <-ing> before it is acquired in the environment of suffixes such as <-ed>. The implication is that what appears to be one and the same rule - consonant doubling - is acquired gradually, starting with the orthographically least complex environments first, then spreading to increasingly more complex domains until native fluency is attained.

"The complexity hypothesis and morphemic spelling" clearly shows that of the three regular allomorphs of the English preterit, /ɪd/:<-ed> is learned before /d/:<-ed>, and /d/:<-ed> is learned before /t/:<-ed>, the hierarchy of learning corresponding to the hierarchy of complexity. This leads to the notion that complexity explains acquisition, the central theme of the work.

"Psycholinguistic determinants of orthography acquisition" shows that age, class, school system, ranked relative frequency, degree of ambiguity, degree of universality, and the phonological relatedness of unfamiliar to familiar words all exercise a determining effect on the acquisition of the long and short vowel spellings. Short vowel spellings are acquired before long vowel spellings, and the dominant effect is the length of the vowel, i.e. that feature which is most complex. Evidently, all the above determinants must be parameters in the theory of learnability and incorporated into the psycholinguistic model of the bilingual speller.

The next paper is a pilot study of the productivity of phonology-free morphographemic alternations (MA) in a developmental setting. We hypothesize that morphographemic productivity is influenced by (1) word-familiarity, (2) part of speech, (3) occurrence in inflected, as opposed to derived words, and (4) MA-type as either non-identical substitution, identical substitution, and addition. We find superiority effects for familiarity, for ADJs over Vs, Vs over Ns, and Ns over ADVs, for inflections over derivations, for non-identical substitutions over identical, and substitutions over additions, with the all-pervasive factor of relative linguistic complexity underlying these effects. These and other results follow from the Law of Contextual Complexity, according to which the complexity of a text is always less than the complexity of its context.

The paper on orthographic complexity and orthography acquisition presents the Praguian theory of complexity in orthography. This consists of a scale or parameter of complexness and a scale or parameter of univocality. The orthography of English inflection and contraction are assigned complexity values along these two parameters and developmental data are assigned to acquisitional stages. It is found that orthographic representations that are 1:1 are acquired before those that are 1:n+1, and that orthographic representations that are 1:n+1 are acquired before those that are either 1:∅ or ∅:1. It is observed that this acquisitional order is perfectly correlated with increasing complexity values on the scales of complexness and univocality and concluded that the theory of complexity explains the acquisitional sequence. Since morphemic complexity also plays a role, it is further concluded that the *nature* of acquisition is *interactive*, rather than modular.

The psycholinguistic model of the bilingual speller differs from the monolingual model in that it provides for the interaction of German phonological processes with English, German phoneme-grapheme correspondences with English, the addition of morphological processes and structures for both monolingual and bilingual processing, a route for the familiarization of unfamiliar words to familiar, and the processing of English false friends (cognates) via German. Proceeding from a German cognate base, it is found that rules of deletion are acquired more readily than rules of addition, a finding also confirmed by our inquiry into morphographemics.

The work concludes with an essay on developmental orthography. Several recent models of the acquisition of reading and writing (= spelling) in monolinguals are compared and our bilingual results are reviewed in a developmental light. Two competing proposals for explaining the developmental sequence are presented and evaluated in terms of their ability to explain the stages observed. One is the Subset Principle of learnability theory, the other the Theory of Complexity. The Theory of Complexity succeeds where the Subset Principle fails, suggesting that the

Subset Principle be abandoned and the Theory of Complexity adopted to explain other areas of bilingual language development.

Sydney   P.A.L.
May 5, 1988

Introduction
Uta Frith

Modern psycholinguistics has been preoccupied with spoken language to the extent of neglecting the study of written language. Yet the investigation of the cognitive and linguistic underpinnings of written words has taken a lead in unravelling developmental processes. Just as for speech, the development of writing is guided by the existence of a grammar. From the outset grammar acts like a theory: it enables the learner to pick up relevant information and to remember it. It leads him to conduct quasi-experiments by use of feedback and to make predictions about novel words. As in science, the abandoning of earlier theories by the aspiring spelling expert is a mark of progress.

Philip Luelsdorff's highly original approach to the grammar of orthography is to analyze in detail how German pupils learn about written English. In this collection of essays and experiments we are presented with the rich finds of a decade of programmatic research. The context is set with an exposition of current cognitive models of reading and spelling. Cognitive psychology and psycholinguistics meet in Luelsdorff's concept of linguistic error. This concept forms the basis from which it is possible to derive the grammar that governs our largely unconscious and vast knowledge of written words. It is proper to talk about a grammar for both orthographic and syntactic aspects of language. This is because spelling knowledge is not piecemeal or erratic but bears all the hallmarks of a system. This insight goes, of course, against the notion beloved of folk-psychology that spelling is simply a matter of rote learning, that rules are a waste of time, and that orthography, English in particular, is illogical.

Luelsdorff and his collaborators demonstrate that spelling of English as a second language is acquired in as lawful a way as it is for native speakers. They show that there is a strong correlation between spelling performance and a new measure of orthographic complexity. In line with current models of acquisition, Luelsdorff distinguishes different stages. However, he goes beyond this initial framework with new evidence to suggest a much more fine-grained sequence of spelling-pattern acquisition. This sequence is determined by a number of factors that are isolated in ingenious experiments.

Research in written language has the arduous task of analyzing, describing and interpreting spelling errors. In this effort the dynamic aspects of spelling-knowledge acquisition and breakdown are often obscured. This problem has been avoided by Luelsdorff who makes acquisition his central theme. The study of second language orthography is not only interesting in its own right, but it greatly benefits the study of first language orthography acquisition. At an age when young learners make very few mistakes in their native language, it is very difficult to probe the strategies that they may be using to spell. They are using truly orthographic skills, over and above merely alphabetic skills for their native language. However, when the second language is encountered many novel spellings have to be learned. What will the learner do in this situation? As a temporary measure, new words may be spelled in the orthographic system of the first language. For instance, as is correct for German spellings, the beginner tends to capitalise nouns in English where only lower case is required. This is an example of negative transfer, but examples of positive transfer exist as well. For instance, many sound-letter correspondences are the same in both languages and used in the same way.

As the orthography of the new language becomes familiar an intriguing phenomenon is observed: transfer of rules may be blocked - even when such a transfer would be helpful. For instance, the doubling of consonants in certain contexts obeys similar rules in German and English, but this similarity is not necessarily recognised. The blocking of transfer reveals a need to keep orthographic systems separate. Correct single consonant spellings are achieved almost from the start, presumably by use of simple alphabetic phoneme-grapheme rules, but double consonants show a pronounced increase in correct performance over time. This separation would be inexplicable if one believed in word-specific learning, where new spellings are learned individually, as they occur in the vocabulary, without an underlying grammar. The consonant doubling rule at morphemic boundaries in English provides a fascinating example. The rule applies equally before -ing as before -ed. So if there is 'batting', for example, then there is 'batted'. Yet, the German school children studied by Luelsdorff 'knew' the rule earlier for the case of -ing than in that of -ed. The conclusion is inevitable that for these children there were two types of doubling rule, learned at different times.

A convincing demonstration of lexical and morphemic strategies in spelling (as opposed to sound-by-sound spelling) is provided by experiments with so-called false friends. Here, semantically and phonologically related words in both English and German are nevertheless spelled differently in the two languages. *Adresse* and 'address', *Galerie* and 'gallery', *Komitee* and 'committee' are notorious examples leading to much confusion. Furthermore data are presented that show that because of well established morphemic spelling patterns perfectly regular words may be spelt as if they were irregular. For instance, 'called' may be spelled *coulled*. There are many other examples of orthographic strategies. They are particularly clear in the very regular order of acquisition of past tense spellings of -ed, -d, and -t. In the area of morphemic knowledge and its acquisition and use by the older child lies the strength of the approach.

We have learned an enormous amount about the beginnings of literacy development through Charles Read's bold methodological advance, which was to investigate very young children's invented spellings. For instance, we know now that preschoolers' understanding of phonology is different from that of adults in certain respects, and that they rationally use letters in sequence in order to represent segmented phonemes. Read's approach was of crucial importance for the conceptualizing of truly alphabetic skills. A similar breakthrough for truly orthographic skills has been due to Philip Luelsdorff. From his analysis of writings of children who are expert spellers in one language but novices in another we have learned a great deal about the growth of the astonishingly creative understanding of morphology and lexical knowledge. The strategies used by the 'novice-experts' prove to be quite different in many ways from what one might have expected. In the empirical studies presented in this volume processes previously only inferred have become observable. Just by looking at concurrent first language spellings in the groups studied nothing much would have been revealed at all.

It has long been a problem to find ways of investigating what processes of literacy development underlie the final stage that I have called 'orthographic'. Through second language orthography Philip

Luelsdorff is showing us a new view of this advanced stage of spelling knowledge and its acquisition. This view is exciting because it seems now possible to form very detailed hypotheses as regards first language spelling about the order in which purely orthographic knowledge is developed. We can look forward to a richer and larger theory of the mental existence of written words.

London
11 January 1989

English Vowel Spellings

Introduction

Confronted with the task of inventing an orthography for English, the theoretical orthographer is faced with a dilemma: there are half as many vowel letters as there are vowel sounds. Various solutions to this problem come to mind, including the assignment of one or several diacritics to the letters to distinctively represent the sounds - the solution adopted by, for example, Czech and Hungarian - duplicating the vowel letter - the solution adopted by, for example, German and Dutch, adding a letter or several letters either before or after the letter in question - a solution adopted by French, or utilizing the context or vowel letter, either in terms of consonantal environment, stress, morphology, syntax, semantics, linguistic history or etymology, all of which are adopted by English, rendering English the most complicated of alphabetic orthographies. In any case, the difference between the number of vowel sounds and the number of vocalic letters - the sound-letter differential or sound-letter duty load - induces a *systematic dynamism* which is an essential fact of not only the core and periphery of English phonology and morphology (Vachek 1983) but of English orthography and phonology as well. The purpose of this paper is to propose a hierarchical description of the orthography of the English vowels which is consistent with this essential dynamism.

1. The prior framework

The most influential treatise on English orthography is Richard L. Venezky's *The Structure of English Orthography* (1970). The author (1970: 101-119) divides the vowel spellings of English into two groups or types, primary and secondary. Primary vowel spellings consist of *one* vowel letter (including <y>), whereas secondary vowel spellings consist of *two or more* (one of which may be <w> or <y>).

Both primary vowel spellings and secondary vowel spellings have major and minor sound correspondences, where the difference between major and minor sound correspondence is the difference between *more and less frequent*. Major correspondences are referred to as 'regular' or 'predictable', minor correspondences as 'irregular' or 'unpredictable', where regularity is sensitive to surrounding consonant and vowel letters, stress and morphemic structure.

The above structure of English orthography we illustrate in the diagram in Figure 1.

Primary Pattern	Secondary Pattern
Major	Major
Minor	Minor

Figure 1. *The structure of English orthography*

Since each of the four resulting patterns - the major primary, the minor primary, the major secondary, and the minor secondary - has its own unique structure, each pattern may be regarded as constituting a 'module', each module containing a unique set of grapheme-phoneme correspondences. In previous work (Luelsdorff 1986) we have shown how each of these modules interact with themselves and each other in the acquisition of English as a foreign orthography and used such inter- and intramodular interaction to explain a very wide variety of developmental errors.

2. A hierarchical framework

The present framework differs from Venezky's in that it is dynamic and hierarchical. It is dynamic in the sense that it views the complicated set of vowel spellings as products of a self-complexing dynamic system (cf. de Beaugrande 1987) emerging as a natural consequence of the above-mentioned sound-letter differential and hierarchical in the sense that it proposes both deep and surface dependency and constituent structure for English orthographic representations. The deep dependency structure is non-linear and the surface constituency structure is linear.

Venezky shows that the vowel spellings <a, e, i/y, o, u>, which he terms "primary vowel spellings", carry the major burden of vowel representations in English, and that each of the primary vowel units corresponds regularly to two different "morphophonemes", a free one and a checked one, according to the morphemic structure of the word in which it occurs and the consonant and vowel units which follow it. These correspondences are given in Table 1, reproduced from Venezky (1970: 102).

Table 1. *Major pattern for primary vowels*

Spelling	Free alternate	Checked alternate
a	{e}	{æ}
	sane	sanity
	mate	mat
	ration	rattle
e	{i}	{ɛ}
	athlete	athletic
	mete	met
	penal	pennant
i	{ai}	{ɪ}
	rise	risen
	malign	malignant
	site	sit
o	{o}	{a}
	cone	conic
	robe	rob
	posy	possible
u	{ju}	{ʌ}
	induce	induction
	rude	rudder
	lucre	luxury

Now the letters of the English alphabet, including the vowel letters, have both names and sounds. In the case of the *major* pattern for the primary vowels, the free alternate pronunciations, i.e. the sounds of the letters, are included (properly in the case of <u>, improperly in the case of <a, e, i, o>) in the names of the letters, while the checked alternate pronunciations are not included in their letter-names. In the former instance, mention = use, in the latter, mention $\neq$ use, where mention = letter-naming and use = letter-sounding.

In order to resolve the discrepancy between mention = use in the free alternate pronunciations and mention $\neq$ use in the checked alternate pronunciations, we introduce a rule associating short checked pronunciations with long free pronunciations and the resultant 'pronunciations' are spelled by the universal means (cf. Volkov 1982) of letter-naming as a spelling strategy, as in (1):

(1)   *Short-long chain*

       $\chi{V} \rightarrow \bar{V}$

The short-long vowel-chain in (1) has the effect of associating the vowel in *sanity*, for example, with the vowel in *sane* and spelling the resultant associate by means of the processing strategy of letter-naming as a spelling strategy. Monomorphemic roots that contain a free alternate, and consequently do not undergo (1), receive a final <e>, as in (2).

(2)   *<e>-Epenthesis*

       $\emptyset \rightarrow$ <e>   / VC$_{o\_\#}$

(2) applies to words like *robe* to introduce the final <e>, thereby orthographically distinguishing it from *rob*, and interestingly, to items like *tie, tee, Mae, toe,* and *due*, but not items such as *to, into, so,* and *hi,* on the one hand, or *sigh, though, thorough,* etc., on the other. This suggests a need for distinguishing deep orthography from surface orthography, function words from major class items, and raises the question of the necessity of ordering orthographic rules (in this case spelling words like *sigh, though,* and *thorough,* etc. before major class items governed by <e>Epenthesis).

The advantages of this system are that it utilizes the names of the letters, which must be in the mental lexicon anyway, for spelling, and is extremely economical in terms of number of rules and elements related by the rules. Most importantly, it accesses information in the orthography/ phonology/morphology interface at the disposal of many, if not most, literate users of English, namely the links in the chains also found in the familiar derivationally related pairs like *sincere~sincerity, sane~sanity, reduce~reduction*, and *divine~divinity*. On the present view, the terms in each pair are related phonologically *because* they are related orthographically (cf. Wang and Derwing 1986 for experimental evidence), which means that phonology is mere guesswork without orthography, in particular, without a linguistics that is experimental.

The system proposed requires that long vowels be derived from short vowels, forming *chains* with short and long vowel *links*. For English such basic chains apparently number seven (3):

(3)　　*Short-long chains*

$$
\begin{array}{llll}
\text{a. } /æ/ - /e/ & \text{m\underline{a}t} & \text{m\underline{a}te} & \text{<a>} \\
\text{b. } /\varepsilon/ - /i/ & \text{m\underline{e}t} & \text{m\underline{e}te} & \text{<e>} \\
\text{c. } /ɪ/ - /ai/ & \text{s\underline{i}t} & \text{s\underline{i}te} & \text{<i>} \\
\text{d. } /a/ - /o/ & \text{r\underline{o}b} & \text{r\underline{o}be} & \text{<o>} \\
\text{e. } /ʌ/ - /u/ & \text{t\underline{u}b} & \text{t\underline{u}be} & \text{<u>} \\
\left\{
\begin{array}{llll}
\text{f. } /u/ - /o/ & \text{l\underline{o}se} & \text{l\underline{o}st} & \text{<o>} \\
\text{g. } /a/ - /æ/ & \text{c\underline{a}r} & \text{c\underline{a}rriage} & \text{<a>}
\end{array}
\right\}
\end{array}
$$

The spelling of words like <car, far, bar> requires that the vowel /a/ be readjusted to /æ/, that this <æ> then be linked with /e/ by (3a), and that this /e/ then be spelled <a> by letter-naming as a spelling strategy. Spellings derived by (3f), such as <moon, soon, goon>, require that the letter <o> be doubled in the systematic environment of /u/ - /o/.

A problem is posed by the sound /ɔ/, which is typically spelled <au> and <ou>, as in <August> and <ought>. These we derive by means of *complex chains*, which we define as chains consisting of two or more simplex chains, where a simplex chain is a pair ordered by one of the associations of (3). Just as the discrepancy between the number of vowel letters and the qualities of the vowel letter-names induces intrasystemic self-organization causing the association of short vowels with long in the form of simplex chains, it also causes the splitting of open /ɔ/ into the *nearest* systemic constituents in the English phonological space, namely /a/ and /o/, which are then spelled by letter-naming as either <a> or <o>, with the following <u> placed as a mark of the movement split, as in (4).

(4)   *The spelling of* /ɔ/

$$/ɔ/ \begin{cases} /a/ \to /æ/ \to /e/ \to <a> \to <au> \\ /o/ \qquad \to \qquad <o> \to <ou> \end{cases}$$

Several advantages are to be derived from the proposed approach. First, it renders unnecessary a long list of so-called 'grapheme-phoneme correspondences', because such lists are derivable from the underlying self-organizing system of autonymic letter-naming. In other words, it replaces a system of lists with a system of conditions displaying the procedural definition of letter-naming as a spelling strategy as its center-piece.

Second, the system is constrained by countenancing only those chains which are motivated by the orthography/grammar interface. In particular, the system admits of only those phonology/orthography/mor-phology relations which are natural, in the sense that they are directly, and to a lesser extent indirectly observable alternations. The central one of these is that of Phonology/Morphology/Orthography Complementarity. Taxonomic phonetically, *mate/mat, mete/met, site/sit, robe/rob, tube/tub, loss/lose* pairwise contrast. Orthographically, however, these pairwise phonetic contrasts are in complementary distribution, with the final marker <e> as the mark of the taxonomic phonemic contrast. The taxonomic phonemes, under orthographic representation, become links in complementarity chains. Note that the links so chained are paradigmatic. In the case of the vowels which have been linked by a putative vowel-shift rule in English derivational morphology (Chomsky and Halle 1968), they are links in chains which are syntagmatic.

Third, it emerges from the above that both English sounds and letters are *variables* whose values are functions of the environments in which they occur. For example, in *mate* and *mat*, the former vowel derives from /e/ and the latter from /æ/ - /e/. Both /e/ and /æ/ are values of the variable /e/, which, by letter-naming, is spelled <a>, which is itself a variable ranging over /e/ and /æ/ - /e/. The status of sound and letters as Variables derives from the absence of systemic biuniqueness in the relata of morphophonemic, phonographemic, and graphophonemic alternations.

As widely discussed, the primary vowel spellings before tauto-syllabic /r/ depend upon the environment following /r/. Venezky (1970: 110) cites three cases (Table 2).

Table 2. *Vowel correspondences before r*

Spelling	Environment 1		Environment 2		Environment 3	
	r	normal	r	normal	r	normal
a	ɛ	e	æ	æ	a	æ
e	ɪ	i	ɛ	ɛ	ə	ɛ
i	aɪ	aɪ	ɪ	ɪ	ə	ɪ
o	ɔ/o	o	a/o	a	o/ɔ	a
u	ju	ju	ə	ə	ə	ə

In environment 1, we require the phonetic adjustment of /ɛ/ and /ɪ/ to /e/ and /i/, respectively, permitting all the vowels in environment 1 to be spelled by means of letter-naming as a spelling strategy. The vowels in environment 2 are, in fact, the vowels we have designated as 'short'. These must be chained together with their long congeners as their second link, and this second link spelled by letter-naming as a spelling strategy. In environment 3 the same applies to /a/ and /o/, as in <alarm>, <adorn>, and <car>, with the proviso that the /a/ in <alarm> be chained to /æ/, which is chained to /e/, then spelled <a>, analogously to <car> (cf. <car-riage>). The problem is with items of the type <erb> and <bird> in environment 3, in which the vowel to be spelled is followed by /r/ + C or ≠. Here, if schwa is permitted to chain with its nearest neighbors, i.e. /ɛ/ and /ɪ/, then regular further linkage to the long vowels /i/ and /ai/, respectively, makes possible the proper spellings with <e> and <i>, respectively.

Venezky (1970: 111-112) cites several exceptions to the normal /r/-rules applying in environments 1, 2, and 3. <delerium>, for example, should be pronounced with an /ai/, <mural> with a schwa, and <scarce> with the same vowel as in <farce>. The advocated approach makes it possible to explain all the listed exceptions, however, by transporting them from the domain of /r/-application altogether and placing them in the domain of chaining, which is not /r/-bound. Thus, <are>, which should be in environment 1, is spelled with an <a> by chaining the vowel /a/ to the vowel /æ/, and then to the vowel /e/. Or, <err>, which should be in environment 2, is spelled by chaining /ɛ/ to /i/ and then spelling /i/ with <e>. Or <scarce>, which should be in environment 3, is spelled by chaining /ɛ/ to /e/, and then spelling /e/ with <a> via letter-naming as a processing strategy. Since vowel chaining and spelling before /r/ is the special case, and vowel chaining and spelling elsewhere the general case, and the special case precedes the default case (Zwicky 1986), our proposal amounts to the requirement that the items listed by Venezky as exceptions be transported from the special to the general or default domain of spelling rule application.

Analogous self-complexing splitting, systemically induced by the letter-name/letter-sound differential, is found in the consonant subsystem in the case of just those consonants whose sounds are not included in the consonant-letter names. For Venezky (1970: 54), the units in question are the simple major relational units <ch, gh, ph, rh, sh, th>, the compound major relational units <ck, dg, tch, wh, x>, the simple minor relational units <kh, sch>, and the compound minor relational unit <gn>.

Our approach differs from Venezky's in that we treat as compound those relational units which he treats as simple. At stake, then, is justifying the analysis of <ch, gh, ph, rh, sh, th> (all major) and <kh, sch> (all minor) as compound. The feasibility of splitting the consonantal molecules into their constituent feature atoms emerges from factoring out the feature differences between the consonant sounds and the names of the letters used to spell them. For example, the sound of the initial letter <s> in <shock> is palatal /š/, while the consonantal sound in the name of the letter <s> is dental /s/. It appears plausible to say that the palatal pronunciation of the letter <s> of <sh> in words of the type <shock> is a dynamic result of the application of <h> to the letter <s> which is normally related to the free syntagmatic dental pronunciation /s/. In other words, the <sh> spelling of /š/ is a complex-action function consisting of the mapping of the letter <s> onto the sound /s/ resulting from the splitting of /š/ into /s/ minus palatality and the subsequent mapping of the letter <h> onto the letter <s>, injecting into the letter <s> a dental function of the letter <h>.

Quite generally, the sound value of the first consonant letter is a function of the second letter, i.e. either <h> or, rarely, <g>. This we notate C = f<g>, C = f<h>, with the result that it is the first consonant that is the dependent term within the dependency framework, i.e., C ← h, C ← g. In the case of both the anonymous (nameless) vowels and the anonymous consonants, the system dynamically selects those letters for orthographic representations whose names are *self-affine* (symmetrically related) with the anonymous sounds the letters are used to represent and selects the redundant letter <h> (cf. Vachek 1987) as the mark of the movement from autonymic to allonymic representation. In this way, orthographic representation is seen to be subject to self-affinity control.

This functional analysis not only results in a smaller inventory of orthographic units but is essentially in line with the general variable nature of English sounds and letters in the English phonology/orthography interface. Moreover, it is further justified by Volkov's (1982) orthographic universal 40, according to which

> "If there is a syntagmatically significant doubling of letters, there are also syntagmatically and nominationally significant combinations of letters within each class forming a free syntagm (cf. French <nn> and <ch>)."

coupled with Volkov's *(op. cit.)* orthographic universal 24, according to which

> "If there is a complex bilateral syntagm, then there is a simple bilateral syntagm."

English disposes of syntagmatically significant doubling of letters in the form of doubled vowel letters, as in <meet> vs. <met>, and doubled consonant letters, as in <wagged> vs. <waged>. Consequently, by universal 40 there must be nominationally significant combinations of letters within a class forming a free syntagm. Indeed these there are, both in the case of vowel letters, such as <ea, eo, ei, oa, ou, ...> and in the case of consonant letters, such as <ch, gh, ph, sh, th, rh, sch, kh>, as listed above. Treating these relational units as free syntagms thus has universal appeal. By universal 24, the fact that English has complex syntagms in the form of consonant singling after complex-vowel sequences, such as in <kneading> and <pouting>, and in the form of consonant doubling after simplex vowels, as in <bidding> and <humming>, implies that there exist simple bilateral syntagms, which indeed there does in cases such as Venezky's simple major and simple minor relational units above. Treating these relational units as simple bilateral syntagms, i.e. as predicate-argument structures with two arguments each of which determines the value of the other also disposes of universal appeal (except <sch>, which is a complex bilateral syntagm, rather than a simple bilateral syntagm, but the analytical reasoning remains the same).

We thus see that in both the case of the alphabetically anonymous vowel sounds and the alphabetically anonymous consonant sounds the linguistic system dynamically selects those letters for use in orthographic representations whose names are *self-affine* with the alphabetically anonymous sounds they are functionally employed to represent. In this sense, as stated above, orthography is a system of representation subject to self-affinity control.

Venezky (1970: 114) points out that the secondary vowel patterns (roughly, sequences of two or more vowel letters) differ from the primary vowel spellings in that they occur less frequently and have a more limited distribution, none occurs before geminate consonant clusters, each has a single major vowel-sound correspondent, and the 'morphophonemic' correspondences tend not to alternate in quality with reduction in stress. The *major* correspondences of the secondary vowels we present in Table 3.

The secondary vowels have been traditionally treated as 'digraphs' because the pronunciations of their wholes were not thought to be compositional functions of the pronunciations of their parts. On the digraph analysis, for example, the pronunciation of <die> cannot be derived from the pronunciation of <i> in <dip> and the pronunciation of <e> in <pep>. The digraphic analysis, however, looses sight of the all-pervasive fact of letter-naming. It is the phenomenon of letter-naming which suggests that the spelling of the English vowels is hierarchical, rather than flat.

Table 3. *Major correspondences of secondary vowels*

Secondary vowels	Correspondences
ai/ay	bait, day
au/aw	cause, law
ea	breach, each
ee	bleed, eel
ei/ey	veil, obey
eu/ew	neutron, pewter
ie	die, achieve, eerie
oa	approach, goal
oi/oy	join, boy
oo	boot, broom
ou/ow	owl, abound
ui	bruise, suitor

Recall that the spellings of the free pronunciations of the primary vowels require the presence of final <e> (or some other letter, if such is required). The free pronunciations of the major correspondences of the secondary vowels also require the presence of a second vowel in spelling whose function is to instruct the reader to pronounce its partner vowel by means of letter-naming as a(n) (oral) reading strategy on the grapheme/ phoneme route to reading. We might call the vowel spelling under letter-naming the 'head' and the instructing vowel the 'specifier'. In <bait>, for example, the <a> is the head and the <i> the specifier, because the name of the letter <a> is the same as the sound of the 'digraph' <ai>. An analogous analysis applies to the <ea> in <breach>, the first <e> in <bleed>, the <i> in <die>, the <o> in <approach>, the <u> in <bruise>, and the <u> in <neutron>.

How does the hierarchical analysis fare with the remaining major correspondences of the secondary vowels?

In <veil> the <e> and the <i> are each spelled as checked alternates, in <join> the <o> is spelled as a free alternate and the <i> as a checked, and in <owl> the <o> is pronounced as a checked alternate and the <w> (= <u>) as a free. Finally, the <o>'s in <boot> are free, derived by the chain (3f), i.e. /u/ - /o/.

We propose to treat the long vowel spellings as follows. For each long vowel slot create two vowel-letter spaces. Spell each long vowel sound with the letter whose name contains that vowel sound, i.e. process each long vowel sound by means of the equation use = mention used as a processing strategy. In the unmarked case, secondary vowel spellings have a left-handed head. If the secondary vowel spelling is unmarked, i.e. if the head is left-handed, and the head is either <e> or <o>, then either double the letter in the first space in the second space *or* write <a> in the second (i.e. right-handed) space; if the head is <u>, then the specifier is <i>. Lastly, in syllable-final position, write <w> for <u> and <y> for <i>, if <u> and <i> are specifiers. If the head is marked, i.e. right-handed, then the specifier is <i> if the head is <e> (e.g. <eerie, achieve>) and <e> if the head is <a> (e.g. <great>).

On this hierarchical analysis, the secondary spellings of vowels, both long (including diphthongs) and short (e.g. <head, weather>) are not unanalyzable digraphs, but complexes derived by means of letter-naming as a spelling strategy within an overarching theory of language as a self-complexing system (cf. de Beaugrande 1987). In <ea, ee, ie, oa, oo, ui> the left-handed, unmarked letter heads are obtained by letter-naming and the right-handed specifiers, which function to indicate that the heads are long, are inscribed by specifier inscription. To the /eɪ/ in <bait> letter-naming applies to produce the <a> and (1) Short-long chaining applies to the /ɪ/ to produce /ai/, which is then spelled <i> by letter-naming. To the /ɪ/ in <veil> (1) Short-long chaining applies twice, once to /ɛ/ to produce /i/, which is then spelled <e>, and once to the /ɪ/ to produce /ai/, which is then spelled <i>. To the /(j)u/ in <neutron>, the /u/ is spelled <u> by use = mention, and the /ɪ/, by (1), is converted to <e> by letter-naming. To the /oi/ in <join>, the /o/ is spelled directly by latter naming, and the /ɪ/, via (1) (= Short-long chaining), becomes /ai/ and is then spelled <i>. In the case of /au/ (<abound>), Rule (1) associates the /a/ with /o/, which is then spelled <o> by letter-naming. The marked (i.e. right-handed) heads in <collie, achieve> are obtained directly by letter-naming and specifier placement.

While the above framework accounts for most of the secondary vowel spellings of the long vowels, it does not offer a plausible account for all. For example, the secondary spellings of the vowels in <cause> and <boot>. Neither the open /ɔ/ in <cause> nor the long /u/ in <boot> may be derived by (1) Short-long chaining and/or letter-naming. Apparently, open /ɔ/ must be resolved by a special rule into /æ/ and /ɪ/, each vowel then undergoing Rule (1) and then letter-naming, and tense /u/ must be rewritten /o/ and then spelled by letter-naming.

The head-specifier analysis of the secondary spellings of the English vowels not only accounts for most of the major correspondences, but many of the minor correspondences as well. <ea>, for example, has its major correspondence in /i/, as in <breach, each, reach, teach>, and minor correspondences in /e/, as in <break, great, steak, yea>, and /e/, as in <health, measure, bread>. On the head-specifier theory of English spelling, <ea>:/i/ is derived by left-head formation, <ea>:/e/ by right-head formation, and <ea>:/e/ by Rule (1) followed by right-head formation. <oi> has its major correspondence in /oi/ and minor correspondences in /ai/ <coyote> and /ɪ/ <chamois>, among others. On this approach, the /aɪ/ contains an /a/ and an /ɪ/, the /a/ becomes /o/ by Rule (1) and is spelled <o> by letter-naming, the <i> then respelled <y> because it is ambisyllabic, with the result that initial /ai/ is correctly spelled <oy>. These are some of the possibilities of the head-specifier approach to the spellings of the English vowels; the obvious potential of the approach makes other possibilities worth exploring.

3.   Orthographic constituent structure

The advocated approach to the spelling of the English vowels - and arguments have also been adduced for the consonant 'digraphs' - emerged from consideration of the difficulty posed by a phonemic orthography containing fewer letters than there are sounds. Although there are several ramifications, modern English is found to solve the problem by spelling short vowels as though they were long vowels and spelling long vowels (and diphthongs) as though they were vowel sequences. In such sequences, one vowel letter is elected head, namely that vowel letter which encodes one of the two arguments in the proposition use = mention, and another vowel letter is elected specifier, namely that vowel letter which elevates the status of its neighbor to that of head. Cast in a different political metaphor, headship encodes an instruction by the speller to the reader to observe the equation mention = use. Pragmatically speaking, headship thus disposes of a certain adhortative illocutionary force. Granting this, then the sound-letter differential, a certain linguistic thermodynamic, *causes* the speller (and the reader) to develop constituent structure, because it, by its very nature, induces the orthographer to represent single segments - sounds - as though they were segment sequences - strings of letters. More accurately, the notion of an alphabet as a collection of discrete letters causes the speller to segment the speech chain into sounds, and the inherited, disadvantageous sound-letter differential becomes the progenitor of plurifunctionality, the plurifunctionality which is the quintessence of English orthography. In other words, the sound-letter differential equation, which performs an impressive semiotic work-load, is responsible for the orthographic complexity that is English.

The orthographic choices that are made are self-organizing in the sense that they are *sein-immanent*, i.e. inherent in the system. Once letter-naming and letter-doubling are selected as strategies for orthographic representation, the nature and extent of the determinacy of English orthography as a self-complexing (cf. de Beaugrande 1987) system becomes established.

While it is too much to expect - at least of me - to incorporate that dynamic complexity of the orthography/grammar manifold into a *formal* theory of grammar, I do not think that such a theory should be immediate constituent analysis, either in it traditional IC version or its more recent redaction in $\overline{X}$ syntax. And this for several reasons.

For one thing, English orthography does contain discontinuous constituents. The final <e> in <rage>, for example, is the encoding by the speller of the length/tenseness of the vowel /e/, which is spelled by letter-naming with the letter <a> (contrast <rag>). The idea of expressing the relationship continuously by the letter sequence <æ> has some appeal, especially because final <e> in the above function does not contrast with the final <e>s in <Mae, flee, pie, woe, blue>. However, this proposal necessitates at least one transformation transposing or extraposing <e> from nuclear to appendical position, i.e. <raeg> → <rage>.

The second reason is more substantial. In *The boy hit the ball*, *The boy* has been treated as an NP (Chomsky 1957), with *The* assigned to the category of Determiner and *boy* to that of Noun. What the associated constituent structure fails to express is that *The* says something about *boy*, namely that it is a specific, possibly presupposed boy, whereas *boy* says nothing about *The*. Analogously, the <e> of the <ea> in <great> says that the <a> should be pronounced by means of letter-naming as a spelling strategy, whereas the <a> of the <ea> in <great> says nothing about the <e>. Here, this topic-comment structure renders <a> a variable, part of whose value is bound by <e>, information that is lost by having <e> and <a> represented as satellite and nucleus sister nodes to a mother node V.

Much of the difficulty is remedied by some form of the $\bar{X}$ approach to syntax applied to the syntax of English orthographic representations. The <e> of the <ea> in <eat> would be dominated by a barless X, and because the distribution of <e> and <ea> are similar and the meaning of <e> and the meaning of <ea> are the same, i.e. /i/, and <ea> contains <e>, <ea> would be dominated by $\bar{X}$. The approach is alluring, but it bristles with problems: the problem of spellings with apparently no heads, like <veil> (cf. above), the problem of spellings with two heads, like <create>, the problem of discontinuous constituents, like <rage> (cf. above), and the quite general problem of one linguist's heads (Zwicky 1986) being another linguist's tails (Hudson 1987).

It is possible that many of these obstacles can be overcome by a dependency analysis. On one formulation (Mel'čuk and Percov 1987), dependency trees are directed graphs consisting of labeled nodes joined by labeled arcs defining relations which are antireflexive, antisymmetric, and antitransitive. Note that linear ordering is not a property of dependency trees.

Within this framework, we distinguish between deep and surface orthography (cf. above), where deep orthographic representations are dependency trees and surface orthographic representations are the trees of $\bar{X}$ syntax. Consider some examples.

The final <e>s in <Mae, flee, pie, toe, due>, etc., are predictable on the basis of their sound-letter pairings without <e> and the morphological fact of their being major class items. The presence of final <e> is predicted by <e>-Epenthesis as stated in (2) above. Accordingly, the <e>-less dependency representation is as in (5), which represents the result of

(5)   <e>-Dependency

a. <C ← a, C ← e, C ← i, C ← o, C ← u>#
          ↓   ↓   ↓   ↓   ↓

b.   e   e   e   e   e

attaching the surface dependency <e> in (5b) to the deep dependency orthographic representations in (5a). After linearization, we obtain the X̄ orthographic representation in (6).

(6)   <e>-X̄

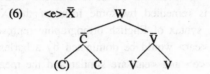

<e> is also epenthesized to otherwise final <u, v>, as stated in (7).

(7)   <e>-Epenthesis II

Ø → <e> / <u, v> __#

This rule relates the deep dependency in (8a) to the surface dependency in (8b)

(8)   <e>-Dependency II

a. u   v >#
     ↓   ↓

b. e   e

Similarly, <e>-Epenthesis I may be expressed as in (9)

(9)   <e>-Dependency I

< V → C >#
     ↓

e

Consonant singling and consonant doubling are given in (10), which applies with exceptions within the morpheme (cf. Venezky 1970:

(10)   Consonant Doubling

Singling   Doubling

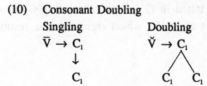

106), but almost without exception across morpheme boundaries. Our preference is to permit the dependencies inherited by the orthography from the phonology to remain as constant as possible and, in the above case, because of consonant letter-doubling in the regular preterit, past participle, comparative, progressive, and gerund, to then delete the doubled letter in stems like <hit, bid, sit>. Spellings like <ebb> would then be excepted from deletion.

To take a final example, if word final /s/ is written <c>, then this <c> must be followed by <e>. This is another <e>-Epenthesis, given in (11) as <e>-Epenthesis III.

(11)   <e>-Epenthesis III

$$\emptyset \rightarrow \text{<e>} \ / \ \text{<c>} \_\_ \ \#$$
$$\uparrow$$
$$\text{/s/}$$

The corresponding dependency is given in (12). Here it will be noted that

(12)   <e>-Dependency III

$$\text{/s/ } \#$$
$$\downarrow$$
$$\text{<c>}$$
$$\downarrow$$
$$\text{<e>}$$

the <e> dependency is in turn dependent upon the dependency of <c> upon /s/ in word final and morpheme-final position.

4. Conclusion

Modern English has more sounds than letters. This sound-letter differential results in short vowels masquerading as long and long vowels masquerading as vowel sequences. It is suggested that the true identities behind the masks may be revealed by placing the short vowels in partnership with the long vowels and deriving their spellings via letter-naming as a spelling strategy. Original long vowels are also spelled by letter-naming as a spelling strategy, with the proviso that additional vowels be added to support their length. The emergent system-driven structure appears hierarchical, but it is not clear if the traditional systems of constituent structure are the correct ones to represent it. What does appear clear is that the letter values of sounds are bound in part by their letter-names in spelling and that the sound values of letters are bound in part by letter-naming in reading. This warrants a more configurational approach to the orthography of English.

A Formal Approach to Error Taxonomy
Wojciech Buszkowski and Philip Luelsdorff

Introduction

Four major anthologies of error analyses have appeared over the past
twelve years (Fromkin 1973, 1980); Coltheart, Patterson and Marshall
(1980; and Cutler 1982) which are a veritable treasure-trove of data and
theory in the domain of linguistic error. The time is right for a major
theoretical synthesis (cf. Luelsdorff 1986, where such a synthesis is
essayed) based on sound empirical footing. Viewed within the context of
knowledge representation and use erroneous patterns are all pervasive;
consequently, linguistic error must be accounted for by an empirically
adequate theory of linguistic structure and process.

We attempt to refine the conceptual apparatus employed in linguistic error analyses and error analyses in general. Our main objective is to
lay the foundation for the formal theory of linguistic deviation as a
necessary complement to current theories of the linguistic norm. Thus
conceived, such a theory should materially contribute to our understanding
of human linguistic competence, our understanding of the interplay
between linguistic competence and performance, language teaching
strategies, etc.

This chapter offers nothing more than a first foray into the pro-
jected field of research. Some quite fundamental notions relevant to error
analyses, especially those of a taxonomic character, will be defined in as
precise a manner as we are able, and several of their principal properties
will be discussed. We abstain from any detailed linguistic illustration (cf.
Luelsdorff 1986 for thousands of examples) and thorough-going empirical
attestation (for which, cf. the items cited above) in the hope that the
considerations articulated are sufficiently self-explanatory in order to
evoke thought about the burning issues at stake.

In section 1 some basic types of competence and performance error
are introduced and briefly examined. Following the error-analytic tradition

we study such error types on the level of segments and segment sequences, identifying various error types with binary relations between them. Certain relevant interconnections between error types are defined and discussed within the framework of relational algebra.

In section 2 we take constituent-structure into account (cf. Gladkij 1970) instead of segments and segment sequences. Beyond the shadow of a doubt constituent structure is the major model of syntactic structure from the standpoint of any current theory of syntactic structure within formal grammar, including Transformational Generative Grammar (TGG), Categorial Grammar (CG), or Dependency Grammar (DG). In the tradition of CG constituent structure is usually related to a functional representation of semantics ("Fregean Semantics", Buszkowski 1985). Though less developed, there have also been interesting attempts to employ constituent structure in morphology (cf. Selkirk 1982, 1984; Toman 1984), phonology (cf. Booij 1984) and orthography (cf. Luelsdorff 1986). The theory of error becomes increasingly more subtle when one considers these levels of representation (cf. Luelsdorff 1985, 1986).

Section 3 is given over to certain formal constraints on the structure of error. From the observation that it seems obvious that not every deviation from a norm (subjective or objective) is performed by the language knower-user it follows that the theory of linguistic error should enable us to distinguish between extant and non-extant and possible and impossible linguistic errors and estimate their relative probabilities. We attempt to achieve this by employing the notion of rank (for the transposition-displacement error) involving a distance function on the constituent structure. Our notion of distance function in fact generalizes the one introduced by Luszczewska-Romahnowa (1961) (cf. also Batóg and Steffan-Batogowa 1980), for an application to phonetics).

Section 4 contains some summary remarks and suggestions for further research.

1. Error taxonomy

The letter 'V' will denote a non-empty set whose members are to be thought of as linguistic atoms (graphemes, phonemes, morphemes, words, depending upon the level of grammar under investigation). By a segment over V we mean a finite string of atoms over V. The empty segment is denoted by 'ʌ'. S(V) denotes the set of all segments over V.

We reserve the variables a, b, c for atoms, and A, B, C for segments (the scope of the latter will be adjusted in the next section). AB denotes the concatenation of A and B in that order. We write A^n for A...A (n times).

The five basic error types (mechanisms) of Transposition (T), Displacement (D), Addition (A), Omission (O), and Substitution (S) can be formally characterized by means of the following schemata:

$$(T) \quad AXBYC \quad \rightarrow \quad AYBXC \quad (X,B,Y \neq \Lambda, X \neq Y),$$
$$(D) \quad AXYB \quad \rightarrow \quad AYXB \quad (X,Y \neq \Lambda, X \neq Y),$$
$$(A) \quad AB \quad \rightarrow \quad AXB \quad (AB \neq \Lambda, X \neq \Lambda),$$
$$(O) \quad AXB \quad \rightarrow \quad AB \quad (AB \neq \Lambda, X \neq \Lambda),$$
$$(S) \quad AXB \quad \rightarrow \quad AYB \quad (AB \neq \Lambda, X,Y \neq \Lambda, X \neq Y).$$

The left-hand segment string represents the correct form (target) and the right-hand segment string stands for the erroneous form (attempt). For the case of (T) and (D) we assume that the attempt differs from the target (this obviously holds for (A), (O), and (S)).

Quite formally, an error of type T, D, etc., is to be defined as a pair (A_1, A_2), where $A_1, A_2 \varepsilon$ S(V), and the above-mentioned conditions are met. For example, (A_1, A_2) is an error of type O if there are A, B, X ε S(V), such that AB $\neq \Lambda$, X Λ, $A_1 = AXB$ and $A_2 = AB$. The letters T, D, etc. will be used to denote the set of all errors of type T, D, etc. As errors are pairs of segment strings, these sets are in fact binary relations between segment strings. Accordingly, 'type of error' means some binary relation between segments (segment strings).

We exemplify with a few errors found in English dictations administered to a 12-year-old pupil in a German *Hauptschule* (cf. Luelsdorff 1986). The pair *<pupil, pilpu>* can be recognized as an error of type T *<p-u-p-il, p-il-p-u>* as well as of type D *<pu-pil, pil-pu>*. To type D we relegate the errors *<every, evrye>*, *<alarm, arlam>*, *<down, donw>*, and *<where, wheer>*. The pairs *<right, righte>*, *<ice-cream, ice-creame>* are examples of errors of type A, *<remembering, rembering>*, *<highest, hiest>* of type O, and *<thinks, sinks>*, *<altogether, altogesser>* of type S.

An error taxonomy, as we understand it, begins and ends with the observation and description of errors. We distinguish between errors as the product of mechanisms ((T), (D), (O), (A), and (S)), on the one hand, and the triggering of mechanisms by processing strategies (= causes), on the other. Mechanisms we liken to rules of grammar, and processing strategies we liken to principles of grammar. While both linguistic and non-linguistic error mechanisms qua mechanisms appear to be identical, irrespective of the level of representation and the nature of the knowledge represented, error processing strategies appear to differ as a function of the type of information being processed. By way of contrast and clarity, we present the major processing strategies which are held to underlie and explain the ca. 1000 vowel and consonant errors detected in over 6000 words of English dictation administered to a 12-year-old incipient English/ German bilingual pupil of English in a *Hauptschule* in Regensburg, the capital of the Upper Palatinate in Bavaria, dispensing with 18 subdivisions of IB and IC. The major processing strategies are grouped as in Table 1, where A = Attempt, T = Target, and :: = corresponds to.

By way of illustration we have presented a sampling of real orthographic errors made by Germans in acquiring English as a foreign language. By *Gedankenexperiment* one may imagine the grammatical error:

(1)   *(Joan smiles charmingly, Joan charmingly smiles)*

which may be qualified as an error of type D. Another example is:

(2)   (p ∧ (q v r), p ∧ q v r)

the latter frequently observed in undergraduate logic courses. (2) can be treated as an error of type S (substitute q v r for (q v r)) or, alternatively, as resulting from a double omission.

In practice we meet many attempts which cannot be traced to any single type T - S or whose assignment to such types would be counterintuitive. As a rule such attempts evidence the effect of several error types. In the preceding paragraphs we mentioned a double omission. According to Luelsdorff 1986 the error <where, weher> should be analyzed as a double displacement <where → wehre → weher>, rather than a single displacement. Similarly, <eight, egth> results from the combination of an omission <eight, eght> and a displacement <eght, egth>.

The relations corresponding to these complex errors can be easily defined from relations T - S by means of composition (relative product).

Recall that if R_1, R_2 are binary relations, then $R_1 \cdot R_2$ (the composition of R_1 and R_2) is a binary relation, satisfying the equivalence

(3) $xR_1.R_2y$ iff there is an x such that xR_1x and xR_2y.

We often write R_1R_2 instead of $R_1.R_2$. Now, double displacement is the type DD; hence, (A_1, A_2) is an error of type DD iff there is a segment B such that (A_1, B) and (B, A_2) are errors of type D. In an analogous fashion we understand errors of type OD (e.g. *(eight, egth)*, and DS (e.g. *twelve, twelef)*, etc.

Table 1.   Transfer

I.   *Intralinguistic*
  A. English letter-naming
    1. Articulation of English letter-name:
         A: \<Her> :: T: \<Here>
    2. Place of articulation of English letter-name:
         A: \<mess> :: T: \<miss>
    3. Sequence of English letter-names:
         A: \<could> :: T: \<cold>
  B. Regularization: A: \<pritty> :: T: \<pretty>
  C. Irregularization: A: \<leate> :: T: \<late>
  D. Simplification: A: \<juse> :: T: \<juice>
  E. Complication: A: \<cload> :: T: \<clothes>

II. *Interlinguistic*
  A. German letter-naming
    1. Articulation of German letter-name:
         A: \<cornfleks> :: T: \<cornflakes>
    2. Place of articulation of German letter-name:
         A: \<Jam> :: T: \<John>
  B. German GPCs: A: \<steschen> :: T: \<station>
  C. Cognatization
    1. Partial: A: \<lauchs> :: T: \<laughs>
    2. Total: A: \<preis> :: T: \<prize>
  D. Decognatization: A: \<schlips> :: T: \<sleeps>

As error types are relations, relational algebra seems to be the proper framework to express and examine their essential properties and interconnections. To this end we need the usual set-theoretic operations: $\cup$ (union), $\cap$ (intersection), the inclusion predicate $\subseteq$, and the empty set symbol $\emptyset$. W^n denotes the set of all n-tuples of elements of the set W. By R^c we denote the converse of the relation R. Thus, xR^cy iff yRx. R^+ denotes the transitive closure of R, i.e. the least transitive relation containing R. Thus, xR^cy iff there are $x_1,...,x_n$ ($n > 1$), such that $x_1 = x$, $x_n = y$ and x_iRy_{i+1}, for all $1 \le i \le n$.

Fact 1: The following formulas are true:

(4) $T^c = T$, $D^c = D$, $S^c = S$, $A^c = O$, $O^c = A$,

(5) $A^c \cap A = \emptyset$, $O^c \cap O = \emptyset$,

(6) $T \cap A = T \cap O = D \cap A = D \cap O = \emptyset$.

In the light of (4) T, D, and S are symmetric relations while A and O are mutually converse and, by (5), antisymmetric. It follows from (5) and (6) that relations T, A, O as well as D, A, O are pairwise disjoint (hence, for instance, no error of type A may be at the same time D, T, or O). We can derive similar properties for complex types. Using the law $(R_1R_2)^c = R_2^cR_1^c$ we easily obtain:

(7) $(DD)^c = DD$, $(AO)^c = AO$, $(OA)^c = OA$, $(DA)^c = OD$

and many other interesting dependencies.

As $T \cap D \ne \emptyset$ (recall *(pupil, pilpu)*), and also $T \cap S \ne \emptyset$, $D \cap S \ne \emptyset$, we are faced with the phenomenon of type ambiguity of error. To embrace this phenomenon in its full generality we must take complex error types into account. The simple calculation:

(8)   AXBYC $\rightarrow$ AYXBC $\rightarrow$ AYBXC

shows that any error of type T is also of type DD, hence $T \subseteq DD$.

We say that a type R is reducible (in a set $U \subseteq S(V)$, respectively) to type R^+ if $R \subseteq R^+$ ($R \cap U^2 \subseteq R^+$). Type R is said to be weakly reducible (in a set $U \subseteq S(V)$) to R^+ if $R \subseteq (R^+)$ ($R \cap U^2 \subseteq (R^+)^+$). Of course reducibility entails weak reducibility, but the converse need not hold. For, if R_1, R_2 are defined as follows:

(9) $a^m R_1 a^n$ iff $n = m+1, a^m R_2 a^n$ iff $m \leq n$,

then R_2 is weakly reducible but not reducible to R_1.

Fact 2:
Each of the types T - S is reducible to AO. T, D, S are reducible to OA. A and O are reducible to OA in the set S(V)-V.

Fact 3:
T is reducible to DD, hence weakly reducible to D. In the set $n \geq U_4 v^n$ D is weakly reducible to T.

Proof.
It is well-known from school algebra that any permutation results from the composition of displacements of adjacent atoms. Accordingly, to verify the second statement, it suffices to prove that in a four-element segment (sequence) any displacement of the latter sort can be obtained by the iteration of transpositions. In fact,

(10)   abcd $\rightarrow$ cdba $\rightarrow$ bdca $\rightarrow$ bacd, dually: abcd $\rightarrow$ ... $\rightarrow$ abdc

(11)   abcd $\rightarrow$ ... (by (10)) $\rightarrow$ abdc $\rightarrow$ acdb $\rightarrow$ ... (by (10)) $\rightarrow$ acbd

Let us mention other cases of reducibility. In S(V) = V types A and O are reducible to S. T and D are reducible to SS. Some general rules may also be obtained, for instance:

(12)   if $R_1, ..., R_n$ are reducible to $R'_1, ..., R'_n$, respectively, then $R_1...R_n$ is reducible to $R'_1...R'_n$,

(13)   if $R_1, ..., R_n$ are weakly reducible to $R'_1, ..., R'_n$, respectively, then $R_1...R_n$ is weakly reducible to $R'_1...R'_n$.

The simple reducibility properties we have discussed above are intended to demonstrate the framework of relational algebra as applied to error theory. It seems evident that a mature theory should provide a much more subtle error taxonomy, more reducibility conditions, etc. A few strides will be made in this direction in the following.

2. Structural errors

In this section we treat error types as binary relations on the set of constituent structures of expressions. We shall see that such a perspective often leads to a different classification of an error than in the preceding section. Moreover, one attains a less ambiguous error taxonomy. Finally, this approach enables us to interpret erroneous attempts as resulting from a deviation from the rules of grammar.

For a set V of atoms, the set C(V) of constituent structures (c-structures) over V is defined by the following induction:

(14) $V \subseteq C(V)$,

(15)   if $A_1,...,A_n \in C(V)$, $n \geq 2$, then $\{A_1...A_n\} \in C(V)$.

We assume, of course, that the symbols '{' and '}' do not belong to V. $A_1,...,A_n$ are called "the immediate constituents of c-structure $\{A_1...A_n\}$". The constituents of $A \in C(V)$ are A, its immediate constituents, the immediate constituents of them, etc. By supp(A), $A \in C(V)$, we denote the support (frontier) of A, i.e. the segment over V that results after one has deleted all the symbols { and } from A.

For example, the sentence *The sun shines all day* is the support of c-structure:

(16)   {{The sun} {shines {all {day}}}},

whose immediate constituents are {The sun} and {shines {all {day}}}. The logical formula p ∧ (q ∨ r) is usually considered as being given in the form of c-structure. This obtains when we respect all the parentheses necessary for the full constituent analysis (except for the outermost ones) of any formula. In case one avails oneself of some conventions for the omission of parentheses, however, it seems more correct to regard the parentheses as constituents of the formula under consideration. Accordingly, we may assign the latter formula the following c-structure:

(17)   {p ∧ {{q ∨ r}}}.

For $A,B \in C(V)$, $a \in V$, by A(B/a) we denote the result of the substitution of B for every occurrence of a in A. We write oc_1 (a,A) if a has exactly one occurrence in A. We also write $C(V, a_1,...a_n)$ instead of

$C(W)$, where $W = V \cup \{a_1,...,a_n\}$. (It is always assumed that $a_1,...,a_n$ are pairwise distinct and that they do not belong to V).

We now formulate precise definitions of the error types $\bar{T}$ - $\bar{S}$, the analogues of T - S, but with c-structures:

($\bar{T}$) $A_1\bar{T}A_2$ iff there are $A \in C(V,a,b)$, $X,Y \in C(V)$, such that $oc_1(a,A)$, $oc_1(b,A)$, a, b, are not adjacent in $supp(A)$, and $A_1 = A(X/a)(Y/b)$, $A_2 = A(Y/a)(X/b)$(also $X \neq Y$).

($\bar{D}$)   differs from ($\bar{T}$) in stipulating: a, b are adjacent in $supp(A)$.

($\bar{A}$) $A_1\bar{A}A_2$ iff there are $A \in C(V,a)$, $B_1,...,B_n$, $X \in C(V)$, and $1 \leq i \leq n$, such that oc_1 (a,A) and there hold: $A_1 = A((B_1...B_n/a)$ $(A_1 = A(B_1/a)$, respectively) and either $A_2 = A((B_1...B_i \ XB_{i+1}...B_n)/a)$ or $A_2 = A((XB_1...B_n)/a)(A_2 = A((XB_1)/a)$ or $A_2 = A((B_1X)/a$, respectively)).

($\bar{O}$) $A_1\bar{O}A_2$ iff $A_2\bar{A}A_1$,

($\bar{S}$) $A_1\bar{S}A_2$ iff there are $A \in C(V.a)$, A non-atomic, and X,Y $\in C(V)$, $X \neq Y$, such that oc_1 (a,A), $A_1 = A(X/a)$, and $A_2 = (Y,a)$.

If A_1RA_2, we say that (A_1,A_2) (also: $A_1 \to A_2$) is an error of type R (where $R = \bar{T},...,\bar{S}$ or R arises as a combination of them). For example, the pair:

{{{The sun}{shines{all{day}}}}→{{all{day}}{shines{the{sun}}}}

is an error of type $\bar{T}$.

Let $\bar{R}$ denote the c-structure analogue of a type R, being defined for strings. We obtain the simple proposition:

Fact 4:

For all $A,B \in C(V)$, if $A\bar{R}B$ then $supp(A)Rsupp(B)$. Furthermore, if $\bar{R}_1$ is (weakly, respectively) reducible to $\bar{R}_2$ then R_1 is also (weakly, respectively) reducible to R_2.

The converse conditionals do not hold, however. Observe that:

(18)   {Joan{smiles charmingly}}→{Charmingly{Joan smiles}}

is an error of type $\bar{D}$ but not $\bar{T}$ though, of course, it is of type D if flattened to segments. Similarly, T is reducible to DD, but not to $\bar{D}\bar{D}$. For in,

(19)   {Joan{smiles charmingly}}→{Charmingly{smiles Joan}}.

to transform the attempt into the target one needs at least three displacements (notice that $\bar{T}$ remains weakly reducible to $\bar{D}$).

It follows from these remarks that the constituent analysis of error structure yields, as a rule, finer stratification and less ambiguity. The more important advantage, however, consists in its direct relation to elementary transformations of grammatical rules.

We have already mentioned that the constituent structure model is a fundamental tool for syntactic analysis within prominent trends in formal linguistics, such as TGG, CG, or DG. As a matter of fact, each of these theories proposes a different categorization of c-structures. In this chapter we follow the categorization stemming from TGG, viz. the phrase-structure grammar framework (cf. Chomsky 1957).

Given a set $L \subseteq C(V)$ the intersubstitutability relation with respect to L, denoted by Int(L), is a binary relation between c-structures over V defined as follows:

(20)   AInt(L)B iff, for any $C \in C(V,a)$, $C(A/a) \in L$ iff $C(B/a)$ $\in$ L.

Int(L) is a congruence on C(V), compatible with L, meaning:

(21)   if $A_iInt(L)B_i$, $1 \leq i \leq n$, then $\{A_1...A_{n}Int(L)(B}1...B_n\}$,

(22)   if AInt(1)B, then $A \in L$ iff $B \in L$,

and, moreover, it is an equivalent relation. The equivalence classes if Int(L) are to be called (syntactic) categories of L. For $A \in C(V)$, by A/L we denote the only category of L containing A. Any formula of the form:

(23) $\{A_1...A_2\}/ L \rightarrow \{A_1/L...A_n/L\}$

is referred to as a basic (grammatical) rule of L. The set of all basic rules of L will be symbolized by BRul(L). The set Rul(D) of all rules of L is defined by the following induction:

(24)   BRul(L) $\subseteq$ Rul(L),

(25)   if $K \rightarrow \{K_1...K_n\}$ and $K_1 \rightarrow \{K'_1...K'_m\}$ belong to Rul(L),
       then $K \rightarrow \{K_1...K_{i-1}\{K'_1...K_m\}K_{i+1}...K_n\}$ also belongs to
       Rul(L)

where K_j, K'_j, K stand for (the names of) categories of L.

For $L \subseteq C(V)$, by CON(L) we denote the set of all constituents of c-structures from L. Observe that, for any $A \in CON(L)$, $A/L = C(V)$. CON/L which means the c-structures $A \in CON(L)$ constitute a single category of L to be termed the nonsense category. The remaining categories of L are said to be relevant to L. A rule of L is said to be relevant to L if its left-most category is relevant to L (hence, all the categories appearing in this rule are relevant). The set of all the basic rules relevant to L will be referred to as the grammar of L, and denoted by G(L). L is said to be finitary if G(L) is finite.

Fact 5:

If $L \subseteq C(V)$ is finitary, then supp(L) = {supp(A): $A \in L$} is a context-free language; in fact G(L) is a context-free grammar generating supp(L) which yields exactly the c-structure from L (rules must be added for substituting atoms for categories).

The converse is also true, namely, any context-free grammar can be reduced to a grammar G(L), for some finitary set L.

For example, consider the set L consisting of the following c-structures:

(26)   *{Joan smiles},*

(27)   *{Joan {smiles charmingly}},*

(28)   *{Joan {smiles charmingly} charmingly},* etc.

One may easily verify that the categories of L are:

(29) $N = \{Joan\}$,

(30) $V = \{smiles, \{smiles\ charmingly\}, \{\{smiles\ charmingly, charmingly\}...\},$

(31) $A = \{charmingly\}$,

(32) $S = L$,

and the nonsense category. The basic relevant rules are:

(33)   S → {NV}, V → {VA},

as a non-basic rule of L we introduce:

(34)   S → {N{VA}}.

Let us consider the error:

(35)   *{Joan {smiles charmingly}}* → *{Joan {charmingly smiles}}*.

Obviously, this error can be analyzed as the result of displacement within the basic rules of L, viz.:

(36)   V → {AV} is used instead of V → {VA}.

On the other hand, the error (18) results by no iteration of displacement within the basic rules. In fact the only attempts available in this way from the left-hand side of (18) are:

(37)   {Joan {charmingly smiles}},

(38)   {{Smiles charmingly} Joan},

(39)   {{Charmingly smiles} Joan}.

Clearly we can treat (18) as resulting from permutation within (34), which admits a reduction to double displacement. Now, if we assume that the performance of language proceeds by applying basic rather than non-basic relevant rules, then the latter analysis seems unsatisfactory as an explanation of (18). More precisely, the above assumption forces one to dismiss errors like (18) from the domain of possible deviations from grammar or, to say the least, consider them to be much less probable than, e.g. (35).

In a natural way we define error types for the rules of L (since their right-hand sides are just some c-structures, one simply adapts the clauses $(\bar{T})$ - $(\bar{S})$). An error (A_1, A_2) is said to be of primary (secondary, respectively) character if A_2 can be derived by means of a deviation (of type $(\bar{T})$ - $(\bar{S})$) from the basic (non-basic, respectively) rules of L (here L stands for a fixed set of targets). Thus, for instance, (35) is of primary character, while (18) is of secondary character. In the above definition we have not referred in an essential manner to A_1. Observe, however, that according to our approach the grammar G(L) is unambiguous (in respect of c-structures), hence it yields exactly one derivation of A_1. Therefore, we consider only those rules of L that participate in the only derivation of A_1 with respect to G(L).

In the light of the above remarks it should be evident that we regard errors of primary character as the most expected in real linguistic experience. In the next section the thesis will be refined by introducing a hierarchy of errors of secondary character.

Prior to this, however, we mention the possibility of analyzing the relation between errors and grammatical rules in a different, perhaps more stimulating, manner. The idea is to describe global effects of enriching the set of targets by an erroneous attempt. As a result, one obtains a larger set of targets with a modified grammar. Thus, the kind of error can be expressed in terms of the relation between the new grammar ('the grammar of that error') and the original one. Let us present one of several possible explications of this idea.

For $L \subseteq C(V)$, $A,B \in C(V)$, the relation ADom(L)B (A dominates B in L) is defined as follows:

(40)   ADom(L)B iff, for any $C \in C(A,a)$, if $C(A/a) \in L$ then $C(B/b) \in L$.

Clearly, Dom(L) is a reflexive and transitive relation on C(V). Moreover,

(41)   AInt(L)B iff both ADom(L)B and BDom(L)A.

Notice also that Dom(L) satisfies:

(42)   if $A_iDom(L)B_i$, $1 \leq i \leq n$, then $\{A_1...A_n\}Dom(L)\{B_1...B_n\}$.

Let $L \subseteq C(V)$ be fixed, and let $A,B \subseteq C(V)$. By Dom(L,A,B) we denote the least reflexive and transitive relation on C(V), such that:

(43) $Dom(L) \subseteq Dom(L,A,B)$

(44)   A Dom(L,A,B)B

and (42) holds with Dom(L) replaced by (Dom(L,A,B). By L(B/A) we denote the set of all $C \in C(V)$, such that $C'Dom (L,A,B)C$, for some C' $\in$ L.

Fact 6:

(i) $\text{Dom}(L(B/A)) = \text{Dom}(L,A,B)$,

(ii) $L \subseteq L(B/A)$,

(iii) $\text{Int}(L) \subseteq \text{Int}(L(B/A))$,

(iv)   If L is finitary, then $L(B/A)$ is also.

We now explain how this construction relates to error analysis. Given an erroneous attempt (A,B), where $A \in L$, $B \notin L$, L being a set of targets, one may assume that the grammar-user is inclined to perform B instead of A in any context. The set $L(B/A)$ consists of all possible performances of that sort. In the light of Fact 6 (iv) $L(B/A)$ is given by means of finitely many grammatical rules (provided L is). Furthermore, by Fact 6 (iii), the categories of $L(B/A)$ can be identified with those of L (though different categories of L may fall into one category of $L(B/A)$). Accordingly, $G(L(B/A))$ admits the same category symbols as $C(L)$ and, possibly, some new ones. One can analyze $G(L(B/A))$ as a transformation of $G(L)$ and classify the error (A,B) with respect to the form of this transformation.

Let us turn back to the example (26)-(28). It is easy to verify that for A = {Joan {smiles charmingly}}, B = {Joan {charmingly smiles}, $L(B/A)$ yields the following relevant rules:

(45)   S → {NV'}, V' → {AV}, V → {VA}, S → {NV},

where V' is the category of c-structures:

(46)   {charmingly smiles},

(47)   {charmingly {smiles charmingly}}, etc.

Thus, $G(L(B/A))$ arises from $G(L)$ in effect introducing a new relevant category, just V', and two new rules. As the first of the rules (45) can be regarded as the result of substitution within the last one, the error under consideration seems to represent an error of substitution on the level of grammar. Notice that our former approach has suggested to us assigning this error to the type displacement.

Of course, the above analysis strongly depends on the assumption that B is to be substituted for A in all targets. Moreover, one regards the modified grammar as containing all the rules of the original one. Clearly, each of these assumptions seems questionable. Our aim has been only to outline a framework to deal with such problems; undoubtedly, the very framework admits of various modifications and refinements. A more thorough presentation of the topics dealt with in this section must be deferred to a later study.

3. Rank hierarchy

In the preceding section we distinguished between errors of primary and errors of secondary character, the former interpreted as resulting from deviations from basic grammatical rules, the latter from non-basic grammatical rules. Now, the distinction will be made more subtle in the corpus of errors of type $\bar{T} \cup \bar{D}$, which we refer to as transpositions (in a generalized sense).

A sequence $A_0, A_1,...,A_n$ of constituents of $A \in C(V)$ is called a path of length n in A (leading from A_0 to A_n), if A_{i+1} is an immediate constituent of A_i, for all $0 \leq 1 \leq n$. By the depth of a constituent A of B $\in C(V)$ ($d_B(A)$) we mean the length of the only path from B to A. If A,B are constituents of $C \in C(V)$, then supp(A,B) denotes the only constituent C' of C, such that there are paths from C' to A as well as to B and, for any C'' having this property, $d_C(C'') \leq d_C(C')$. We define $d_1^c(A,B)$ (($1_2^c(A,B)$, respectively) as the length of the path from supp(A,B) to A (to B, respectively). Finally, we put:

(48) $d^s(A,B) = d_1^c(A,B) + d_2^c(A,B)$,

where A,B are constituents of C. The number $d^c(A,B)$ is called the distance between A and B within C.

Fact 7:
For any $C \in C(V)$, d^c is a distance function on a set of constituents of C. This means, for all constituents A_1, A_2, A_3 of C, the following conditions hold true:

(49) $d^c(A_1, A_2) = 0$ iff $A_1 = A_2$ (they are equal as constituents!)

(50) $d^c(A_1, A_2) = d^c(A_2, A_1)$

(51) $d^c(A_1, A_3) \leq d^c(A_1, A_2) + d^c(A_2, A_3)$

A c-structure is said to be regular if all its atomic constituents have the same depth. It is readily seen that if C is regular and a,b are atomic constituents of C, then:

(52) $d_1^c(a, b) = d_2^c(a, b)$

According to Luszczewska-Romahnowa (1961), the distance between two atomic constituents of C is to be measured by d_1^c rather than d^c, provided that C is regular (strictly speaking, the author was concerned with classifications, not c-structures, but this distinction is immaterial here). So, $d^c = 2d_1^c$ in the scope of atomic constituents of a regular C; since the constant factor does not affect the mathematically essential properties of distance functions, we may regard our notion of distance as generalizing that given by Luszczewska-Romahnowa (1961).

Let us turn back to the clauses ($\bar{T}$) - ($\bar{D}$) of the definition of (structural) error types. A pair (A_1, A_2) is a transposition (i.e. a $\bar{T} \cup \bar{D}$ error) if there are $A \in C(V,a,b)$, $X,y \in C(V)$, $X \neq Y$, such that $oc_i(a, A)$, $oa_i(a, A)$, and $A_1 = A(X/a)(Y/b)$, $A_2 = A(Y/a)(X/b)$. In what follows we additionally assume X,Y are minimal (i.e. the least complex) c-structures satisfying those equalities, and consequently, there is only one A fulfilling them. By the rank of a transposition (A_1, A_2) we simply mean the distance between a and b or, equivalently, between X and Y within A_1 (or A_2).

Fact 8:
The transpositions of rank 2 are exactly those of primary character. More exactly, (A_1, A_2), where $A_1 \in L$, $A_2 \in L$, is of rank 2 iff it can be derived by applying a single transposition of a basic rule of L.

Consequently, transpositions of rank greater than 2 correspond to deviations from non-basic rules. The higher the rank, the more complex must be the non-basic rules under deviation. Hence, the appearance of such transpositions in linguistic data seems less probable. If p_n represented the frequency of the transpositions, one would expect the formula:

(53) $p_n = 1/2^{n-1}$

Of course, any serious prediction of this sort should be based on empirical investigations.

Errors of type $(\bar{T} \cup \bar{D})$ are called iterated transpositions. Thus, (A,B) is an iterated transposition iff there is a sequence (A_1, A_{i+1}), $1 \leq i \leq n$, such that $A_1 = A.A_{n+1} = B$, and (A_1, A_{i+1}) is a transposition, for all $1 \leq i \leq n$. For any such sequence, the maximal rank of its term is referred to as the rank of the sequence. Finally, by the rank of iterated transposition (A,B) we mean the minimal rank of sequence (A_i, A_{i+1}) fulfilling the above condition.

Fact 9:
The iterated transpositions of rank 2 are exactly those of primary character. More precisely (A_1, A_2), where $A_1 \in L$, $A_2 \notin L$ is an iterated transposition of rank 2 iff it can be derived by applying basic transpositions of some basic rules of L.

Clearly the remarks we have formulated above for the case of transposition probability pertain to the case of iterated transposition. Our final task consists of discussing the somewhat sophisticated matter of generating errors of an *a priori* bounded rank. Notice first, that by iterated transposition of atoms one is able to obtain an arbitrary permutation of a given segment. On the level of c-structures, however, this usually involves transpositions of arbitrarily high rank. We know that context-free languages are not closed under permutation (cf. Gladkij 1970). That is, there exists a set $C \subseteq S(V)$ which is generated by a context-free grammar, such that the set of all permutations of the segments from C is not context-free (take $C = ((a, b)^n C^n: n \geq 1)$. On the other hand, we obtain:

Fact 10:
Let $L \subseteq C(V)$ be finitary. For every $n \geq a$, the let L_n, consisting of all c-structures derivable from those in L by iterated transposition of rank not greater than n, is also finitary, hence $\text{supp}(L_n)$ is a context-free language.

Accordingly, restricting the rank of possible error one gains an effective procedure for generating the expected erroneous performances which still dwells within the realm of context-free grammar. This strongly motivates our interest in the rank hierarchy as yielding some natural constraints necessary for a practically manageable error description.

4. Final remarks

In section 1 (Error taxonomy) we define the five major linguistic error types: Transposition (T), Displacement (D), Addition (A), Omission (O), and Substitution (S). By "type of error" we mean a certain binary relation among segments or segment sequences. Simplex errors, the products of just one error operation, are distinguished from complex errors, the products of several error operations. We introduce the notion of the converse of a relation, thereby establishing T, D, and S as symmetric, A and O as mutually converse and antisymmetric, and T, A, O and D, A, O as pairwise disjoint. Finally, the notions reducibility and weak reducibility are introduced and the distinction between error mechanism and error cause drawn and exemplified.

Section 2 (Structural errors) treats error types as binary relations on the set of constituent structures of expressions. We present an error classification alternative to section 1, a less ambiguous error taxonomy, and the interpretation of erroneous attempts as resulting from a deviation from the rules of grammar.

In a treatment more comprehensive than the one here possible, the crucial *psycholinguistic* (as opposed to logical) distinction between competence and performance errors (cf. Luelsdorff 1986) should be made and exemplified. In competence errors the left coordinate of a pair of speaker trees is not necessarily identified with the community norm, whereas in performance errors the left coordinate may or may not be identified with the community norm.

Crucial to the argument is the notion that orthographic structure is hierarchical, the orthographic representation inheriting the c-structure of the phonological representation (cf. Luelsdorff 1985). The inherited c-structure is then used as a basis for pairs of trees whose structure reflects the constraints on error variables (cf. Luelsdorff 1986, chs. I-VIII).

Precise definitions of the error types $\bar{T}$ - $\bar{S}$, the analogues of T - S, are formulated and it is then shown that the constituent structure of errors yields, as a rule, finer stratification and less ambiguity. Furthermore, it is demonstrated that constituent analysis bears a direct relation to elementary transformations of grammatical rules. A distinction between errors of primary and errors of secondary character is drawn, the former resulting from a deviation from elementary grammatical rules, the latter from non-basic grammatical rules.

In section 3 (Rank hierarchy) we introduce the notion of rank hierarchy, where by the rank of a transposition (A_1, A_2) we mean the distance between a and b within A. Iterated transpositions of rank 2 are just those of a primary character. This distinction between error types and distances should be supplemented by the development of the *modus errans et corrigens*, i.e. the theory of linguistic error and repair (cf. Luelsdorff 1986).

Processing Strategies in Bilingual Spellers*

Introduction

This study and the study on which it is based deviate in four major respects from the norm for the study of spelling errors. First, they are studies of target-language, rather than native-language, spelling errors. Second, they are based on not only an inquiry into the number of misspellings and the number of different forms of misspelling, but also an investigation of types of misspelling and their causes. Third, the corpus consists of words misspelled to dictation of sentences at grade-level, rather than above grade-level. Fourth, they are rooted in in-depth, single-subject investigations which yield a misspelling profile for a single informant, rather than characteristics of the misspelling behaviour of a group, rooted in the notion that the locus of language is the individual (Luelsdorff 1982), rather than the community, although the two intricately interact.

This chapter presents a summary statement of the major, but by no means only, processing strategies which are held to underlie and explain the 977 vowel and consonant "substitution" errors - excluding those found in the *conduits d'approche* - detected in 6,162 words of English dictation administered over a 14-month period to a 12-year-old male second-year student of English in a German *Hauptschule* in Regensburg, the capital of the Upper-Palatinate in Bavaria. Bernhard and I met once, sometimes twice a week for a period of from 1/2 to 3/4 of an hour, with lessons focussing on dictation from his first and second year English textbooks *English H 1* and *English H 2* (Friedrichs 1970, 1971) and composition, in this case writing letter to a pen-friend in the United-States, Lisa, from Tuscumbia, Alabama, age 14. Bernhard was failing English, although he was doing very well in most of his other subjects, especially math, and was referred to me by his parents for remedial work. His main problem with English seemed to me to be his inability to concentrate, although others remarked that he could concentrate if he wanted to. My own experience with Bernard was that he was often distracted, forgetting pens, pencils, books, notebooks, and appointments, and insofar as his dictations were concerned, frustratingly absent-minded, often forgetting to do his homework, which typically consisted in reading the passage to be dictated and writing 5-50 times words which he had misspelled. Especially exasperating was Bernhard's tendency to persist in misspelling words which he had just written, sometimes as many as 5-50 times. The dictation procedure followed the recommendations of Deyes (1972b), namely, reading the text three times:

(1)   When the dictation is given, the pupil should listen in order to get a general idea of its content without writing;

(2)   When the dictation is to be written, the teacher should divide the text into convenient groups of four or five words each. They must be read, however, as connected groups and not as separate words;

(3)   The teacher has to be careful to use the weak forms of *can, to, at, of,* etc., when the context calls for them;

(4)   The third reading should be done at the same speed as the first reading, but with breaks at the end of every sentence or two sentences. In this case the students have time to correct a sentence just read without being distracted by the need to listen to the next sentence at the same time.

Since my interest was not only in helping Bernhard overcome his deficiencies in English orthography but also in ascertaining the causes of these deficiencies, Deyes' further recommendation of a fourth reading with the students' having a copy of the correct text in hand was not adopted, since this fourth step would have obviously led to the staggering of the statistics on the *conduits d'approche.*

The study of vowel and consonant "substitution" (see below) errors is a major part of a larger study of putative "transpositions", errors of addition and omission, errors of anticipation and perseveration, and orthographic *conduits d'approche.* The fundamental distinction between errors of substitution, on the one hand, and errors of displacement, transposition, addition and omission, on the other, justifies their being the exclusive subject of discussion in this summary statement of processing strategies, where segments are subordinated to strategies, rather than strategies to segments. Compared with the results of studies of the spelling performance of different categories of monolingual and bilingual learners conducted within an identical framework, the conclusions drawn in these investigations could be used to determine those error types which are characteristic of the class of German learners of English as a whole; could serve as a basis for a general typology of orthographic errors in English made by foreign learners; could contribute to a general theory of orthographic error; take a step in the direction of the study of the acquisition of spelling skills by Germans and bilinguals in general; and they could be used as a basis for the development of materials for teaching the structure of English orthography to Germans and others designed to prevent and remediate errors potential and actual.

Drawing on Chomsky and Halle (1965), we sharply distinguish among three levels of adequacy in the study of errors, the observational, the descriptive, and the explanatory. The first, temporally and logically, entails the observation of a set of deviations between the form produced and the community production norm, noting, for example, that the suffix in *appearence* is spelled with an <e>, as opposed to the community-normative *appearance*, in which the suffix is spelled with an <a>. The second, the description of errors entails a statement of the correct relationship between the discrepant production and the community norm. In the above example, the second <e> in the deviant production is said to *correspond* to the third <a> in the norm. Notice that it would be incorrect to conceptualize the relationship between deviant <e> and normative <a> as one of *substitution*, since substitution, either conscious or subconscious, implies a processual view according to which normative <a> has been replaced by discrepant <e> which in the instance of a speller unaware of the normative spelling could in principle not be the case. Three reasons occur to us why an analyst might wish to consider an error of the above type an instantiation of a substitution operation. First, observation of the productions in an *independent* corpus in which normative <a> occurs, leading to the norm-centered view that non-normative <e> has been substituted for normative <a>. Second, the observation that <e> varies with <a> in the spelling productions of the informant. In the former case, the postulation of <e> as the deviate of <a> violates what has been called the "Independence Principle" (cf. Luelsdorff 1975), resulting in the assignment of a norm-deviate structure, namely <a> → <e>, which cannot be justified on the basis of observations of the productions of the informant viewed independently of the community norm. In the latter case, the relationship may be expressed by <a> ~ <e>, since the alternation under discussion is to be observed in the protocol for the informant in question. Since our interest in this study is in the nature and causes of deviant productions in the spelling of an incipient German/English bilingual speller who had had exposure to the British English spelling norms of the words he was required to spell in sentences to dictation, i.e. *the mechanisms involved in long- and short-term memory loss*, we view the deviations produced in terms of the processes of the addition, omission, substitution, and displacement of phoneme/grapheme correspondences in the norm as revelatory of the processes of *memory loss*, and in this sense as psychologically real, yielding an insight into the quality and quantity of those processes which should be accorded special attention in programs designed to prevent and remediate spelling errors, without concomitantly claiming that these processes are psychologically real in any sense other than the one intended, for example, that they were still active in the processing of the errors involved at the time the dictations were administered. The complementary, equally viable, approach, is to treat the erroneous products as functions in the application of non-standard GPCs assignable to different sets of processing strategies available to the language user, dispensing entirely, *from this perspective*, with the most misleading labels "substitution", "addition", "omission", "displacement", etc., and the concepts behind them, since, from this latter perspective, the introduction of such notions reflects incredible confusion. The importance of this difference in perspective cannot be overestimated. The third level of adequacy is the explanation of errors, entailing a statement of the cause(s) of the relationships yielded by the descriptive level of adequacy. In English orthography, for example, overgeneralization is fostered by system-internal irregularity such as the one-many phoneme/grapheme correspondence in

$$/w/ \rightarrow \left\{ \begin{matrix} <wh> \\ <w> \\ \cdot \\ \cdot \end{matrix} \right\}$$

whose failure to be committed to lexical memory explains why a spelling error of the type <w> for <wh>, as in <wich> for <which>, occurs. The importance of distinguishing between the description of an error and its explanation, between the mechanism by which it occurs and the cause of its occurrence, has been stressed in the most recent error-analytic literature (Cutler 1981), where it is claimed that statements of cause and statements of mechanism are logically independent and suggested (Cutler 1980) that whereas causes of errors might differ across languages, individuals and occasions, error mechanisms ought to be speaker- and language-universal.

1. Processing strategies

We proceed with an examination of the major types of processing strategies underlying the "substitution" errors in our corpus, using "substitution" in the above-qualified sense, as part of our ongoing attempt to specify the entire set of strategies employed by German learners of English.

1.1 *Letter-naming*

Recapitulating Luelsdorff (1984a), letter-naming, i.e. pronouncing the names of the letters of the alphabet, e.g. English <a> = [ei̯], <e> = [Ii̯], <i> = [ai̯], <o> = [oʊ̯], <u> = [ju̯], or German <a> = [aː], <e> = [eː], <i> = [iː], <o> = [oː], <u> = [uː] has been described as one of the devices characteristic of the invented spelling of young children (Read 1971, Schreiber and Read 1980, Cook 1981) where letter symbols are generated on the basis of preliterate children's phonetic analysis of the spoken word and their knowledge of the written alphabet and letter-names.

We place three conditions on a theory of letter-naming used as a strategy for spelling: (1) that the informant know the names of the letters; (2) that the names of the letters be either identical with, closely approximate, or contain the sounds of the words they are used to represent; and (3) that the letters do not correspond to those used in the standard spelling. (If the letters do correspond to those in the standard spelling, it is clearly impossible to distinguish between letter-naming used as a spelling strategy, on the one hand, and letter-sounding used as a spelling strategy, on the other.) We view this phenomenon as an overgeneralization of those instances where the names of the letters partially resemble the sounds the letters are used to legitimately represent, hence the abilities to (1) letter-name and (2) use letter-naming as a spelling strategy as constituent components of the spelling competence of the normal, fluent writer. Since this relationship is one of similarity between the sound of the letter-name and the sound of the words the letter-name or the sequence of letter-names is used to represent, it is echoic. Were this relationship completely regular, whereby the names of the letters were identical with the constituent sounds of the words, or the sounds of the words predictably derivable from the names of the letters, such as appears to be the case, or nearly the case, in Japanese *kana*, the orthography would be optimally echoic.

Clear examples of English letter-naming in the Bernhard corpus include the vowels <a>, <e>, <i>, and <u> (see Table 1).

Table 1. *English Letter-naming*

Vowel	Target	Attempt	Page
<a>	paints	pans	A 2(2)
<e>	Here	Her	A 6, A 9(2)
	jeans	jens	A 75
<i>	likes	liks	A 5
	nine	nin	A 9
<u>	juice	just	A 20

Unambiguous examples of German letter-naming include the letters <a>, <e>, <i> and <u> (Table 2).

Apparently interpretable as examples of either English or German letter-naming are English or German <o>, which were pronounced virtually the same by the person administering the dictations:

<o>	Toast	Tost	A 6
	bones	Bons	A 49

Table 2. *German Letter-naming*

Vowel	Target	Attempt	Page
<a>	John	Jan	A 14
<e>	cornflakes	cornfleks	A 2
	eighth	egth	A 11
<i>	evening	ivening	A 1
	sleeps	shlips	A 5
<u>	to	tu	A 9
	soup	sup	A 49

Lax /ɛ/ is misrepresented in 69% of the error tokens by either <a> or <e>. The high frequency of <a> appears all the more enigmatic, since *<a> → /ɛ/ is not a regular GPC in either English or German. We find a plausible explanation for <a> → /ɛ/ in an *extended* use of the concept of letter-name. Ordinarily, when one speaks of letter-naming used as a spelling strategy (cf. above) one refers to using a letter to represent a sound which is identical to the sound of the name of the letter, justifying the assertion that this phenomenon is based on the equation use = mention, where use is the letter-sound and mention is the letter-name, as in attempt: <spek> for target: <speak> or attempt: <spik> for target: <spike>. Were we now to center upon just those articulatory features which the name of the letter <a>, i.e. /e/, has in common with the target vowel /ɛ/, i.e. the intersection of the set of features defining /e/ with the set of features defining /ɛ/, thereby arriving at the archisegment /E/, we would find that /ɛ/ would be just as likely to be represented by <a> as would /e/, under a spelling strategy based on letter-naming. We do in fact find <a> → /e/, letter-naming used as a spelling strategy for /e/ (cf. Table 1). Succinctly stated, the data (cf. attempt: <whan> for target: <when> (A 78), attempt: <allrady> for target: <already> (A 89), attempt: <thar> for target: <there> (A 19), attempt: <sad> for target: <said> (A 96), attempt: <thar> for target: <their> (A 8)) dictate introducing in bilingual contexts the notion of *the place of articulation of a letter-name* as the basis of a spelling strategy in addition to letter-naming proper. This is not to claim that the informant perceptually identifies /ɛ/ with /e/, but that he judges them articulatorily sufficiently similar to assign them identical representa-

tions under a letter-naming strategy. It is also to claim that vowel similarity judgments assign priority to *place of articulation* (in this case front
central) over manner of articulation (in this case tense/lax), yielding the
prediction that /e/, for example, will be judged more similar to /ɛ/ than to
either /i/ or /ɪ/, a prediction borne out by the fact that <a> is not among
the 21 types of misrepresentations of /i/ and /ɪ/, with the sole exception
of the lone example <a> → /i/ in attempt: <plase> for target: <please>
which we analyzed as a slip of the pen.

Precisely this abstract sense of letter-naming as a spelling strategy
has been attested in studies of children's acquisition of their native
orthographies. In an investigation of developmental strategies of spelling
competence in primary school children, Beers (1980: 38-39), for example,
notes three and two stages in the acquisition of short <e> = /ɛ/ and short
<i> = /ɪ/, respectively:

A. Short <e> as in <met>
   (1) <a> for <e> - <gat> for <get>
   (2) <i> for <e> - <wint> for <went>
   (3) correct form

B. Short <i> as in <sit>
   (1) <e> for <i> - <mes> for <miss>
   (2) correct form

where (A1) and (B1) confirm place of articulation of letter-names as a
spelling strategy, which we have referred to above as "abstract" in the
sense that its effective utilization entails abstracting away from the tenseness vs. laxness which phonetically differentiates these vowels. Note that
(A2), <wint> for <went>, might have constituted a counterexample, since
the features distinguishing the letter-name of <i> (= /ay/) and /ɛ/ include
that of place of articulation, were it not for our suspicion that <went> is
typically pronounced [wɪnt] and not [wɛ=nt] in this part of the States, i.e
Laurel, Maryland, bordering on the south. Our suspicion is strengthened
by Beers' report (1980: 39) that <many> was spelled <mene>, <e> by
the author's own account (see above) constituting the first step in the
acquisition of the correct orthographic representation for short <i> (= /ɪ/),
cf. <mes> for <miss>.

Finally, we introduce the notion of a sequence of letter-names as a
spelling strategy. Not predicted by the interlinguistic transfer theory of

error is the representation <ou> for English /ow/, amply in evidence in the error data and exemplified as in Table 3.

Table 3.

Error Type	Frequency	Target	Attempt	Page
<ou> for <oa>	3	<Goal>	<Goul>	A 66(2)
<o>	3	<cold>	<could>	A 76
<ow>	2	<showed>	<shoud>	A 75(2)
<oCe>	1	<clothes>	<couse>	A 78

The transfer theory of error must be modified accordingly so as to include the principle that a native-language grapheme *sequence* may be used to represent a target-language sound even in the presence of native-language single graphemes corresponding to native-language phonemes similar to the target-language single phonemes to be represented should the combined phonetic effect of articulating the names of the graphemes in such a sequence be similar to the target-language sound under representation. Here by "native-language grapheme sequence" we do not mean only a sequence of graphemes adhering to the graphotactic conventions of the native language, such as German <ei, ai>, as in <Meister> 'master' and <Kaiser>, but also grapheme sequences, impermissible in the native language, whose composite pronunciation is roughly similar to the native language sound under representation such as *<ou> in native German vocabulary used as an invented spelling for English [oʊ], "invented" because although the informant had been exposed to some of the major and minor correspondences of the English secondary vowel pattern <ou/ow>, for example, [aʊ]: <mountain>, [ʌ]: <cousin>, [ʊ]: <could>, he had no introduction to the correspondence [oʊ] as in <cantaloup>, <shoulder>, <poultice>, <soul>, <thorough>, etc.

1.2 *Overgeneralization*

If <X> → /Y/ and <Z> → /Y/ in the standard orthography, where <X> ≠ <Z>, the use of <X> for <Z> constitutes an overgeneralization. Attempt

<Mery> for target: <Mary> (A 80) is an overgeneralization of the regular pattern for the representation of the checked alternate of English <e> to environments which intersect with those in which <e> regularly represents /i/. <or> → /ɜ:/ evidenced in attempt: <borstey> for target: <birthday> (A 9(2)) must be an overgeneralization of unstressed <or> → /ɜ:/, such as the agentive, to stressed syllables since the exceptional <or> → /ɜ:/ in stressed syllables is found in words which were not part of the informant's vocabulary, e.g., <borough>, <thorough>, and <worry>. Negative transfer from German is ruled out as a possible explanation for the use of <o> for either <a> or <oh>, as in attempt: <wont> for target: <want> (A 6) and attempt: <Jon> for target: <John> (A 14(2)) because there is no *<o> → /a/ GPC in German; the errors involved are attributable rather to the overgeneralization of the predictable major pattern for the checked alternate of English <o>, as in <conic>, <rob>, <possible>, etc., to cases which are unpredictable. Inasmuch as the misspellings exemplifying the use of <o> for either <a> or <oh> recur, and in the instance of attempt: <wont> for target: <want> (A 6) recur throughout the 14-month dictation period, we are dealing with a conventional error. We distinguish between (1) *lexical conventional errors* and (2) *rule-governed conventional errors*, the former referring to a consistently incorrect graphemic representation <G₁> → /P₁/ whereby there are other representations in the corpus <G₂> → /P₂/ where <G₁> ≠ <G₂>, the latter referring to the consistently incorrect graphemic representation <G₁> → /P₁/ for all occurrences of /P₁/. The conventional error attempt: <wont> for target: <want> for example, is a lexical conventional error, since /a/ (= P₁) is represented by <a> (= G₂) in attempt: <an> for target: <on>. Rule-governed conventional errors are unattested in the author's own field experience, but are in evidence in studies of the early acquisition of native orthographies (cf. Beers 1980 where short <e> [= /ɛ/] is consistently incorrectly represented by <a>, as in attempt: <gat> for target: <get>).

Regularization and irregularization are special instances of overgeneralization, the former referring to the overgeneralization of the predictable pattern to the unpredictable, the latter to the overgeneralization of the unpredictable pattern to the predictable. The qualitatively and quantitatively most frequent misrepresentation of /ɪ/ in our corpus consists in the use of <i> for <o>, <a>, <e> and <iCe>, as in attempt: <wimen> for target: <women> (A 55), attempt: <sausitches> for target: <sausages> (A

56), attempt: <pritty> for target: <pretty> (A 75(2)), and attempt: <givs> for target: <gives>. We interpret all of these instances of <i>-representation, with the exception of attempt: <wimen> for target: <women>, as regularizations to the checked alternate representations of the major pattern for the vowel /ɪ/, which, like the remainder of the primary vowel representations, corresponds to its checked alternate when followed by (1), a functionally compound consonant unit, e.g., <x, dg>, (2) a cluster of consonant units, e.g., <-nn, -lth> (<sausitches, pritty>) or (3) a word-final consonant unit or units (<givs>). <women>, analyzable into at least two morphemes, does not follow the pattern for the free alternate pronunciation of a primary spelling unit in monomorphemic words, in which case it would be pronounced [wóʊmən], is hence unique in its spelling. The informant's <wimen> is a closer approximation to its pronunciation, and <wimmen> would have been even closer, since, as noted above, the checked pronunciation occurs before word-internal *clusters*. Remarkable about the total set of misrepresentations of [e] is the fact that they are not restricted to misrepresentations of the unpredictable cases, 1/3 (17/51) misspelling the regular representation <aCe>, for example, attempt: <leate> for target: <late>. We thus note a strong tendency to *irregularize* the regular cases in addition to the intuitively more anticipatable but weaker tendency to regularize the irregular cases, for example, attempt: <stake> for target: <steak>. Interestingly enough, this latter strategy is restricted to the regularization of <ea>, suggesting the notion of a regularization-prone orthographic representation, but leaving unexplained why some irregular orthographic representations should be more regularization-prone than others. One hypothesis which readily suggests itself is that there is an inverse relationship between regularization-proneness and frequency of irregular spelling-type, but the testing of this hypothesis lies beyond the scope of this study. Suffice it to say, pending detailed investigation of this question, that /e/, together with /ɛ/, is a *minor* correspondence of the secondary vowel pattern <ea>, the major correspondence being /i/, while the major correspondence of both <ei/ey> and <ai/ay> is /e/. The hypothesis predicts that words of the type <break>, <great>, <steak>, and <yea>, containing the minor correspondence <ea> → /e/, will be more frequently regularized to sequences containing <aCe> than words of the type <abeyance>, <obey>, <reign>, and <veil>, on the one hand,

and <bait>, <day>, <player>, and <wait>, on the other, containing the major correspondences <ei/ey>, <ai/ay> → /e/, respectively.

Two further special cases of overgeneralization we term "simplification" and "complication", the former referring to the use of a major primary vowel pattern for a major secondary vowel pattern, the latter to the use of a major secondary vowel pattern for a major primary vowel pattern. Note that simplification and complication are not to be equated with regularization and irregularization, respectively, since both simplification and complication are regular, referring as they do to *major* patterns. The major correspondences of the secondary vowel patterns <ui> and <oo> are /(j)u/ and /u/, respectively. Hence, we interpret attempt: <juse> for target: <juice> (A 30) and attempt: <Pure> for target: <Poor> (A 92) as simplifications consisting in the assimilation of major secondary vowel patterns to a major primary vowel pattern. Of the error types characteristic of the misrepresentations of /ow/ we attribute the use of <oCe> for <oa>, as in attempt: <Prarkrode> (A 32) for target: <Park Road> to the overgeneralization of the major correspondence of the primary vowel pattern to the major correspondence of the secondary vowel pattern, hence to simplification, and the use of <oa> for <oCe>, as in attempt: <cload> for target: <clothes> (A 78) to the converse, i.e., the overgeneralization of the major correspondence of the secondary vowel pattern to the major correspondence of the primary vowel pattern, hence to complication. <f> for <gh>, as in attempt: <laft> for target: <laughed> (A 89), is a simplification - one letter for two - and a regularization - the representation of /f/ by regular <f>, rather than irregular <gh>.

1.3 *Transfer*

Our error corpus is replete with examples which support the transfer theory of error, which we regard as a necessary but by no means sufficient theory of errors encountered in the target language competence and performance of bi- and multilinguals (see below). We present several examples in the domain of vowel and consonant-letter substitution errors which support the transfer theory of error, and an extended example of a consonant error which does not. Several of the examples are illustrative of the "collaboration", or, better, "collusion", of several strategies held to account for the erroneous output.

Thirty-five per cent of the misspellings of English /i/, namely, <i> → /i/, as in attempt: <Hi> for target: <He> (A 36), attempt: <wir> for target: <We're> (A 70), attempt: <filds> for target: <fields> (A 7), attempt: <chise> for target: <cheese> (A 49), and attempt: <lori> for target: <lorry> (A 55), we interpret as resulting from the misemployment of the German GPC <i> → /i:/ transfer strategy, as in <dir>: [di:r] 'to you' or <mir>: [mi:R] 'to me', in English or misemploying the strategy of German letter-naming - the name of the German letter <i> is [i:] - in English, not excluding the possibility of these two strategies conspiring. A further 12% of the misspellings of English /i/, as in attempt:. <bie> for target: <be> (A 95) and attempt: <kiep> for target: <keep> (A 34) to the negative transfer of the GPC <ie> → /i:/ from German.

Renderings of <i> by <e> for /ɪ/, as in attempt: <thes> for target: <this> (A 6) and attempt: <sex> for target: <six> (A 17) although very few in number, are of theoretical interest. Since they are related to attempt: <wiesit> for target: <visit> (A 43), they will be discussed together. It is informally widely noted that English orthographic <i> is frequently pronounced [i:] by beginning German learners of English. This we trace to the fact that <i> is pronounced [i:] in a few frequent German monosyllabic words, e.g. <dir>: [di:R] and <mir>: [mi:R] glossed as above. Reading English as though it were German thus results in a pronunciation of <this> and <will> containing [i:], and this is indeed the way in which the informant pronounced these words, supporting our repeated observation that spelling errors cannot be understood unless the informants' actual pronunciations are taken into consideration as opposed to the standard pronunciation norms. Note that there is nothing necessary about the <i> → [i:] pronunciation in German, since <i> is also articulated [ɪ], namely before two consonants, as in <Kinder>: [kɪndəR] 'children' and in monosyllables, in fact most monosyllables, as in <mit>: [mɪt] 'with' and <in>: [ɪn] 'in', so that the negative transfer of <i> → [i:] is the exercise of just one of two options. The pronunciations [zi:s] for <this> and [vi:l] for <will> we thus derive from German letter-naming and/or letter-sounding as a pronunciation strategy and the misspellings <thes> and <well> for <this> and <will> from English letter-naming as a spelling strategy. The misspelling attempt: <wiesit> for target: <visit> is relevant inasmuch as it is an unambiguous piece of orthographic evidence for the fact that there exists a German spelling-pronunciation in English words corresponding to the standard pronunciation [ɪ]. The important question of which factors, if any, enable one to predict whether [ɪ] will be correctly spelled, or misspelled as a product of English letter-naming based on German letter-naming/sounding in a given case, must, for lack of an adequate understanding of the processes involved, remain un-answered.

<t> is most frequently misrepresented by <d>, and then only post-tonically: <gardengad> for <garden gate> (A 9), <jamtords> for <jam-torts> (A 11), <god> for <got> (A 32(2)), <frond> for <front> (A 44), <mead> for <meat> (A 51), <wrid> for <write> (A 61), etc. We posit the combined effect of two processes in order to explain this all-pervasive post-tonic voicing: (1) the negative transfer of the German rule of syl-lable-final obstruent devoicing to English and (2) orthographic hypercor-rection consisting in the voiced misrepresentation of obstruents which are devoiced in standard. In order to show that the German rule of syllable-final obstruent devoicing is operant in the informant's English, we point to the observations that (1) standard English syllable-final obstruents are often phonetically devoiced and (2) this devoicing is very frequently reflected in the informant's English misspelling of standard voiced obstru-ents by letters corresponding to voiceless, e.g., <picturekat> for <picture card> (A 9), <fint> for <find> (A 11(2)), <salet> for <salad> (A 57), <pont> for <pound> (A 51), etc. Representations of the type voiceless consonant for voiced are in fact so frequent that the negative transfer of the German rule of syllable-final obstruent devoicing should be regarded as the primary process underlying the misrepresentation of the English voiced obstruents. The hypercorrection is explained by the informant's accommodating himself to his teacher's corrections of his misrepresenta-tion of voiced consonantism in pronunciation and spelling. It is conceiv-able that even at least some of the correct representations of the English voiced obstruents originate via this route - devoicing then hypercorrec-tion - resulting in the correct representations for the wrong reasons.

Of those misspellings of the past tense which are most plausible - <Vt>, <d>, and <t> - all are represented in the data:

<it> for <ed>: <paintit> for <painted>   (A 52)
<d> for <ed>: <colld> for <called>   (A 71)
<t> for <ed>: <laught> for <laughed>   (A 75(2))

The overwhelming majority of these misrepresentations may be accounted for by either phonetic spelling <Watcht> for <watched> [A 76]) or phonetic spelling subsequent to the negative transfer of the German rule of syllable-final obstruent devoicing (<inveitet> for <invited> [A 78]). It is the rare exception such as <Parkd> for <parked> (A 68) which cannot be completely accounted for by either. <Parkd> reflects only partial application of phonetic spelling, namely the omission of <e> from preterit <-ed>.

We point to a parallel between the misrepresentation of the preterit discussed above and a category of non-standard spelling which frequently appears in the writing of native speakers in kindergarten and the first and second grades, namely the use of <t> to render <ed> in the past tense form of certain verbs, namely just those which undergo vowel deletion and regressive assimilation (cf. Luelsdorff 1969), as in <likt> for <liked>, <lockt> for <looked>, <pikt> for <picked>, etc. (Gentry and Henderson 1980: 118).

Inasmuch as the regular correspondence of <t> and <d> are sounds which are contained in their letter-names, i.e. [t] in [ti:] and [d] in [di:], respectively, the phenomenon referred to above as "phonetic spelling" is also an example of letter-naming - phonetic spelling, letter-naming, and obstruent devoicing conspiring to yield the misrepresenting product.

We proceed to an extended example of a consonant error which the transfer theory of error does not explain, namely, the non-transfer of the German rule of consonant-doubling. In German the shortness of vowels is often designated by the doubling of the following consonant, as in *Pfiff* 'whistle', *Metall* 'metal', *Egge* 'harrow', *Gewitter* 'storm', *Paddel* 'paddle', *Schrott* 'scrap-metal', *Etappe* 'stage', etc. Were this German regularity transferred to English, it would facilitate spellings in which short vowels are followed by geminates and interfere with spellings in which short vowels are followed by single consonants. Since all of the examples of <t> for <tt> involve instances in which <t> is preceded by a *short* vowel, as in <beter> for <better>, <leters> for <letters>, <litel> for <little>, however, we clearly cannot attribute these misspellings to the negative transfer of the German consonant-doubling rule. Furthermore, since the misspellings *recur* and *persist* throughout the entire duration of the dictations, they also cannot be considered unmonitored slips of the pen. In view of these latter two features, recurrence and persistence, we relegate them to the category of conventional errors.

If erroneous consonant singling cannot be accounted for by negative transfer of the German rule of consonant-doubling, neither can erroneous consonant-doubling. The 4 cases of <mm> for <m>, e.g., <hammster> for <hamster> (A 5) and <Kammara> for <camera> (A 11(2)), may not be traced to the transfer of the German rule of consonant-doubling which requires the doubling of a consonant in stems ending in a consonant if the preceding vowel is short and stressed (<Scheffel> 'bushel', <Lappen> 'rag'), except <k> and <z>, which in such cases are written <ck> and <tz>, respectively (<Kuckuck> 'cuckoo', <Schwätzer> 'gossip'), although there are exceptions (cf. Schmidt and Volk 1976: 18-19), and even exceptions not among those listed as such (e.g., <Kanne> 'can', <Wanne> 'tub'), because more than one stem consonant follows <m> in <hamster> and <camera> ends in a vowel. As in the case of <mm> for <m>, the instances of <nn> for <n> also cannot be explained by the negative transfer of the consonant-doubling rule from German, since, in addition to cases which meet the structural description of the rule and are doubled (e.g., <runns> for <runs> (A 11)), there are cases which do not meet the structural description of the rule but which are doubled anyway (e.g., <evenning> for <evening> (A 2)), <dinning> for <dining> (A 2)) and cases which do meet the structural description of the rule but are not doubled (e.g., <runing> for <running> (A 72)). The examples of <nn> for <n> do however amply evidence total cognatization (see below), e.g. <winn> for <win> (A 65), cf. German *gewinnen* 'win', <beginn> for <begin>, cf. German *beginnen* 'begin', <Kann> for <can>, cf. German *kann* 'can', and the identification of English <when> with German <wenn> 'if', even though they differ in meaning.

By orthographic "cognatization" we understand the partial or total orthographic assimilation of a target cognate to the corresponding native language cognate. The four occurrences of <ch> for <gh> in <lauchs> for <laughs> exemplify partial cognatization where the misrepresentation of the target is a partial recapitulation of the spelling of the corresponding native-language cognate cf. German <lacht> 'laughs'. The two occurrences <shwans> for <swans> (A 76) and <schwam> for <swam> (A

89(2)) exhibit at once partial cognatization, with the English spelling <sh> of /š/ in the German initial cluster /šv/ and negative transfer of the German initial cluster /šv/, there being no initial /šw/-cluster in German. <Dezember> for <December> (A 66), on the other hand, instantiates total cognatization, cf. German *Dezember* 'December' as does <Preis> for <Prize>, cf. German *Preis* 'prize' (A 17). <ä> in attempt: <Bäter> for target: <better> clearly reflects negative transfer from German, where <ä> → /ɛ:/, as in *Bär* 'bear'. We do not regard <Bäter> as an instance of cognatization of English <better> to German <besser>, however, since (1) adjectives are not capitalized in German unless they are substantivized or occur in sentence-initial position, (2) German <besser> is written with an <e> in the stressed syllable, not an <ä>, and (3) cognatization would have entailed a representation with <-s-> or <-ss-> for English <-tt->. On the contrary, it rather dramatically illustrates what might be termed "decognatization", reflecting as it does a dissimilation of the standard representations of the respective cognates, and instantiates transfer only insofar as it contains the German vowel <ä>. The case of attempt: <prais> for target: <prize> (A 14(2)), where the vowel spelling in <prais> is the vowel spelling of neither the native nor the target representation, while the final consonant is that of the native, underscores the gradient, rather than categorial nature of cognatization as a processing strategy.

2. Summary and conclusion

Both orthography and the study of orthographic error have been grossly neglected in the linguistic literature, possibly traceable to the unjustified absence of an orthographic component in the more popular theories of grammar.

The major processing strategies are grouped as in the formal approach to error taxonomy given in Ch. 2, Table 1.

Although the corpus is replete with examples which support the transfer theory of error, which is thus a necessary subtheory of the theory of constraints on bi- and multilingual spelling errors, it is by no means sufficient.

Prideaux (1987) develops the thesis that a set of factors has emerged within psycholinguistics which reflects and highlights the earlier

Praguian concern with functional considerations, in particular, that the Prague School notion of "cooperation of means" has developed independently within psycholinguistics, and "that such 'means' as the psychological analogues of communicative dynamism, the role of context, and the importance of grammatical structure, along with specific processing heuristics, all interact as the language user goes about tasks of language comprehension and production". In the above, we have cited several independently motivated examples of how spelling strategies and strategies related to spelling conspire in written bilingual production, confirming the Praguian functionalist credo of the cooperation of means, the functional unity of orthographic rules.

Note

*   Orthographic representations are enclosed in angle brackets (< >), autonomous (unless otherwise noted) phonemic representations in slashes (/ /), and phonetic representations in square brackets ([ ]). 'GPC' abbreviates grapheme/phoneme correspondence, 'PGC' phoneme/grapheme correspondence, and an asterisk prefixed to either a GPC or a PGC stands for a non-correspondence in English or German, depending on the case.

Bilingual Intralinguistic Orthographic Interference

Introduction

The following remarks are intended as a refinement of our taxonomy of processing strategies leading to bilingual intralinguistic orthographic interference errors (Luelsdorff 1986; chapter 3, this volume). We begin with a brief discussion of the experiment used to elicit the data, proceed with a presentation and exemplification of the refined error framework, and conclude with a summary of three of the major conclusions reached.

1. The group experiment

Until 1983 our analysis had been an extensive and intensive inquiry into the spelling errors made in English by one native-speaking German pupil in the *Hauptschule*, grades 6 and 7, age 12, on grade-level English dictations administered privately over a 14-month period. This analysis indicated massive interlinguistic and intralinguistic interference. In order to assess the extent to which these interactions are shared, it was necessary to test a large number of subjects in the German school systems at various stages in the acquisition of English spelling. Pursuant to this goal, the following testing procedure was devised.[1]

1. Two groups of subjects were drawn from intact classes in both grades 7 and 9 in each of the three schooltypes comprising the German system of secondary education, the *Hauptschule* (H), the *Realschule* (R), and the *Gymnasium* (G). Within each grade and each school, one group was administered a grade-level dictation followed by an error-correction exercise. The other group was administered the same two tasks, but in the reverse order. 248 pupils were tested, 59 from H, 90 from R, and 99 from G. This procedure yielded data on the development of orthographic and metaorthographic processing strategies.

2. The grade-level dictations were administered in British English by the regular teachers of the respective classes in order to avoid the possible effect of an unfamiliar face in the classroom. Normally, dictation as a teaching device is discontinued by G9. The dictation procedure followed the recommendations of Deyes (1972a) and the words selected from the standard textbooks for H6/H7 (Friedrichs 1970, 1971) were known in advance to be error-prone from the errors in the individual data. All of the pupils had had prior exposure to all of the words dictated, except <juice, salad, store, gate, movie>, which were unfamiliar to the pupils in G. The dictation consisted of three short paragraphs, segmented into short phrases, which the teacher read aloud three times, before the dictation, during the dictation, and after the dictation. The pupils were asked to write on alternating lines of the response sheet and told not to make any corrections during their initial transcriptions. Allowance for corrections was made during the final reading by the teacher after the dictation had been written.

3. Following the initial writing, the pupils were asked to edit their own work by underlining the words they thought to be misspelled and writing the versions they thought to be correct beneath them. This yielded data on ego-errors and ego-corrigibility.

4. The error-correction exercise, which will be of no further concern to us here, was a written version of the dictation laden with many real errors extracted from the individual data. The errors ranged from obvious to subtle deviations from the standard spellings. Pupils were asked to listen to the dictation, scan the text for errors, underline the spellings thought to be errors, and transcribe the spelling thought to be correct under the spelling thought to be wrong. This yielded data on the pupils' ability to alter-monitor, to detect errors made by others.

The following is a report on the errors made only in the dictations, administered both before and after the error-correction exercise, after the pupils had had a chance to correct their errors. The discussion is restricted to vowel misspellings of the substitution type which are held to be the product of the use of intralinguistic orthographic processing strategies.

In general, our conclusions on processing strategies are thought to be valid only insofar as (1) the subjects had had prior exposure to the normative spellings of the words in the texts dictated and (2) the distribution of the major and minor primary and secondary vowel spelling patterns in the experience of the informants parallels their distribution in the language. Absolute certainty on this latter issue would require familiarity with the history of each informant's exposure to the spellings of each of the items dictated, a familiarity which we do not and could not have.

2. The error framework

Venezky (1970: 101-119) divides the vowel spellings of English into two groups or types, primary and secondary. Primary vowel spellings consist of *one* vowel letter (including <y>), whereas secondary vowel spellings consist of *two or more* (one of which may be <w> or <y>).

Both primary vowel spellings and secondary vowel spellings have major and minor sound correspondences, where the difference between major and minor sound correspondence is the difference between *more* and *less frequent*. Major correspondences are referred to as 'regular' or 'predictable', minor correspondences as 'irregular' or 'unpredictable', where regularity is sensitive to surrounding consonant and vowel letters, stress, and morphemic structure.

The above structure of English orthography we present in the diagram in Figure 1.

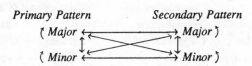

Figure 1. *The structure of English orthography*

Since each of the four resulting patterns - the major primary, the minor primary, the major secondary, and the minor secondary - has its own unique characteristic structure, including letters, sound correspondences, distribution, and frequency, we regard each pattern as constituting a module, each module containing a unique set of grapheme-phoneme correspondences.

Errors of substitution occur when two different members of the same module are substituted for one another or when a member of one module is substituted for a member of another. All of the possible substitution error types are presented in the diagram in Fig. 1, where x → Y is to be read: 'X is substituted for Y'. In our individual study (cf. Luelsdorff 1986) and in the following our understanding of regularity and irregularity is based on Venezky (1970) and Wełna (1982).

Inter- and intramodular interaction yields the following 16 substitution error types, listed and exemplified in Table 1.

Table 1. *Intralinguistic substitution error types*

Error Type	Attempt	Target
1. Primary Regularization	\<Camebridge\>	\<Cambridge\>
2. Primary Reregularization	\<jame\>	\<jam\>
3. Primary Irregularization	\<sommer\>	\<summer\>
4. Primary Re-irregularization	\<pollover\>	\<pullover\>
5. Secondary Regularization	\<braught\>	\<brought\>
6. Secondary Reregularization	\<enjoied\>	\<enjoyed\>
7. Secondary Irregularization	\<movey\>	\<movie\>
8. Secondary Re-irregularization	\<broaght\>	\<brought\>
9. Regularization cum Simplification	\<wer\>	\<wear\>
10. Reregularization cum Simplification	\<movi\>	\<movie\>
11. Irregularization cum Simplification	\<pice\>	\<piece\>
12. Re-irregularization cum Simplification	\<laghe\>	\<laugh\>
13. Regularization cum Complication	\<Caimbridge\>	\<Cambridge\>
14. Reregularization cum Complication	\<geit\>	\<gate\>
15. Irregularization cum Complication	\<coulled\>	\<called\>
16. Re-irregularization cum Complication	\<wear\>	\<were\>

1. *Primary Regularization* (Major Primary → Minor Primary). Primary Regularization refers to the substitution of a Major Primary pattern for a Minor Primary pattern. \<aCe\> is the Major Primary pattern for /e/ in \<came\> and \<a\> is the Minor Primary pattern for /e/ in \<Cambridge\>. Attempt: \<Camebridge\> for Target: \<Cambridge\> is therefore the substitution of a Major Primary pattern for a Minor Primary pattern, a Primary Regularization.

2. *Primary Reregularization* (Major Primary → Major Primary). Primary Reregularization refers to the substitution of a Major Primary pattern for another Major Primary pattern. <aCe> is the Major Primary pattern for /e/ in <came>, while <a> is the Major Primary pattern for /æ/ in <jam>. Attempt: <jame> for Target: <jam> is therefore the substitution of one Major Primary pattern for another Major Primary pattern, a Primary Reregularization.

3. *Primary Irregularization* (Minor Primary → Major Primary). Primary Irregularization refers to the substitution of a Minor Primary pattern for a Major Primary pattern. /ʌ/ is the Major correspondence of the Primary vowel pattern <u> when <u> is followed by a single consonantal, as in <fun, hut, cup>, or a consonantal cluster C_1C_2, where $C_1 \neq$ <r>, as in <summer, butter, custom>. /ʌ/ is the Minor correspondence of the Primary vowel pattern <o> when <o> occurs before <m, n, v>, <th>, and other consonantals, as in <comfort, son, another>. Thus, Attempt: <sommer> for Target: <summer> is the substitution of a Minor Primary pattern for a Major Primary, a Primary Irregularization, reinforced, in this case, by Partial Cognatization to German <Sommer>.

4. *Primary Re-irregularization* (Minor Primary → Minor Primary). Primary Re-irregularization refers to the substitution of a Minor Primary pattern for another Minor Primary pattern. /ʊ/ is the Minor correspondence of the Primary pattern <o> in apparently only <bosom> and <woman>. Since <u>:/ʊ/ is itself a Minor Primary pattern, Attempt: <pollover> for Target: <pullover> is the substitution of one Minor Primary pattern for another Minor Primary pattern, a Primary Re-irregularization.

5. *Secondary Regularization* (Major Secondary → Minor Secondary). Secondary Regularization refers to the substitution of a Major Secondary pattern for a Minor Secondary pattern. /ɔ/ is the Major correspondence of the Secondary pattern <au, aw>, as in <taught, craw> and the Minor correspondence of the Secondary pattern <ou>, as in <brought>. Attempts: <braught, brawght> for Target: <brought> are therefore substitutions of Major Secondary patterns for a Minor Secondary pattern, each a Secondary Regularization.

6. *Secondary Reregularization* (Major Secondary → Major Secondary). Secondary Reregularization refers to the substitution of a Major Secondary pattern for another Major Secondary pattern. <oi> for /oy/ is

written in morpheme-medial position, whereas <oy> for /oy/ is written morpheme-finally, with exceptions (e.g. <oyster, royal>, etc.). Attempt: <enjoied> for Target: <enjoyed> is thus the substitution of one Major Secondary pattern for another Major Secondary pattern, a Secondary Reregularization.

7. *Secondary Irregularization* (Minor Secondary → Major Secondary). Secondary Irregularization refers to the substitution of a Minor Secondary pattern for a Major Secondary pattern. The Secondary pattern <ey> has the Minor correspondence /i/ in words like <key> and <monkey>. The Major correspondence of Secondary <ie> is /i/, as in <achieve, niece>. Thus, Attempt: <movey> for Target: <movie> is the substitution of a Minor Secondary correspondence for a Major Secondary correspondence, a Secondary Irregularization.

8. *Secondary Re-irregularization* (Minor Secondary → Minor Secondary). The substitution of one Minor Secondary pattern for another Minor Secondary pattern constitutes a Secondary Re-irregularization. /ɔ/ is the Minor correspondence of the Secondary pattern <oa>, as in <broad, board, oar>, the Minor correspondence of <oo>, as in <door, floor>, and the Minor correspondence of the Secondary pattern <ou/ow>, as in <cough, trough>. Thus, Attempts: <broaght, brooght> for Target: <brought> exemplify the substitutions of Minor Secondary patterns for a Minor Secondary pattern, each a Secondary Re-irregularization.

9. *Regularization cum Simplification* (Major Primary → Minor Secondary). Regularization cum Simplification is the substitution of a Major Primary pattern for a Minor Secondary. /ɛ/ is the Major correspondence of the Primary pattern <e>, as in <let, bet, wet> and the Minor correspondence of the Secondary pattern <ea>, as in <wear, tear>. Attempt: <wer> for Target: <wear> is thus the substitution of a Major Primary pattern for a Minor Secondary pattern, an example of Regularization cum Simplification.

10. *Reregularization cum Simplification* (Major Primary → Major Secondary). Reregularization cum Simplification refers to the substitution of a Major Primary pattern for a Major Secondary. <i> and <y> most frequently correspond to /i/ in unstressed position, as in <taxi, city>. As noted above, the Major correspondence of the Secondary pattern <ie> is /i/, as in <achieve, piece>. Attempts: <movi, movy> for Target: <movie>

are thus examples of the substitution of a Major Primary pattern for a Major Secondary, Reregularization cum Simplification.

11. *Irregularization cum Simplification* (Minor Primary → Major Secondary). Irregularization cum Simplification is the substitution of a Minor Primary pattern for a Major Secondary pattern. The Minor correspondence of the Primary pattern <iCe> is /i/, as in <machine, ravine>, and the Major correspondence of the Secondary medial pattern <ie> is /i/, as in <achieve, piece>. Attempt: <pice> for Target: <piece> thus exemplifies the substitution of a Minor Primary pattern for a Major Secondary pattern, an Irregularization cum Simplification.

12. *Re-irregularization cum Simplification* (Minor Primary → Minor Secondary). Re-irregularization cum Simplification refers to the substitution of a Minor Primary pattern for a Minor Secondary. /a/ is the Minor correspondence of the Primary pattern <aCe>, as in <are, massage, corsage> and the Minor correspondence of the Secondary pattern <au>, as in <laugh>. Attempt: <laghe> for Target: <laugh> thus exemplifies the substitution of a Minor Primary pattern for a Minor Secondary pattern, a Re-irregularization cum Simplification.

13. *Regularization cum Complication* (Major Secondary → Minor Primary). Regularization cum Complication refers to the substitution of a Major Secondary pattern for a Minor Primary. /e/ is the Major correspondence of the Secondary pattern <ai>, as in <wait, rain> and the Minor correspondence of the Primary pattern <a>, as in <Cambridge>. Attempt: <Caimbridge> for Target: <Cambridge> thus illustrates the substitution of a Major Secondary pattern for a Minor Primary pattern, a Regularization cum Complication.

14. *Reregularization cum Complication* (Major Secondary → Major Primary). Reregularization cum Complication refers to the substitution of a Major Secondary pattern for a Major Primary. /e/ is the Major correspondence of the Secondary pattern <ei>, as in <weight>, and the Major correspondence of the Primary pattern <aCV>, as in <potato>. Attempts: <geit, poteito> for Targets: <gate, potato> are therefore examples of the substitution of a Major Secondary pattern for a Major Primary, Reregularization cum Complication.

15. *Irregularization cum Complication* (Minor Secondary → Major Primary). Irregularization cum Complication refers to the substitution of a Minor Secondary pattern for a Major Primary. /ɔ/ is the Minor correspon-

dence of the Secondary pattern <ou/ow>, as in <c<u>ou</u>gh, tr<u>ou</u>gh> and the Major correspondence of the Primary pattern <a> directly after <w>, as in <w<u>a</u>nt, w<u>a</u>sh, w<u>a</u>tch>, and before a final or preconsonantal <l>, as in <c<u>a</u>ll, s<u>a</u>lt, w<u>a</u>lk>. Thus, Attempt: <c<u>ou</u>lled> for Target: <c<u>a</u>lled> illustrates the substitution of a Minor Secondary pattern for a Major Primary pattern, as Irregularization cum Complication.

16. *Re-irregularization cum Complication* (Minor Secondary → Minor Primary). Re-irregularization cum Complication refers to the substitution of a Minor Secondary pattern for a Minor Primary. /ɜ:/ corresponds regularly to <ea> before <r> followed by a consonantal, as in <p<u>ea</u>rl, h<u>ea</u>rd, s<u>ea</u>rch> and is the Minor correspondence of Secondary <ea>, as in <y<u>ea</u>r>. Moreover, /ɜ:/ is a Minor correspondence of Primary <e> in <w<u>e</u>re>. Attempt: <w<u>ea</u>r> for Target: <w<u>e</u>re> thus exemplifies the substitution of a Minor Secondary pattern for a Minor Primary, a Re-irregularization cum Complication.

3. Some conclusions

We have presented a description of our group experiment used to elicit our error data and a finely graded taxonomy of the processing strategies held to underlie the intralinguistic vowel spelling errors of the substitution type. We end with a brief summary of three of the major conclusions reached.

1. The same sound in different words may be spelling-error prone in different ways. The /ɔ/ in <walk>, for example, was misspelled <oo, o, oa, Acce>, while the /ɔ/ in <called> was misspelled <ou, o, au, oa>. Moreover, the same sound with the same normative spelling may be spelling-error prone in different ways in different words. For example, the /o/ in <woke>, with the normative spelling <oCe>, was misspelled <ooC, oC, ouC, oaC, owC, a(C)C, uCC, oo, e>, while the /o/ in <wrote>, with the same normative spelling <oCe>, was misspelled <ou, oa, o, oo, oe>. Furthermore, the same normative spellings of different sounds in different words may be spelling-error prone in different ways. For example, the <ie> for /i/ in <piece> was misspelled <eaCe, iC(C)e, ie, ea, ee, eCe, eeCe, e>, while the <ie> for /ɛ/ in <girlfriend> was misspelled <e, ee, i, eeCe, ae>. Finally, even in those cases where the set of spelling-error

types for a vowel in one word is properly included in the set of spelling-error types for the same vowel in a different word, the members of each set of spelling error types for each word may exhibit different absolute frequencies and these frequencies may appear in different ranks. For example, the set of misspellings of the /i/ in <cheese> is properly included in the set of misspellings of the /i/ in <piece>, but whereas <ee> is the most frequent misspelling of the /i/ in <cheese> (18.78%), it is the fifth most frequent misspelling of the /i/ in <piece> (.81%).

These (rather discouraging) observations lead us to conclude that it is not just sounds, nor just letters, nor even letter-sound correspondences, which are misspelling-prone in certain ways, but letter-sound correspondences *in individual words*. This we refer to as the "word-effect for spelling errors".

2. Statements of the form 'X is substituted for Y by means of the processing strategy Z', as in <uCe> is substituted for <uiCe> by means of Reregularization cum Simplification, miss an important generalization, in fact the most important generalization about errors of the substitution type. The fundamental fact about such errors is that any letter(s) X may be substituted for *any* letter(s) Y on the condition that X and Y stand for the *same sound* in the standard orthography. Casting this sufficient constraint on error variables of the substitution type in semiotic terms, the signifiants of two different signs may be substituted for one another if they have the same signifiés. Call this condition on substitution error variables the 'Identical *Signifié* Constraint'. We are thus left with the notion of the general operation of substitution (a *mechanism* in the terminology of this investigation) being subject to conditions or constraints (*processing strategies* in the terminology of this study), i.e. of rules or rule-like operations interacting with principles. On this theory, the substitution of letter-naming is subject to the constraint that the letter-sound be contained in the letter-name, i.e. that the letter X may be substituted for the letter Y if the signifiant of X (the letter-name) properly or improperly includes the *signifié* of Y (the letter-sound). The negative transfer of a native language GPC to the target language, on the same theory, is subject to the constraint that a native letter(s) X may be substituted for a target letter(s) Y if X and Y have identical or similar *signifiés*. Thus viewed, the development of spelling skills is the development of condi-

tions on rules, some conditions becoming less general, others more general, some added, others lifted.

The 'Identical *Signifié* Constraint' must be supplemented with two additional minor, but important, constraints, called the 'Near Neighbor Constraint' and the 'Close Relative Constraint', both with domains in interlingual, rather than intralingual transfer. For the details, I refer the interested party to *Constraints on error variables in grammar* (Luelsdorff 1986).

3. Several recent models of English contain two routes to oral reading, called the *lexical* and the *non-lexical* (Coltheart 1984: 68-69). On the lexical route, a word-specific input letter pattern is matched with the same word-specific letter pattern in the mental lexicon and associated with its phonological representation. On the non-lexical route, letter patterns serve as the input to a set of regular grapheme-phoneme correspondences whose successive applications assemble the pronunciations of the graphemically parsed strings.

Henderson (1984: 2-4) points out that the distinction between a lexical and a non-lexical route to oral reading is based on the dichotomization of the English vocabulary into *regular* and *exception* words, where a word is regular if its pronunciation is predictable from its spelling by means of the most frequently occurring GPCs in the language. According to the dual-route hypothesis, irregular words or irregular portions of words are read orally on the lexical route, whereas pseudowords, regular words, or regular portions of words or pseudowords are read orally on the non-lexical, rule-governed route.

Now, were one to apply the dual-route hypothesis to spelling, then pseudowords, regular words and sounds with regular letter correspondences would be processed non-lexically, i.e. by means of PGCs, while irregularly spelled words or sounds with exceptional letter correspondences would be processed lexically, in a manner that is word specific. While this hypothesis predicts the occurrence of spelling errors of the reregularization type, it fails to predict errors of regularization, irregularization, and re-irregularization, however, because, on this hypothesis, irregular spelling patterns are *lexical*, not rule-governed, i.e. word-specific, not rule-general. The abundance of spelling errors of regularization, irregularization, and re-irregularization, however, argues strongly against the hypothesis of a dual-route to spelling and strongly in favor of the hypothesis that irregularly spelled words, like regularly spelled words, are spelled by means of rules, i.e. PGCs. On this hypothesis, the difference between spelling a regular and an irregular word is not that the former is rule-governed, and the latter lexical, but that the former is word-general, i.e. controlled by processes affecting the majority of the occurrences of the sound-type being spelled, and the latter word-specific, i.e. controlled by processes affecting the minority of the occurrences of the sound-type being spelled, with both regular and irregular spellings being rule-governed. Since this latter hypothesis - call it the 'Dual Word Hypothesis' - predicts errors of regularization, irregularization, and re-irregularization, in addition, of course, to errors of reregularization, i.e. all and only the substitution error types in this investigation, we consider it confirmed.

The Dual Word Hypothesis on spelling may have implications for the Dual Route Hypothesis on reading. If, for example, spelled pseudowords are orally read irregularly, say <preat> as [pret], it must mean that they are being read via a non-lexical route. But if a reader is reading pseudowords via the non-lexical route, it must mean that the irregular spellings themselves are not lexical, but rule-governed.

Note

1.   Thanks are due to Wm.J. Baker for discussion leading to the design of this experiment.

The Complexity Hypothesis and Graphemic Ambiguity

Philip A. Luelsdorff and E. Ann Eyland

Systemic deviation from phoneme-grapheme biuniqueness is a major source of error in the acquisition of a native or foreign alphabetic script. Such deviation is graphemically ambiguous if the relation between grapheme and phoneme is many-to-one and phonetically ambiguous if the relationship between grapheme and phoneme is one-to-many. Previous research has shown that the acquisitional order of the resolution of phonetic ambiguity is predictable on the basis of the degree of complexity of the relation between orthography and phonology in the case of German learners of English. The present study shows that the acquisitional order of the resolution of graphemic ambiguity follows the same pattern for the same population. Although German and English have similar rules of consonant singling and doubling, it is shown that German pupils acquire English consonant doubling later than English consonant singling and later before some suffixes than before others. It is argued that these differential acquisitional orders cannot be explained by transfer but by the fact that consonant doubling is more complex than consonant singling and the hypothesis that different doubling rules are acquired for different suffixes.

1. Introduction

1.1 Review of the literature

According to the alphabetic principle, graphemes stand for phonemes. In the ideal case, for every grapheme there is a phoneme, and for every phoneme there is a grapheme. We call such an unambiguous case "biunique". Real alphabetic scripts, however, deviate from biuniqueness to a greater or lesser extent, and such deviation is the major cause of errors in the acquisition of a native or foreign alphabetic orthography.

Orthographic deviations from biuniqueness have been divided into two major types: graphemic ambiguity (Bierwisch 1972: 75) and phonetic ambiguity (Luelsdorff 1987a). A phonetic representation is considered graphemically ambiguous if, and only if, it has at least two graphemic representations. In German, graphemic ambiguities include <a, aa, ah> for /a:/, as in <R<u>a</u>t, S<u>aa</u>l, Z<u>ah</u>l> and <ch, g, k, ck> for /k/, as in <Wa<u>ch</u>s, Teig, <u>K</u>ind, A<u>ck</u>er> (Sommerfeldt *et al.* 1981: 254-255), and such ambiguity has been shown to be a source of frequent error, as in <das> for <daß>, <krigt> for <kriegt>, and <Ermel> for <Ärmel> (Menzel 1985: 12). On the other hand, a graphemic representation is considered phonetically ambiguous if, and only if, it has at least two phonetic representations. In English, phonetic ambiguity is found in homographs, like <P<u>o</u>lish, p<u>o</u>lish>, in prefixes like <tele->, as in <tel<u>e</u>graph, tel<u>e</u>graphy>, in the roots of some derivationally related words, such as <sinc<u>e</u>re, sinc<u>e</u>rity>, and in the spelling of inflectional morphemes, such as possessive <'s>, as in <Ross'<u>s</u>, Jack'<u>s</u>, John'<u>s</u>>.

In a study of the acquisition of the <-ed> spelling of the *phonetically ambiguous* English regular past tense morpheme (Luelsdorff 1987a) we found fairly consistently better performance on /ɪd/ than on /d/ and on /d/ than on /t/. In order to explain this distribution we advanced the Complexity Hypothesis according to which orthographic representations which are less complex are acquired earlier than those which are more complex, where complexity is measured in terms of the number of nodes required to relate the orthographic representations to the phonetic. We thus have some evidence in support of the view that the acquisition of the orthographic resolution of phonetic ambiguity is controlled by a hierarchy of complexity.

1.2 *Purpose*

This study is an exploration of the acquisition of the spelling of *graphemically ambiguous* English consonants by German learners of English in the German school systems. In both German and English a consonant sound is orthographically either singled or doubled depending on the environment in which it occurs. After surveying the facts of consonant doubling in German an English, describing our experiment and stating the hypotheses on which it was based, we present results suggesting that the resolution of graphemic ambiguity, like the resolution of phonetic ambiguity, is controlled by a hierarchy of complexity.

2. Consonant doubling in German and English

In this section we survey the basic facts of consonant doubling in German and English, relying on Mentrup (1981: 21-22) for German and Venezky (1970: 106 fn.) for English.

2.1 German consonant doubling

In German a consonant sound is spelled with doubled consonantal letters if it follows a vowel sound which is (1) short and (2) in most cases stressed, (3) unless it occurs in a consonant cluster within the stem. <ck> is written instead of <kk> and <tz> instead of <zz>. We thus have <robben> 'to crawl', <buddeln> 'to dig', <hemmen> 'to slow down', <blicken> 'to glance', <ritzen> 'to scratch', in which the doubled consonantal letter occurs after a stressed short vowel, but <Gunst> 'favor', <Hast> 'haste', <Wirt> 'landlord', <Zapfen> 'stopper', in which the consonant following the short stressed vowel is a term in a stem-internal cluster, and <renn + st> 'runs (2sg)', <dünn + ste> 'thinnest', <kann + st> 'can (2sg)', in which the consonant following the stressed short vowel ends the stem. Exceptions include: (1) a group of monosyllabic words, e.g. <ab> 'from', <an, am> 'on', <um> 'at', <zur> 'to'; (2) several old words like <Brombeere> 'blackberry', <Himbeere> 'raspberry', <Herberge> 'lodging', <Herzog> 'duke', <Lorbeer> 'laurel'; (3) many foreign words like <Offizíer> 'officer', <Billíon> 'trillion', in which consonantal letters are doubled after a vowel which is unstressed, and <Ánanas> 'pineapple', <Chéf> 'boss' and <Jánuar> 'January', in which consonantal letters are not doubled after a vowel which is stressed.

2.2 *English consonant doubling*

According to one version of English consonant doubling (Reid and Hresko 1981: 268), there are two rules for the doubling of final consonants, one for monosyllabic stems, the other for stems which are polysyllabic, where the terms 'consonant' and 'vowel' refer to letters, not sounds:

> *Rule 1:*
> Words of one syllable ending in one consonant after one vowel double the final consonant before a suffix beginning with a vowel, but do not double it when the suffix begins with a consonant: *bigger, biggest,* but *bigness.*

> *Rule 2:*
> Words of more than one syllable, ending in one consonant after one vowel, double the final consonant before a suffix beginning with a vowel, if the main stress is on the final syllable: *begín, begínning,* but *open, opening.*

Venezky (1970: 106 fn.) notes that exceptions to the rule of consonant gemination are plentiful and that usage is divided on whether or not to double final \<l\>. He further notes that geminate consonants frequently occur medially and finally after the primary spellings \<a, e, i, o, u\>, in which case the primary vowel spellings correspond as a rule to their checked alternates, as in \<a̱bbess\>, \<be̱ggar\>, \<bli̱zzard\>, \<co̱llar\>, \<bu̱tton\>, and \<a̱dd\>, \<e̱bb\>, \<whi̱rr\>, \<boyco̱tt\>, and \<fu̱zz\>.

Note that the proper application of both the German rule and the English rule requires simultaneous discrimination of quite similar elements. Correct application of the German rule presupposes the ability to simultaneously distinguish (1) short and long vowels, (2) stressed and unstressed vowels, (3) single consonants and consonant clusters, and (4) stem-internal and stem-external clusters. Similarly, correct application of the English rule presupposes the ability to simultaneously distinguish (1) simple vowel letters from digraphs, (2) stressed from unstressed vowels, (3) single consonant letters from consonant-letter clusters, and (4) stems from suffixes.

Moreover, the conditions on the application of consonant doubling in German and English are similar in that both rules apply after short stressed vowels. German consonant doubling is more general, however, in that it applies after short stressed vowels everywhere, not just in the environment of a following vowel-initial suffix, unless the consonant is the first term in a stem-internal cluster.

Previous investigations indicate that L1-German learners have difficulties with the acquisition of both German and English consonant doubling, the large number of errors bearing witness to the complexity of the trees involved. Menzel (1985: 12), in an investigation of over 20,000 spelling errors made by German school children, reports that 8.6% of the errors made involve either single consonants for double <nim + t, fäl + t> or double consonants for single <bekamm, darann>. Luelsdorff (1986: 125), in a study of the constraints on spelling errors made by L1-German learners of English, notes many cases of improper consonant doubling and singling and concludes that such errors cannot be explained by the negative transfer of the consonant-doubling rule from German, since, in addition to cases which meet the structural description of the rule and are doubled (<runns> for <runs>, there are instances which do not meet the structural description of the rule but are doubled anyway (<evenning> for <evening>, <dinning> for <dining>) and instances which do meet the structural description of the rule but are not doubled (<runing> for <running>).

3. Method

3.1 Subjects

The subjects for this experiment were 525 German pupils taking English as a foreign language in regular, intact classes in each of the grades of each of the schools comprising the German system of secondary education, the *Hauptschule* (H), the *Realschule* (R), and the *Gymnasium* (G). The distribution of the cases for this study by grade, school system, and sex is given in Table 1.

Table 1. *Distribution of cases*

Grade	Hauptschule		Realschule		Gymnasium	
	M	F	M	F	M	F
5	7	6	-	-	37	20
6	8	5	-	-	19	11
7	8	11	-	28	18	16
8	6	7	61	6	18	9
9	8	6	-	22	23	7
10	-	-	16	29	14	13
11	-	-	-	-	34	21
12	-	-	-	-	9	5
13	-	-	-	-	13	4
Total	37	35	77	85	185	106

Comparisons across sex were dispensed with due to the absence of male subjects in R7 and R9.

3.2 Design

According to the transfer theory of learning, the transfer of the German rules of consonant singling and consonant doubling to English should uniformly facilitate consonant singling and doubling in English in those environments which the rules of the two languages have in common. Several hypotheses emerge.

According to the first hypothesis, there is a similarity between the orders of acquisition of (1) single consonants after long vowels and (2) doubled consonants after short vowels, since in both English and German a stem-final single consonant following a stressed vowel in the environment of a vowel-initial suffix remains single if the preceding vowel is long and doubles if the preceding vowel is short. *This hypothesis predicts, for example, that there are within-grade similarities for each of the grades in each of the school systems between (1) the spelling performances on <wading, dining, striped>, in which the consonants are not normatively* *doubled, and (2) the spelling performances on <humming, trimmed, flopped>, in which the consonants are normatively doubled.*

According to the second hypothesis, there is a similarity between the orders of acquisition of consonant doubling of stem-final single consonants after stressed short vowels before *different* vowel-initial suffixes, since in both English and German a stem-final single consonant following a stressed vowel in the environment of a vowel-initial suffix remains single if the preceding vowel is long and doubles if the preceding vowel is short. *This hypothesis predicts, for example, that there are within-grade similarities for each of the grades in each of the school systems between (1) the performance on consonant doubling in <trimmed, flopped>, in which the stem-final consonant doubles after a short stressed vowel before the vowel-initial suffix <-ed>, and (2) the performance on consonant doubling in <humming>, in which the stem-final consonant doubles after a short stressed vowel before the vowel-initial suffix <-ing>.*

3.3 *Materials*

The materials consisted in a portion of a 36-item word-list dictation designed to elicit data on the acquisition of the spelling of the long and short vowels (Luelsdorff and Eyland, forthcoming) derivationally related words, the past tense (Luelsdorff 1987a), and consonant doubling. The dictated items relevant to consonant-doubling acquisition - unfamiliar real words of very low frequencies - were <wading, dining, striped>, in which the stem-final consonants are not normatively doubled because the stem vowels, although stressed, are long, and <humming, trimmed, flopped>, in which the stem-final consonants are normatively doubled, because the stem vowels are both short and stressed, and the consonants precede suffixes beginning in vowels.

3.4 *Procedure*

The 36-item word-list dictation was administered to intact classes by the regular teachers in order to avoid the possible effect of an unfamiliar face in the classroom. The items were arranged in two lists of 18 items each and the teachers were instructed to dictate each of the items on each of the lists, in the sequence presented, beginning with list 1, to repeat each word twice and allow their pupils sufficient time to write their responses on the answer sheets provided.

4. Results

4.1 *Hypothesis 1*

In Figure 1 we compare pupils' performance on consonant doubling after short vowels in <humming, trimmed, flopped> with pupils' performance on consonant singling after long vowels in <wading, dining, striped> in each class in each school system. Note that performance is uniformly better in each grade on consonant singling than on consonant doubling and consonant doubling is uniformly better in G than in R and better in R than in H. Furthermore, with the exception of G8, R10, and G10, performance within each school system consistently improves from grade to grade. If hypothesis 1 is correct, then differences between the proportions of correct spellings on the singling and doubling tasks are due to chance fluctuations. A statistical model describing the pattern of changes can be used to test this hypothesis.

Inspection of the data immediately suggests that the hypothesis is incorrect, and this is confirmed by the fitted model (for details, cf. Appendix I). The model expresses the log-odds of being correct as a linear function of grade for each school-word type combination. Log-odds is the logarithm of the proportion correct to the proportion incorrect. Comparison of the singling model with the doubling model for each school indicates that, except for the senior years of the *Gymnasium*, performance on consonant singling after long vowels is superior to performance on consonant doubling after short vowels. The model confirms additional impressions. In the *Hauptschule*, consonant singling worsens with time, while consonant doubling improves. In the *Realschule*, there is very little improvement in time. In the *Gymnasium*, consonant singling is generally correct through all grades, and consonant doubling improves significantly with time.

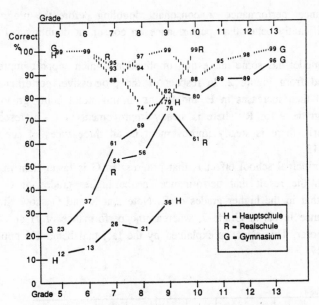

Figure 1.   *Consonant doubling after short vowels and consonant singling after long vowels*

...... = After long vowel ——— = After short vowel

4.2 *Hypothesis 2*

In Figure 2 we compare pupils' performance on consonant doubling before preterit <-ed> in <trimmed, flopped> with pupils' performance on consonant doubling before progressive <-ing> in <humming> in each class in each school system. Note that performance before <-ing> is consistently superior to that before <-ed> in H and R, with the exception of H/R9, and in G5-8.

In order to decide if the differences between doubling before the progressive and doubling before the preterit can be explained in terms of chance fluctuations in sampling, we modelled the log-odds of being correct in terms of grade, school type, and word type. The best model is set out in Appendix II. If hypothesis 2 is correct, then the type of ending (progressive vs. preterit) should not make a significant contribution to the model. In point of fact, however, the type of ending has the most impact on performance: performance on consonant doubling before the progressive is significantly better than performance on consonant doubling before the preterit.

The model has some interesting implications which support impressions derived from Figure 2. In respect of the progressive, performance declines and then increases in H and R, the turning point being grade 6 for H and grade 9 for R. There is steady improvement in G. In respect of the preterit, there is steady improvement in all three types of school until G11-G13.

The principal school effect is that progress in G is faster than in H and R, with the result that performance in the higher grades of G is superior to that in the higher grades of R. Note that R and G show similar performance levels at Grade 7, whereas the performance of H at 7 is markedly poorer. This effect is explained by the fact that better H6 pupils may enter R7.

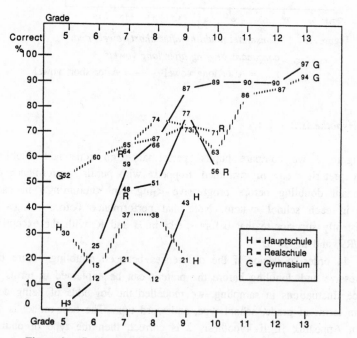

Figure 2. *Consonant doubling: preterit vs. progressive*
..... = Before progressive   —— = Before preterit

5. Discussion

5.1 *Hypothesis 1*

The single most important conclusion to emerge from a comparison of the data presented in Figure 1 is that consonant doubling is acquired later than consonant singling uniformly in each grade in each school system. This conclusion contradicts the prediction of *transfer theory* according to which English consonant singling and doubling should be acquired by native writers of German with equal ease, since, in the environments studied, the German consonants are also orthographically singled and doubled. These observations require an explanation.

We noted above that German school children experience difficulty with the acquisition of even German consonant singling and doubling, writing doubled consonants for single and single consonants for doubled at the same time they are acquiring the corresponding rules for English. After errors in capitalization (25.38%), misspelling of inflectional endings (12.50%), and the mutual confounding of <das> and <daß> (9.22%), errors in consonant singling and doubling (8.59%) are among the most frequent native misspellings of German, with single consonants for double (5.83%) over twice as frequent as double consonants for single (2.76%). This testifies to the relative complexity of doubling as opposed to singling in both L1-German and L2-English irrespective of the similarity in the rules of the two languages involved.

There are several reasons for this observed acquisitional complexity, each having to do with the nature of the orthography/phonology interface in German and English.

First, in both languages there is a phonetic basis for singling, but no such basis for doubling: single consonant sounds are spelled with a single consonant letter after long vowels, whereas single consonant sounds after a short vowel are spelled with a double consonant letter. In the first case the relationship is 1:1, in the second it is 1:2, the former unmarked, the latter marked. Thus, consonant doubling is acquired later than consonant singling, because doubling is marked, whereas singling is unmarked.

Second, the typical relationship between sound and letter is linear, with temporally earlier sounds represented by letters to the left and temporally later sounds represented by letters to the right. While this direct relationship is observed by consonant singling, it is violated by consonant doubling. For example the temporal sequence of the sounds in /h + ʌ + m/ *hum* is directly reflected by the spatial array of the letters in <h + u + m>, but the temporal sequence of the sounds in /h + ʌ + m + ɪ + ŋ/ is indirectly reflected by the spatial array of the letters in <h + u + m + m + i + n + g>, since the fact that the stressed vowel, phonetically represented in second position, is short, is orthographically marked by the second <m>, which appears in fourth position. Hence, while consonant singling is linear consonant doubling is non-linear, the former unmarked, the latter marked. Consonant doubling is acquired later than consonant singling, because doubling is marked, singling unmarked. Incidentally, since orthographic doubling derives from information contained in the preceding vowel, we have an argument in support of grouping the vowel letter and following consonant letter(s) as constituent of the same construction, say, vowel letter nucleus and consonant letter offset as constituents of the construction orthographic rhyme.

Third, consonant doubling is more complex than consonant singling. Consonant singling involves the assignment of a single consonant letter to a single consonant sound, e.g. spelling the /m/ of *hum* by means of the letter <m>, expressible by means of the phoneme-grapheme correspondence /m/ → <m>. Consonant doubling, on the other hand, involves the doubling of a consonant letter obtained by the application of a phoneme-grapheme correspondence, e.g. doubling the <m> in <humming>, obtained as a result of the application of /m/ → <m> to yield <mm>, expressible by means of the grapheme-grapheme correspondence <m> → <mm> in a certain environment. Phoneme-grapheme correspondences are operations on phonemes which yield graphemes, while grapheme-grapheme correspondences are operations on graphemes which yield graphemes. Grapheme-grapheme correspondences are more abstract than phoneme-grapheme correspondences in that the proper operation of the former presupposes the proper operation of the latter and each operates on entities of a different type, the former graphemes, the latter phonemes.

Thus, on the basis of the above, consonant doubling is learned later than consonant singling because it lacks a phonetic basis, is non-linear, and metaorthographic, i.e. because it is more complex.

5.2 Hypothesis 2

The most important conclusions to emerge from a consideration of the data presented in Figure 2 are (1) performance on consonant doubling before <-ing> is on the whole superior to performance on consonant doubling before <-ed>, with the exceptions noted in § 3.2, and (2) doubling before <-ing> and doubling before <-ed> are independent. Both facts require an explanation.

An explanation for the superior performance on doubling before <-ing> suggests itself from a consideration of the instructional sequence in which the progressive and preterit are taught, namely, the progressive before the preterit. In H, for example, the present continuous is taught around the start of grade 5 (the first year of English), while the regular past is taught towards the end of grade 6 (the second year of English). This differential instructional sequencing accounts for the discrepancy in <-ing> and <-ed> performance in H5 (30% correct vs. 3% correct) and virtual identity in <-ing> and <-ed> performance in H6 (15% correct vs. 12% correct), but fails to explain the relatively superior performance on doubling before <-ed> in H/R9.

The independence of doubling before <-ing> and doubling before <-ed> appears to imply that, for the class of learners studied, there is not one doubling rule, but several. That is, if there were one doubling rule being acquired, depending on whether or not it was learned one would expect it either to be applied or not applied to an equal extent, which is clearly not the case except in grades G11-13 in which a single rule may be assumed. The existence of several doubling rules, say, one for the progressive, one for the comparative/superlative, one for the preterit, etc., makes especially good psycholinguistic sense in the context of teaching materials in which the relevant structures are so vastly discontiguous and the relevant spelling generalization never presented. We thus envision an acquisitional routine in which doubling is, at best, learned separately, without subsequent conflation of the rules in question until G11, around the age of 17.

6. Conclusion

Systemic deviation from phoneme-grapheme biuniqueness is responsible for many of the errors made in the acquisition of native and foreign alphabetic orthographies. Such deviation assumes two basic forms: phonetic ambiguity, in which there is a one-many relation between grapheme and phoneme, and graphemic ambiguity, in which the relation between grapheme and phoneme is many-one.

The resolution of phonetic ambiguity (Luelsdorff 1987a) observes an L2-acquisition order predictable by the degree of complexity of the relation between orthography and phonology. In the acquisition of English by German school children, for example, regular preterit <-ed>:/ɪd/ is learned before <-ed>:/d/, and <-ed>:/d/ is learned before <-ed>:/t/.

The resolution of graphemic ambiguity also observes an L2-acquisition order predictable by the degree of complexity of the phonology/orthography interface. German learners of English spelling, for example, acquire <C>:/C/ before <CC>:/C/ and <CC>:/C/ in the environment of <-ing> sooner than <CC>:/C/ in the environment of <-ed>.

The lack of correlation between performance on <C>:/C/ and <CC>:/C/ and between performance on <CC>:/C/ before <-ing> and <CC>:/C/ before <-ed>, in all but the most advanced classes of the *Gymnasium*, suggests that each term in each pair is governed by its own rule.

A contrastive analysis based on descriptions of English and German qua *language grammars* fails to predict these results, since the rules governing consonant doubling and singling in these two languages are very similar. Possibly, a transfer hypothesis based on the contrastive analysis of German and English qua *speaker grammars* would be more productive, especially since it is known that German consonant singling and doubling are native learner error-prone.

In addition to correlating L1-German and L2-English performance on consonant singling and doubling, further research must consider the fact that several word-final consonant clusters ending in /-t/ or /-d/ are two-ways ambiguous in word, as opposed to sentence, dictations: either they are intramorphemic, as in <past, pact>, or they are intermorphemic, as in <pass + ed, pack + ed>. Furthermore, there are intermorphemic word-final clusters in English, such as the /m + d/ in <humm + ed>, which may easily appear intramorphemic to L1-German learners of English, cf. German <Hemd> 'shirt'. In either case, such ambiguous clusters, especially if they appear in unfamiliar real words or possible non-words to dictation, may legitimately be interpreted by German and other learners of English as intramorphemic and the post-vocalic consonant spelled accordingly with a single rather than double consonant. In such instances, the experimenter must avoid the danger of categorizing such singled orthographic representations as errors in consonant doubling. This state of affairs speaks in favor of sentence dictations with unambiguous contextual cues on grammatical category or word dictations requiring subjects to categorize the items dictated. For a variety of reasons, the former alternative appears much more attractive.

A comprehensive contrastive analysis of consonant doubling in German and English would include all the environments in which consonants are normatively doubled - stem-medially, word-finally, and, for English, before all vowel-initial suffixes. Such promising areas for further research would shed additional light on the complexity hypothesis and graphemic ambiguity.

APPENDIX I

Model to assess Hypothesis 1

Response variable   = log (# correct spellings / # incorrect spellings)
Error distribution   = binomial

Parameter	Estimate	Est./s.e.	p-value
constant	8.70	4.89	0.00
grade	- 0.39	- 3.99	0.00
REAL	- 7.26	- 3.09	0.01
GYM	- 5.16	- 2.69	0.01
LONG	-12.47	- 6.09	0.00
grade*REAL	1.01	3.57	0.00
grade*GYM	0.81	3.51	0.00
grade*LONG	1.21	4.73	0.00
REAL*LONG	10.04	3.80	0.00
GYM*LONG	5.07	2.35	0.03
grade*REAL*LONG	- 1.20	- 3.71	0.00
grade*GYM*LONG	- 0.60	- 2.25	0.03

scaled deviance = 86.24   df = 24

Notes

1.   grade is used as a continuous variable
2.   REAL = 1 if *Realschule*, 0 otherwise
3.   GYM = 1 if *Gymnasium*, 0 otherwise
4.   LONG = 1 if after long vowel, 0 otherwise
5.   From notes (2), (3) and (4), the reference group is *Hauptschule* and consonant located after a short vowel
6.   From the scaled deviance and the degrees of freedom, it appears that the model is not a very good fit. However, only 3 of the 36 points had large residuals (max standardised + 2.7). Of these, one point had 3 incorrect out of a possible 28.
7.   The model was fitted using GLIM 3.77 (1985, NAG, Royal Statistical Society, London).

APPENDIX II

Model to assess Hypothesis 2

Response variable = log (# correct spellings / # incorrect spellings)
Error distribution = binomial

Parameter	Estimate	Est./s.e.	p-value
constant	0.06	0.04	.97
grade	- 0.25	0.61	.55
grade^2	0.02	0.63	.53
REAL	2.70	2.04	.05
GYM	- 0.39	0.37	.72
PRET	-11.00	4.81	.00
grade*REAL	- 0.12	0.73	.47
grade*GYM	0.26	1.75	.09
grade*PRET	2.25	4.06	.00
grade^{2*PRET}	- 0.11	3.33	.00
REAL*PRET	- 0.59	1.40	.18
GYM*PRET	0.25	0.61	.55

scaled deviance = 29.03   df = 24

Notes
1. grade is used as a continuous variable
2. REAL = 1 if *Realschule*, 0 otherwise
3. GYM = 1 if *Gymnasium*, 0 otherwise
4. PRET = 1 if before preterit, 0 otherwise
5. From notes (2), (3) and (4), the reference group is *Hauptschule* and consonant located before progressive
6. Omission of REAL*PRET and GYM*PRET gives scaled deviance of 36.57 with 26 df. The difference in deviances, 7.54 with 2 df, has p-value .02. Hence, these terms have been retained.
7. The model was fitted using GLIM 3.77 (1985, NAG, Royal Statistical Society, London).

The Complexity Hypothesis and Morphemic Spelling*

Introduction

Much if not most of the trouble encountered in the acquisition of a native or foreign alphabetic script is traceable to what has been termed "graphemic ambiguity". A phonetic representation is considered graphemically ambiguous if, and only if, it has at least two graphemic representations (Bierwisch 1972: 75, cited in Eisenberg 1983: 69). Among L1-German spellers in grades 2-10 (Menzel 1985: 12), for example, frequent errors include <s> for <ß>, as in <das> for <daß>, <i> for <ie>, as in <krigt> for <kriegt>, and <e> for <ä>, as in <Ermel> for <Ärmel>. Or, among L1-Spanish-English bilinguals in *kindergarten* through university (Staczek 1981: 149) graphemic ambiguity accounts for errors such as <b> for <v>, as in <bisitan> for <visitan>, <j> for <g>, as in <ajente> for <agente>, or <i> for <y>, as in <mui> for <muy>.

A neglected source of difficulty is what might be termed "phonetic ambiguity", where an orthographic representation is considered phonetically ambiguous if, and only if, it has at least two phonetic representations. In English, phonetic ambiguity is found in the major and minor vowel and consonant patterns, such as <breach, break, health; thief, of>, in homographs, such as <Polish, polish>, in prefixes like <tele->, as in <telegraph, telegraphy>, in the roots of some derivationally related words such as <sincere, sincerity>, and in the spelling of inflectional morphemes such as possessive <'s>, as in <Ross's, Jack's, John's>.

This paper is a foray into the acquisition of the phonetically ambiguous English regular past tense spelling <ed> (where <ed> is also morphemically ambiguous, since it may also stand for the past participle) by German learners of English in the German school system. Here, the spelling situation is at the crossroads between tutored and natural, since the pupils are not given the benefit of much explicit instruction in the principles underlying systematic aspects of English orthography.

After completing the *Grundschule* (grades 1-4), pupils either enter the *Hauptschule* (grades 5-9), or, if their grades in German and math are high enough, the *Gymnasium* (grades 5-13). Pupils with superior performance in the first two years of the *Hauptschule* may enter the *Realschule* (grades 7-10). Instruction in English spelling is increasingly more explicit from the *Hauptschule* to the *Realschule* to the *Gymnasium*. In the case in point, the regular past tense is introduced in the *Hauptschule* at the very end of the second year (H6), in the *Realschule* halfway through the first year (R7), these pupils already having had two years of English in the *Hauptschule* grades H5 and H6, and in the *Gymnasium* halfway through the first year (G5). In the *Hauptschule* there is no explicit instruction in English spelling and reading; whatever the pupils learn about English orthography they must induce from the printed page, listening to their teachers' pronunciation in oral reading, and from dictations. In the *Realschule* instruction in reading and spelling the regular past tense consists of explicit rules for pronouncing <ed> after voiced and voiceless sounds and [t, d], dropping the <e> after words ending in <e>, doubling the consonant after a single stressed vowel, and changing the <y> after a consonant into <i> before adding <-ed>, accompanied by a few exercises in which the application of these rules is drilled. Instruction on <-ed> in the *Gymnasium* is similar to that of the *Realschule*, but with cross-references to parallel reading and spelling processes in the plural, present participle, the genitive, the 3rd singular, and the comparison of adjectives. Those instructional passages immediately relevant to the teaching input on <-ed> in each of the three school systems are reproduced in the Appendix.

The method of this study is discussed in chapter 4, § 3.3.

The dictated items relevant to regular past tense spelling acquisition - mostly unfamiliar real words of very low frequencies - were <dented, cheated>, with the regular allomorph /ɪd/ after dental stems, <bragged, stabbed>, with the regular allomorph /d/ after voiced stems, and <cramped, raked>, with the regular allomorph /t/ after voiceless stems. We were interested in ascertaining if the <ed> spellings of these three allomorphs improved grade by grade in each of the three school systems, if performance was better in one school system than another, if the uniform spelling of these allomorphs exhibited any characteristic order of acquisition, if the allomorphs underwent any typical misspellings, and, if so, why.

The distribution of the cases for this study by grade, school systems and sex is given in chapter 5, Table 1. Comparisons across sex were dispensed with due to the absence of male informants in R7 and R9.

1. Received developmental patterns

There are two widespread beliefs concerning tutored L2-acquisition which bear closer examination. The first of these is that pupils' performance improves through time, such that the higher the grade the better the performance. Call this the received developmental pattern for grades. The second is that, other things being equal, performance improves from H to R and from R to G. Call this the received developmental pattern for school systems.

We tested the received developmental hypothesis for grades by comparing pupils' performance on past tense <ed> in each grade and each school system. We computed the percentages of the correct spellings of past tense <ed> for each of the regular past tense allomorphs /ɪd/, /d/, and /t/. The results are presented in Figures 1-3. In Figure 1 *(Hauptschule)* we note deviations from the received developmental pattern for grades in the spelling of /ɪd/ in grades 6 and 8, and in the spelling of /d/ and /t/ in grade 6. Maximally regression prone in H is thus grade 6. In Figure 2 *(Realschule)* we note deviations in the spelling of /ɪd/ in grade 9, in the spelling of /d/ in grade 10, and in the spelling of /t/ in grades 8 and 9. In Figure 3 *(Gymnasium)* we observe deviations in the spelling of /ɪd/ in grade 9, in the spelling of /d/ in grades 11 and 12, and in the spelling of /t/ in grades 9, 10, 11, 12, and 13. Of 45 possible deviations we thus register 16, or 36%, and consider this sufficient evidence for rejecting the hypothesis of a received developmental pattern for grades, at least in the domain of the spelling of past tense <ed>.

The most rapid grade-to-grade developments are in the spelling of /ɪd/ from grade H6 to H7 (53% improvement), in the spelling of /t/ from R9 to R10 (44% improvement), and in the spelling of /d/ from G5 to G6 (73% improvement).

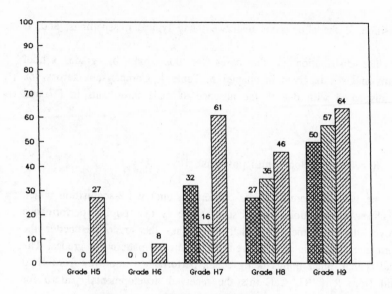

Figure 1.   *Hauptschule:* % Correct <ed>

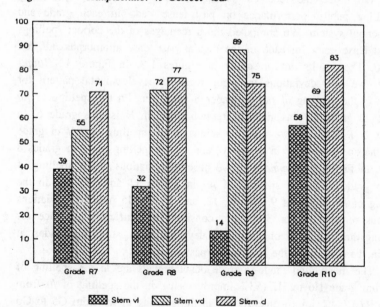

Figure 2.   *Realschule:* % Correct <ed>

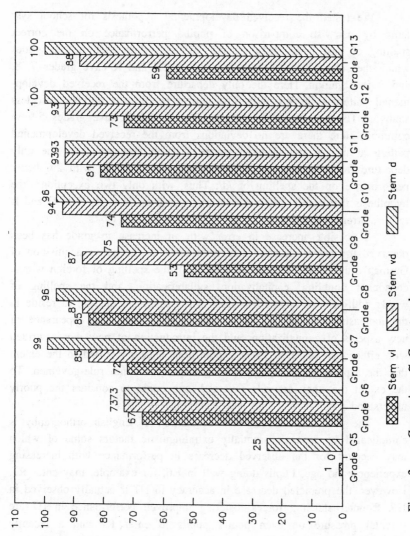

Figure 3.   *Gymnasium: % Correct <ed>*

We tested the received developmental hypothesis for school systems by pairwise comparison of pupils' performance on the correct spelling of past tense <ed> for /ɪd/, /d/ and /t/ in each of the grades which the school systems have in common. H and R have grades 7, 8, and 9 in common. Here the only departure from the received developmental pattern is in R9, with 50% correct spelling of /t/ after voiceless stems in H9 as opposed to 14% in R9. H and G have grades 5-9 in common. Here there are no deviations from the received developmental pattern at all. R and G have grades 7-10 in common; here the only departure from the received developmental pattern is G9 with 2% better performance on the spelling of /d/. Thus, with only two exceptions, the hypothesis that pupils' performance improves from H to R, H to G and R to G is strongly confirmed.

A possible increase in error with an increase in grade has been observed for several categories of error made in the native acquisition of German orthography (Eichler 1978: 82-83): the spelling of foreign words, consonant doubling, capitalization, syllabification, and the spelling of words with <z> as opposed to <tz>. The causes are thought to reside in the increasing use of foreign vocabulary in writing, the appearance of new aspects of capitalization, and the introduction of new words written with either <z> or <tz>. These explanations appear justified to the extent that the aspects of orthography being acquired are not rule-governed. To the extent that they are rule-governed, one ought to consider the poorly understood possibility of rule loss (Luelsdorff 1984b).

The picture of the German acquisition of English orthography is complicated by several essentially extralinguistic factors some of which may account for the observed decrease in performance with increasing experience and age. Pupils doing well in H6, for example, may enter R7. However, the predicted decrease in accuracy in H7 is actually observed in H6. Counterbalancing forces fostering improved performance in H7 are parental pressure on even poorer pupils to enter R7 and a recently introduced provision making it possible for pupils so disposed to discontinue English after H6. Apparently, linguistic pieces alone are insufficient for putting together the developmental puzzle.

2.   Learning morphemic spelling

It is common knowledge that the English past tense morpheme has the three regular allomorphs /ɪd/, /d/, and /t/ and that these have the uniform spelling <ed>. The uniform orthographic representation of a morpheme having different allomorphs is frequently referred to as "morphemic spelling". The past tense and past participle morphemes are among the most morphemically spelled morphemes of English.

We hypothesized that there are differences among the accuracy orders of the <ed> spellings of /ɪd/, /d/, and /t/ in each of the grades in each of the school systems. In order to test this hypothesis we calculated the percentages of correct spellings for the past tense morpheme for each of the pairs <dented, cheated> (dental stems), <bragged, stabbed> (voiced stems) and <cramped, raked> (voiceless stems). The results are depicted in Figures 1-3.

In Figure 1 (Hauptschule) we note that <ed> performance is better on dental stems than on voiced stems and better on voiced stems than on voiceless - the only deviation from this pattern is H7, where the performance is 16% worse after voiced stems than voiceless.

In Figure 2 (Realschule) we again note that <ed> performance improves from voiceless stems to voiced and from voiced stems to dental, with the sole exception of R9 which shows 14% better performance after voiced stems than after dental. Thus, for both H and R the central accuracy tendency is first dental, then voiced, then voiceless.

In Figure 3 (Gymnasium) we note the same trend, with the exceptions of G9, in which performance is better after voiced stems than dental, and G5, in which performance is slightly better after voiceless stems than voiced.

We explain this central tendency as follows. Of the three regular attempts of the past tense, the past tense spelling <ed> most closely resembles /ɪd/, since both <ed> and /ɪd/ consist of two segments and the regular phoneme correspondences of <d> and unstressed <e> are /d/ and /ɪ/. Of the two allomorphs /t/ and /d/, the past tense spelling <ed> more closely resembles /d/, since the regular phoneme correspondence of the grapheme <d> is /d/. In other words, the three regular past tense allomorphs /ɪd/, /d/, and /t/ appear in a hierarchy of complexity relative to their uniform spelling <ed>:/t/ is more complex than /d/ and /d/ is more complex than /ɪd/. From the hypothesis that orthographic accuracy order is governed by the degree of complexity of the relation between orthography and phonology, such that the more complex the relation between a grapheme and a phoneme the less the accuracy, it follows that the <ed> spelling of /t/ will be less accurate than the <ed> spelling of /d/ and that the <ed> spelling of /d/ will be less accurate than the <ed> spelling of /ɪd/.

We note a striking similarity in all three school systems in the relative heights of the boxes representing the accuracy of <ed> after dental stems and after voiceless stems. In each school system both dental stems and voiceless stems exhibit roughly the same zigzag patterns, with an increase or decrease in one corresponding to an increase or decrease in the other. In other words, the better (or poorer) the performance on dental stems, the better (or poorer) the performance on voiceless stems, and vice versa. At least as concerns the <ed> spelling of the past tense after dental stems and after voiceless stems mastery of the morphemic principle exhibits roughly proportional growth.

Recall that for most of the subjects the words dictated were unfamiliar real words of very low frequencies. Hence, the recognition of the presence of the past tense morpheme for such subjects depends upon their perception of the terminal phonetic properties of the words, rather than on their familiarity with the meanings of the stems. This means the assignment to the past tense of the /ɪd/ of <dented, cheated> in the case of dental stems, of the /d/ of <bragged, stabbed> in the case of voiced stems, and of the /t/ of <cramped, raked> in the case of voiceless stems. The assignment of /ɪd/ to the past tense morpheme is fairly straightforward, since there are only a few uncommon words ending in /ɪd/ preceded by a dental non-nasal stop which are not verbs, e.g. <fetid, sordid>. The assignment of /d/ in /-gd, -bd/ to the past tense morpheme is even more straightforward, since there are no English words ending in /-gd, -bd/ which are not the past tense/past participle forms of verbs. A truly ambiguous case is that of /t/, however, since /-pt, -kt/ may either end a morpheme, e.g. <rapt, act>, or cross the past tense or past participle morpheme boundaries, e.g. <cramped, raked>. Thus, some of the misspellings of final /t/ by means of <t> must be attributed to attempts to spell <cramped> and <raked> as though they were monomorphemic. This is another explanation, we submit, for the higher error rate on voiceless stems than on stems that are dental or voiced.

Apropos morpheme recognition, it must be mentioned that spelling a final /t/ or /d/ with <ed> is conclusive evidence in support of the claim that the final /t/ or /d/ has been recognized as the past tense/past participle ending. Spelling a final /ɪd/ with <ed>, however, means either that the /ɪd/ has been recognized as the past tense/past participle *or* that it has been phonetically spelled without having been morphemically identified. This ambiguity is due to the fact that the words dictated were mainly unfamiliar real words. The same would apply to analogous pseudowords (possible non-words). It appears that the ambiguities of final /ɪd/ and obstruent clusters in final /t/ can only be resolved if the words dictated are familiar or if they are unfamiliar but indexed with information on part of speech and grammatical category (e.g. verb, past tense) or appear in sentences in which information on part of speech and grammatical category is predictable from the context. Either case, of course, excludes the possibility of morpheme recognition solely on the basis of phonetic cues. Alternatively, the relevant items could remain ambiguous and the subjects asked to (1) identify past tense items as such and (2) spell them accordingly. In this case, only those items correctly identified as a possible past tense *and* correctly spelled would count as correct.

Data on the acquisition of the morphemic spelling <ed> for the regular past tense allomorphs /d/ and /t/ was collected incidental to an experiment designed to elicit data on the developmental of vowel spellings *in unambiguous sentence contexts* in H7/9, R7/9, and G7/9 (for methodological details, cf. Luelsdorff 1986: chapter VIII). This data is summarized in Table 1, where the percentages given are percentages of error.

Table 1.   *Error % on /-d/ and /-t/ allomorphs in sentence dictation*

Item	<enjoyed>		<remembered>		<called>		<watched>
Grade	<-d>	<-t>	<-d>	<-t>	<-d>	<-t>	<-t>
H7	67	4	52	26	52	28	11
H9	50	3	19	13	31	3	9
R7	35	0	17	8	38	6	6
R9	17	0	7	0	14	0	5
G7	12	0	4	0	2	0	0
G9	0	0	0	0	0	0	0

Here it will be observed that the spellings of the /d/ and /t/ allomorphs to sentence dictations invariably follow both the received developmental pattern for schools and the received developmental pattern for grades, i.e. the higher the grade and the higher the school, the better the performance on <ed> for /d/ and /t/. Furthermore, the prototypical error on <ed> for /d/ is <d>, a result which squares with the results of the error analysis of the word-list dictation reported below. Interestingly enough, however, /t/ proved itself to be consistently less error-prone than /d/ across both grades and school systems in contradiction to the prediction of the Complexity Hypothesis on morphemic spelling. This may have something to do with the intimate familiarity of the test item <watched> in the experience of the learners and/or the strangeness of the appearance of a would-be error <watcht> relative to <crampt> for <cramped> or <rakt> for <raked>. Further research in this area, analogous to the case of the L1-English acquisition of the regular allomorphs of the plural (cf. Baker and Derwing 1982), may show that differently spelled stems with the same regular allomorph of the past tense undergo significantly different orders of acquisition, some, such as <-tch-> in <watch>, complicating the overall pattern of first <ed>:/ɪd/, second <ed>:/d/, third <ed>:/t/.

In order to resolve the issue of the stem-internal vs. stem-external status of terminal /ɪd/ and /t/, we administered *sentence* dictations containing <dented, cheated>, <bragged, stabbed>, and <cramped, raked>, in which it was clear from the context (past time adverbials) that the past tense was intended, in grades R7' (N = 32), R8' (N = 22), and R9' (N = 23). The outcome is depicted in Figure 2'.

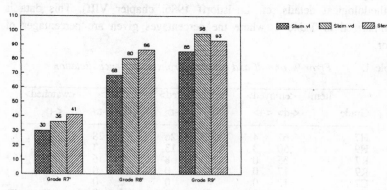

Figure 2'.   *Realschule:* % Correct <ed> in sentences

It will be noted that the results of the sentence dictation in Figure 2'
parallel the results of the word dictation in Figure 2 in the sense that the
respective percentages of correct representations are proportional, even
including the interesting case of R9' and R9 in both of which performance is better on <ed>:/d/ than on <ed>:/ɪd/. Furthermore, whereas
performance on all three categories is consistently better in R8' and R9'
than in R8 and R9, corresponding to our intuition that unambiguous
sentence contexts aid the correct spelling of past tense <ed>, it is interesting that performance is consistently *worse* in R7' than in R7. Apparently,
in the early grades, the presence of context reduces absolute accuracy
while relative accuracy is preserved.

3.   Hierarchies of accuracy vs. hierarchies of acquisition

It was noted over a decade ago (Larsen-Freeman 1976) that orders of
accuracy are *not* to be identified with orders of acquisition. In the case at
hand, it would be a mistake to *assume* that the order of acquisition of the
<ed> spelling of the three regular past tense allomorphs was necessarily
the same as their order of accuracy. The reason for this is that most of
the individuals who spelled /t/ correctly may have spelled /d/ or /ɪd/
wrong, or /d/ correctly and /ɪd/ wrong. Clearly, the group means of
correct representations should not be used as the basis for establishing
orders of acquisition.

In order to ascertain the acquisition hierarchy of the <ed> spellings
of the regular allomorphs of the past tense morpheme, we adopted the
ordering-theoretic method (Dulay, Burt and Krashen 1982: 222-225)
according to which a structure A is acquired before a structure B if the
percentage of disconfirming cases (where B is right and A is wrong) is
"sufficiently small" (5% to 7%). Furthermore, structures form an unordered pair (are acquired at the same time) if they exhibit a small
percentage of disconfirming cases in *both* directions (7% in one direction
and not more than 14% in the other).

We adopted the more liberal criteria of grouping if the difference
in both directions was 5% or less and otherwise ordering A before B if
the percentage of disconfirming cases was less than that of B before A.
The results are presented in Table 2, where '1' stands for <ed>:/ɪd/, '2'

stands for <ed>:/d/, and '3' stands for <ed>:/t/, and the numbers in the cells are the percentages of the cases which disconfirm the hypothesis that the items on the left precedes <'>') the item on the right.

Table 2.   *Disconfirmation percentages on acquisition orders*

Order Grade	1 > 2	2 > 1	1 > 3	3 > 1	2 > 3	3 > 2	Order
H5	0	46	0	46	0	0	1 > 2 + 3
H6	0	15	0	15	0	0	1 > 2 + 3
H7	5	74	5	36	37	5	1 > 3 > 2
H8	23	31	8	38	8	23	1 > 2 > 3
H9	21	21	14	43	29	43	1 + 2 > 3
R7	21	39	11	54	7	32	1 > 2 > 3
R7'	16	28	13	34	16	31	1 > 2 > 3
R8	22	30	1	61	3	64	1 > 2 > 3
R8'	18	27	14	36	18	27	1 > 2 > 3
R9	36	9	0	91	0	100	2 > 1 > 3
R9'	13	4	13	26	0	22	2 > 1 > 3
R10	11	36	4	49	9	31	1 > 2 > 3
G5	0	40	0	39	2	0	1 > 2 + 3
G6	23	20	20	27	7	23	1 + 2 > 3
G7	0	24	0	41	9	29	1 > 2 > 3
G8	4	22	7	22	19	19	1 > 2 + 3
G9	37	10	3	37	0	53	2 > 1 > 3
G10	4	7	4	44	4	41	1 + 2 > 3
G11	13	9	11	33	4	27	1 + 2 > 3
G12	0	13	0	53	0	40	1 > 2 > 3
G13	0	24	0	82	6	65	1 > 2 > 3

Ignoring the unordered pairs, comparison of the results obtained by the ordering theoretic method for acquisitional hierarchies with those obtained by the group means method for accuracy hierarchies yields the interesting conclusion that they are identical. Thus, whereas a given accuracy hierarchy does not necessarily imply the same acquisition hierarchy - in fact we have elsewhere found ample examples to the contrary - a given acquisition hierarchy (apart from the unordered pairs) does necessarily imply the same accuracy hierarchy. The accuracy hierarchy follows from the acquisition hierarchy, and the acquisition hierarchy follows from the complexity hypothesis on the relation between the language acquisition device and the linguistic analysis of morphemic spelling. Hence, both the accuracy hierarchy and the acquisition hierarchy appear epiphenomenal in relation to the learner and the structures being learned.

4.   Error patterns in morphemic spelling

The spelling of familiar words to dictation may be the product of the processing strategies of phoneme-grapheme correspondence application, memorization, or spelling by analogy. Spelling unfamiliar real words or possible non-words, on the other hand, excludes the possibility of their being orthographically processed by memorization. In either case, the errors produced are windows opening onto the processing strategies in spelling production, and this is one of the main reasons the study of linguistic error is of interest.

We investigated the main misspelling types and frequencies of the three regular allomorphs of the past tense morpheme in all the grades and school systems, restricting ourselves to errors on <dented> for the dental stems, <bragged> for the voiced stems, and <cramped> for the voiceless stems. Our hypotheses were: (1) that the major misspellings would be based on the processing strategy of phonetic spelling, (2) that the major misspelling of /t/ would be more frequent than the major misspelling of /d/ and that the major misspelling of /d/ would be more frequent than the major misspelling of /ɪd/, and (3) that the frequencies of the major misspellings would decrease with experience in time. The results are presented in Figures 4-6.

In Figure 4 (Hauptschule) we note that the major misspelling of the past tense after voiceless stems is <t> for all grades. Since the allomorph of the past tense morpheme after voiceless stems is /t/, and the letter <t> is the regular correspondence of the phoneme /t/, we attribute the misspelling of the phoneme /t/ by the letter <t> to the processing strategy of phonetic spelling. After voiced stems the major misspellings of the past tense morpheme are <d> (in H6 and H8) and <t> (in H5, H7,

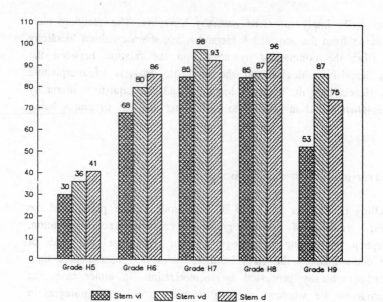

Figure 4. *Hauptschule:* % Prototypical error for <ed>

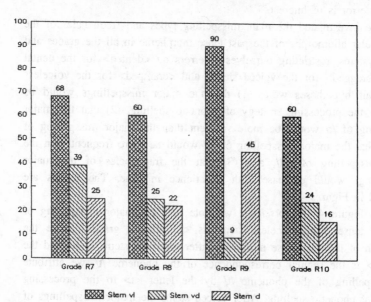

Figure 5. *Realschule:* % Prototypical error for <ed>

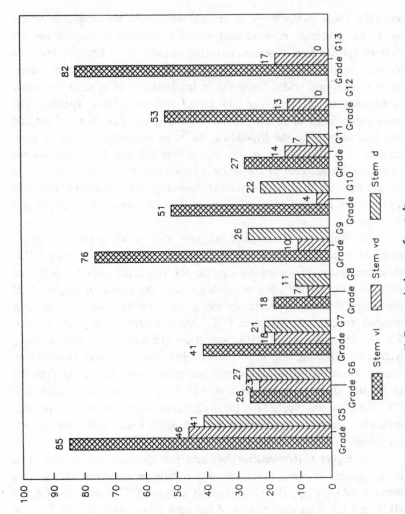

Figure 6.   *Gymnasium:* % Prototypical error for <ed>

and H9). These misspellings in <t> we attribute to the combined effects of (1) the devoicing of word-final voiced consonants in English and (2) German syllable-final obstruent devoicing transferred to English, hence to phonetic spelling. The major misspelling of the past tense after dental stems is uniformly <id>. Since <i> in unstressed position most frequently corresponds to /ɪ/, we assign <i> for /ɪ/ also to phonetic spelling. The main misspellings of /t/ are indeed more frequent than those of /d/ and /ɪd/, but, contrary to the hypothesis, the main misspelling of /ɪd/ is more frequent than that of /d/ in the later grades H8 and H9. Next, on the whole, the frequencies of the major misspellings of the past tense in the *Hauptschule* decrease with experience in time, with exceptional increases noted in the misspelling of /t/ in H8 and in the misspellings of /ɪd/ and /d/ in H6.

In Figure 5 *(Realschule)* we note that in all grades the major misspelling of /t/ is <t>, which is attributable to phonetic spelling. /d/ is most frequently misspelled by <t> (in R8 and R10), <d> (in R7), and <dt> (in R9), also all phonetic spellings after the effects of English final devoicing, German obstruent devoicing, and, in the case of <dt>, the negative transfer of a German PGC. /ɪd/ is misspelled by <id> (in R7, R8, and R9) and <it> (in R10), both errors grounded in phonetic spelling, with <it> reflecting the effects of English devoicing and German obstruent devoicing. /t/ is consistently misspelled more frequently than /ɪd/ or /d/ and /d/ more frequently than /ɪd/, the latter with the exception of R9. Then, in the *Realschule* the frequencies of the major misspellings somewhat decrease with experience through time, with the notable exceptions of /t/ and /ɪd/ in R9.

In Figure 6 *(Gymnasium)* we note that the main misspelling of /t/ in all grades is <t>, while the major misrepresentations of /d/ vary between <d> (in G5, G6, G7, G9, G10, G11, and G13) and <t> (G8 and G12), and the main misspellings of /ɪd/ vary among <id> (in G5, G6, and G11), <ied> (in G7, G8, and G10), and <y> (in G9). With the exception of errors in <ied> and <y> for /ɪd/ all these misspellings are traceable to phonetic spelling as a processing strategy. Excepting a negligible deviation in G6, the most frequently misspelled allomorph of the past tense is /t/, but, contrary to the hypothesis, in more than half the *Gymnasium* grades the prototypical misspelling of /ɪd/ is more frequent than that of

/d/. Finally, performance on all allomorphs ultimately improves with experience through time, with /t/ undergoing radical oscillations.

In sum, of the prototypical errors in spelling of the regular allomorphs of the past tense, those with the highest frequency in all grades (except G6) misspell /t/. Contrary to the hypothesis, the typical misspelling of the past tense of dental stems is more frequent than that of voiced stems in the *Hauptschule* 8 and 9, and the frequencies of the major misspellings of dental stems and voiced stems vie for second place in the *Realschule* and *Gymnasium*. The vast majority of the misspellings indicate that they are the products of phonetic spelling as a processing strategy.

5.   Summary and prospects

In this paper we studied the acquisition of the <ed> spellings of the regular allomorphs of the English past tense morpheme, /ɪd/, /d/, and /t/, by German school children in all the grades of the three systems of secondary education, the *Hauptschule*, the *Realschule*, and the *Gymnasium*.

We began by testing the validity of the view that pupils' performance consistently improves from grade to grade - the received developmental hypothesis on grades - and the view that performance consistently improves from the *Hauptschule* to the *Realschule* and from the *Realschule* to the *Gymnasium* - the received developmental hypothesis on schools. Whereas the received developmental pattern for grades must be rejected, we do find support for a received developmental pattern for school systems (but cf. Luelsdorff 1986 for a different position on the acquisition of some vowel spellings). At least in the domain of the spelling of past tense <ed> in a quasi-instructional setting, there is no basis in fact for the expectation of consistent grade-to-grade improvement.

We then looked into the order of acquisition of the spellings of the regular past tense allomorphs, fairly consistently finding better performance on /ɪd/ than /d/ and on /d/ than /t/. In order to explain this distribution we advanced the Complexity Hypothesis according to which orthographic representations which are less complex are acquired earlier than those which are more complex, where complexity is measured in terms of the number of rules relating the orthographic representations to the phonetic. Also influencing the slow development of <ed> for /t/ is the fact that most /t/s ending word-final obstruent clusters are either past tense/past participle, in which case /t/ is spelled <ed>, *or* stem constituents, in which case /t/ is spelled <t>.

Just as the Complexity Hypothesis on morphemic spelling predicts the order of acquisition of the <ed> spellings of the regular past tense allomorphs - first /ɪd/, second /d/, third /t/ - it naturally also predicts the relative frequencies with which these allomorphs will be misspelled - first /t/, second /d/, third /ɪd/. Furthermore, the Complexity Hypothesis on morphemic spelling, augmented by a theory of phonetic spelling and a theory of transfer, also predicts the actual major misspelling types of the regular allomorphs of the past tense morpheme themselves: <t> for /t/, <d/t> for /d/, and <id/it> for /ɪd/.

It must be emphasized that the above facts on the acquisition of morphemic spelling support a universalist, rather than structuralist, approach to the phonology/orthography interface, since of the two it is the universalist which delivers the levels of complexity necessary to explain the observed orders of acquisition. Structurally, <ed> is realized /ɪd/, /d/, or /t/ in reading, and /ɪd/, /d/, and /t/ are realized <ed> in spelling, with no given realization any more complex than any other. Universally, <ed> is realized /ɪd/, /d/ via /ɪd/, and /t/ via /d/ via /ɪd/ in reading, and /ɪd/, /d/ via /ɪd/, and /t/ via /d/ via /ɪd/ are realized <ed> in spelling (for a theory of the phonology of English inflection, cf. Luelsdorff 1969). By equating depth of derivation with level of complexity and prototypical errors with phonetic spelling, universal orthography succeeds in predicting both the order of acquisition and major misspellings of the normative spellings of the regular past tense. We suspect that a study of the early reading behavior of German learners of English would confirm the hypothesis that past tense <ed> for /d/ and /t/ is first read /ɪd/.

If the Complexity Hypothesis on the acquisition of morphemic spelling predicts the order of acquisition, error types and relative error frequencies of the <ed> spellings of the regular past tense allomorphs of English, then it should also serve to predict the acquisition orders, error types, and relative misspelling frequencies of other allomorphs which are morphemically spelled, such as the <', 's> spellings of the possessive allomorphs /s, z, ɪz/ and the <es, s> spellings of the third singular allomorphs /s, z, ɪz/. Such studies would be of interest in their own right, may lend independent support to the Complexity Hypothesis on morphemic spelling, and shed further light on the orthography/morphology/phonology interface in language acquisition.

Note

* An abbreviated version of this paper appeared as 'The abstractness hypothesis and morphemic spelling' in *Second Language Research* 3 (1), 1987, pp. 76-87.

APPENDIX: **Instruction on the pronunciation and spelling of the regular past tense**

Hauptschule (Learning English HS2, 1975: 85)

Girl:	Excuse me, I'm looking for a young man with long black hair and glasses. He's wearing jeans and a black jacket, and he's got a brown suitcase with him.
Mr Jackson:	Well, a few minutes ago there were a lot of people in here. I think they were passengers for the boat to France. Let me see. Oh yes, of course. There was a young man with a brown suitcase, and I think he had long black hair. He looked a bit like a student.
Girl:	Yes, that was him. He's my brother. I must find him.
Mr Jackson:	Well, he's not here now. He rushed off in a taxi about ten minutes ago.
Girl:	In a taxi?
Mr Jackson:	Yes. It was funny. He ordered a cup of coffee. Then he looked in all his pockets and emptied them. After that he opened his suitcase and looked in that, too. Then he called me and asked me for some small change. He had a £5 note, and I changed it for him. After that he telephoned for a taxi, and when the taxi arrived he hurried out of the café and jumped into the taxi. That was about ten minutes ago.
Girl:	Oh no! I bet he's on his way home to fetch his passport. He can't get on the 10 o'clock boat to France without it - and I've got it here!

Gymnasium (Learning English A1, Grammatisches Beiheft, 1972: 25)

3. Das Präteritum der regelmäßigen Verben

I	looked	ich schaute	we looked	Das Präteritum der regelmäßigen
you	looked	du schautest	you looked	Verben wird durch Anhängung der
he			they looked	Endung *ed* an den Infinitiv gebildet.
she	looked			Es hat für alle Personen dieselbe
it				Form.

Beachte die Schreibregeln:

to wipe - I wiped	1. die **Regel vom stummen**	§ 11, 2.
to arrive - I arrived	**End-e**	§ 37 (Beachte 1).
to race - I raced		
to rub - I rubbed	2. die **Verdoppelungsregel**	§ 11, 1.
to stop - I stopped		§ 37 (Beachte 2).
to trap - I trapped		
to try - I tried	3. die **y-Regel**	§ 16, 2.
to hurry - I hurried		§ 37 (Beachte 3).
to carry - I carried		

Beachte die Ausspracheregeln:

to jump - I jumped [-t]	1. die **Angleichungsregel**	§ 2, § 7, § 14.
to ask - I asked [-t]	[t] nach stimmlosen Kon-	
to reach - I reached [-t]	sonanten stimmlos	
to climb - I climbed [-d]	[d] nach Vokalen und	
to play - I played [-d]	stimmhaften Konso-	
to call - I called [-d]	nanten stimmhaft	
to shout - I shouted [-id]	2. die **Regel vom silbischen**	§ 5, § 16.
to hand - I handed [-id]	**Auslaut**	
to want - I wanted [-id]	nach *t* und *d* [id]	

Psycholinguistic determinants of orthography acquisition*
Philip A. Luelsdorff and E. Ann Eyland

Introduction

Previous studies have shown that the growth of morphemic spelling and consonant doubling is subject to the laws of orthographic complexity. In the present study we answer the questions: who acquires the short and long vowel spellings <a, e, i> when and what governs their order of acquisition? In particular, we investigate the acquisition of selected English short and long vowel spellings by German learners of English also in the three main German secondary school systems, the *Hauptschule* (H), the *Realschule* (R), and the *Gymnasium* (G).

We were interested in whether there are sequencing differences in the acquisition of long and short <a, e, i> and, if so, advancing and testing hypotheses capable of explaining such differences.

Four causal hypotheses appeared worth testing. On the first hypothesis, there are no differences between the acquisition accuracy orders for the vowel spellings and the *type* frequency orders of the main spelling of each vowel in the pupils' texts. Call this the *Frequency Hypothesis* (FH). The FH emerged from the apparently reasonable assumption that exposure to phoneme-grapheme correspondences (PGCs) that are more frequent will result in better learning than exposure to PGCs that are less frequent. On this hypothesis, for example, it is easier to acquire the <a> spelling of the vowel in <man> than it is to acquire the <a-e> spelling of the vowel in <mane>, since the /æ/ → <a> PGC in <man> is roughly five times more frequent than the /ej/ → <a-e> PGC in <mane> (cf. Hanna *et al.* 1966).

On the second hypothesis, there are no differences between the acquisition accuracy orders and the orders of phoneme-grapheme ratios, i.e. the extent of graphemic ambiguity, where graphemic ambiguity is measured by the number of different graphemes used to represent a particular phoneme. Call this the *Univocality Hypothesis* (UH). The UH emerges from the assumption that PGCs that are less ambiguous are easier to learn than those that are more ambiguous. On this hypothesis, for example, it is easier to acquire the <i-e> spelling of the /aj/ in <mine> than the <a-e> spelling of the /ej/ in <mane> because /aj/ has a phoneme-grapheme ratio of 1:8 whereas /ej/ has a phoneme-grapheme ratio of 1:12 (cf. Hanna *et al.* 1966).

The third hypothesis follows from the conjunction of contrastive analysis (CA) and universal grammar (UG) and has been called the *Complexness Hypothesis* (CH) (Eckman 1977). A phenomenon A in some language is more marked than B if the presence of A implies the presence of B, but the presence of B does *not* imply the presence of A.

On the CH a foreign language learner's difficulties are predictable from a CA of L1 and L2 and the markedness relations of UG such that structures that are more marked in L2 than in L1 will be more difficult to learn.

The fourth hypothesis, the *Word Hypothesis* (WH), is more elusive. We have repeatedly noticed (Luelsdorff 1986: 271) that the same sound in different words is spelling-error prone in different ways, confirming for L2-English spellers Nelson's observation (1980: 477) about L1-English spellers: "... some words are especially prone to a particular type of error, e.g. 'son' is often misspelled as <sun> but other misspellings of 'son' are extremely rare. Thus, if error types obtained from different words are compared, such error tendencies of specific words may seriously bias the results." For example, given the fact that /i/ in <cheese> is most frequently misspelled <eeC>, one might be disposed to conclude that all /i/s are most frequently misspelled <eeC>, a conclusion patently contradicted by the most frequent misspellings of the /i/s in <piece> and <movie>. Or, for example, given the fact that the <ie> (= /i/) in <movie> is most frequently misspelled <i>, one might conclude that all <ie>s (= /i/) are most frequently misspelled <i>, a conclusion falsified by the most frequent misspelling of the <ieCe> in <piece>, namely <eaCe>. Thus, among the several determinants of spelling errors, in addition to the sound being spelled and its environment, is the word being spelled itself. We accordingly hypothesized that the members of each pair of unfamiliar words containing the same long or short vowel phoneme-grapheme correspondence exhibit the same quantity and quality of error, in this case that <hem, speck>, <drift, skid>, <tame, scrape>, and <spike, slime> each contain items that are error-prone in the same way and to the same extent. If it can be shown that the members of such pairs exhibit differential error-proneness which is either quantitative or qualitative or both, this would have the interesting result that error is not only a function of frequency, complexness, and uniqueness of PGCs but of analogy of unfamiliar words to words that are familiar.

Clearly, the testing of the above four hypotheses requires a great deal of information. The Frequency Hypothesis demands knowledge of the frequencies of PGCs in different words (type frequencies) and/or texts (token frequencies). Very fortunately, such frequency tabulations are available for English (Hanna *et al.* 1966) and German (Ortmann 1976a, b). It is a serious mistake, however, to equate such frequencies *a priori*, since they were tabulated on the basis of a variety of texts from the adult standard languages, not on the basis of the frequencies of PGCs occurring in the second language learners' texts, where the vocabulary is severely restricted. For this important reason we undertook the extremely arduous task of counting all the PGCs for the vowel spellings examined in each of the textbooks in each of the tested grades in each of the school systems. In general, we found the relative frequencies of the PGCs to be fairly close to, but not identical with, the adult standard language norm, but the PGC ratios, i.e. the degrees of ambiguity, were frequently found to be smaller in the learners' textbooks than in the standard language norm. Clearly, this state-of-affairs would have biased the results of the testing of the Univocality Hypothesis, and it is therefore recommended that future investigations in this area continue to be predicated on textbook statistics.

The testing of the Complexness Hypothesis is even more demanding, requiring as it does not only intimate familiarity with the phonologies and orthographies of the languages contrasted but acquaintance with the (few) studies of orthographic universals (Justeson 1976, Volkov 1982), supplemented by a theory of orthographic markedness or complexity. A few examples should serve to illustrate what is involved. Volkov's (1982: 168) Universal 19 states that if there is a progressive syntagm, there is also a regressive syntagm (a regressive syntagm may be found without a progressive, but not vice-versa). English <Wang>, for instance, contains the progressive syntagm <Wa>, which is progressive because the letter <W> influences the pronunciation of the letter <a> to rhyme with <bong> rather than <bang>. By Volkov's Universal 19, English must also have a regressive syntagm, and, in fact, it has many. The final geminate <-ll>'s in <ball, tall, fall>, for example, require the preceding <a>'s to rhyme with the vowel in <pall>, rather than <pal>. By the Complexness Hypothesis, native readers and writers should have a harder time with <Wang> than <wing> and with <ball, tall, fall> than <pal, cal, gal> and foreign learners without either progressive or regressive syntagms, in this case Germans, should have problems with <ball, tall, fall> and even greater problems with <Wang>. To take another example, Volkov's Universal 20 states that if there is a non-contact syntagm, then there is also a contact syntagm. English has a non-contact syntagm in <mate>, where the <a> rhymes with <fate>, rather than <fat>, due to the presence of the final <-e>. Since non-contact syntagms are more marked than contact syntagms, they are more complex, learned later, and more error-prone, for both native and foreign learners.

Testing the Word Hypothesis requires familiarity with the quantity and quality of errors made on the members of each pair and assessing the differences for significance. In order to explain the differences, recourse must apparently be had to familiar words which bear an intimate similarity to the unfamiliar dictated. The familiar words serving as the basis for analogy may be either native or foreign. For example, performance on <speck> is invariably significantly better than performance on <hem>. Presumably this differential error-proneness is due to spelling unfamiliar English <speck> by analogy to familiar German <Speck> or to familiar English <speak>, and unfamiliar English <hem> by analogy to familiar English <ham>. Spelling English <speck> by analogy to German <Speck> 'bacon' results in the correct spelling for the wrong reason, and shows that either German PGCs or lexical orthographic representations may be accessed in the spelling of English, and spelling English <hem> by analogy to English <ham> results in an incorrect spelling due to familiarity with <ham> and the proximity of the sound in the word <hem> to the sound of the word <ham>.

1.   Method

The distribution of pupils by grade and school systems is given in Table 1 in Appendix I. The reader is referred to chapter 5 § 3.3 for a description of the method used.

Embedded in the dictation were 12 words containing 7 different vowel sounds. The spellings of these sounds reflect the traditional educationalist distinction between short and long vowels. These are given in Table 2 in Appendix I.

Both long and short <a, e, i> are represented. For each grade, the percentage of correct spellings for each phoneme were recorded. Other orthographic data was collected for each phoneme for each grade, the relevant variables being:

(a)   phoneme/grapheme ratio, i.e. the inverse of the number of different ways of spelling a given sound in the actual textbooks;

(b)   the absolute frequency of occurrence of a PGC (irrespective of its spelling) in the classroom text-books;

(c)   the relative frequency of occurrence, i.e. the ratio of the number of type occurrences in the text-books, including the phoneme most frequently spelled with a given grapheme(s), to the number of type occurrences in the text-books including the phoneme.

2.   Purpose

The data set was collected in order to explore the determinants of differential acquisition of orthographic representation. Four hypotheses were tested.

Hypothesis 1:   Performance improves with phoneme frequency.

Hypothesis 2:   Performance decreases with graphemic ambiguity.

Hypothesis 3:   Performance decreases as a function of the degree of contrast between the PGCs of English and German.

Hypothesis 4:   Performance on a given normative PGC varies with the words containing it.

Hence, the following independent variables were considered as possible correlates of performance:

af: absolute frequency of occurrence of a particular PGC
rf: relative frequency of occurrence of a particular PGC
pg: phoneme/grapheme ratio
vowel: 1=short, 2=diphthong, 3=long

School type and grade were also considered as possible correlates.

3. Procedure

Statistical methods were used to clarify patterns in the data. These deliver ways of summarizing the data and hence provide tools for assessing the validity of the four hypotheses. Hypothesis testing can be viewed as fitting a parametric model based on the hypothesis to the data and deciding whether the model is "closer" to the data than a competing model. This means that we have some way of measuring distance between the model and the data and the distance between two models. Interpretation of the measure of distance is based on the assumptions about the probability distribution of the variables which have been measured. There were various steps in the data analysis.

1. The data were graphed by sound, grade, and school type. In order to summarize the data, the following model was fitted:

(a)   Performance as measured by the percentage of correct spellings for a particular class was expressed as a function of phoneme, grade, and school type.

(b)   The probability model used is the binomial model. Formally the number of correct spellings of sound i is assumed to be a binomial random variable with probability of success in grade j of school type k equal to π_{ijk} and with the number of trials equal to the number of children in grade j of school type k.

(c)   The probability model in (b) specifies the appropriate function to consider in (a). That function is the inverse logit function of a linear combination of variables representing grade and school type, i.e.

$$\log(\pi_{ijk}/(1-\pi_{ijk})) = \text{linear combination of } S_i, G_j, SCH_k \text{ and the cross-products of these variables.}$$

where S_i takes value 1 for sound i, 0 otherwise
G_j takes value 1 for grade j, 0 otherwise
SCH_k takes value 1 for schooltype k, 0 otherwise
Therefore i = 1,..., 7, j = 5,..., 10, k = 1,...,3

The purpose of this model is to clarify the nature of the differences in orthographic performance between grades and school systems.

2. Each hypothesis was investigated in turn using a model similar to that in (1), but with replacing the sound variables, $\{S_i\}$, with the characteristics of those sounds which are the foci of the four hypotheses.

3. If each hypothesis holds, then the question arises as to whether some hypotheses are more dominant than others. For example, it may be that graphemic ambiguity is associated with vowel length, the conclusion that spelling performance is higher in words with short vowels may simply be another way of saying that spelling performance on the vowels with less ambiguity is higher if short vowels are the less ambiguous vowels. Hence, it is important to investigate the combined effects of the four hypotheses. These were investigated by fitting models similar to that set out in (1) but with the sound variables replaced by their characteristics as specified in the five hypotheses. In addition, relationships among the characteristics were investigated by using correlation and regression techniques.

Statistical analysis was carried out using the Minitab statistical software and GLIM.

4.   Results

1.   *Summary of data in terms of sound, grade and school type*

The graphs in Appendix II show, for each sound, the percentages of correct spellings plotted against grade or year at school for each school type. Modelling these data in terms of sound, grade and school type as in Section 3 Step 1 confirms the following:

(a) *performance differs by sound.* In year 5, the level of performance for the 7 sounds is: sound 7 < sound 6 < sound 4 < sound 2 < sound 1 for both *Hauptschule* and *Gymnasium.* Sound 5 and sound 3 slot in at different levels for the two school types. In other years, differences occur but the ordering changes.

(b) *performance differs by school type.* In general, and surprisingly, *Hauptschule* < *Gymnasium* < *Realschule.*

(c) *performance differs by year at school.* In general, performance improves with time. There are some notable exceptions, e.g.

- performance on sound 1 at H and G see-saws
- performance on sound 4 at R decreases
- performance on sound 5 remains steady

Performance, then, improves by year at school but the rate of improvement varies between school types and between sounds, the rate of improvement for a given sound being a function of school type.

2.   *Investigation of each hypothesis separately*

Hypothesis 1

"Performance improves with phoneme frequency." Four measures of phoneme frequency were used

i   absolute frequency of phoneme-grapheme occurrence
ii   the rank within each class of the absolute frequency of phoneme-grapheme occurrence
iii   the relative frequency of phoneme-grapheme occurrence
iv   the rank within each class of the relative frequency of phoneme-grapheme occurrence

Since we had established in Step 1 that performance differed between school types and between years, the statistical analysis was adjusted for these differences, i.e. we investigated the effect of phoneme frequency over and above effects due to the class environment. From the statistical analysis, we found that the best specification of phoneme-grapheme frequency was the ranked relative frequency. (By best, we mean that this specification produced models which more closely represented the data than other models.) Goodman and Caramazza (1986: 317) arrive at a similar conclusion in a study of three acquired dysgraphics, namely that the probability of activating a particular phoneme-grapheme conversion rule is a function of the frequency of occurrence of that phoneme-grapheme mapping option in English orthography.

In general, we found support for the hypothesis viz. as ranked relative frequency increases so did performance (the higher the rank the higher the relative frequency of phoneme occurrence). There were exceptions as follows:

- years 7 and 9 in the *Hauptschule*
- year 10 in the *Realschule*
- all years in the *Gymnasium*

In each of these cases, phoneme-grapheme frequency had no impact on performance.

Hypothesis 2

"Performance decreases with grapheme ambiguity", i.e. the more alternative ways there are of spelling a particular phoneme, the poorer performance is expected to be.

This result does not appear to hold in three of the thirteen classes surveyed, viz. years 6 and 9 at the *Hauptschule* and year 8 at the *Gymnasium*.

Hypothesis 3

"Acquisition of spelling of short vowels precedes that of diphthongs and long vowels."

As can be seen from Figure 1, this hypothesis has some merit. In general, for each class, performance on long vowels is poorer than on short vowels and diphthongs. In G8, performance on diphthongs is better than on short vowels. Otherwise, there is little difference between short and diphthongal vowels although short vowels have the edge.

Hypothesis 4

"The same vowels with the same spellings in different words are misspelled in different ways." Under discussion here are the items in the pairs <hem, speck>, <drift, skid>, <tame, scrape>, and <spike, slime>. The pair <craft, damp> was excluded, since the words did not have the same vocalic pronunciation in the speech of the teachers (RP). So was the pair <creep, thief>, because the words do not have the same vowel spellings. The results are shown in Appendix II. Here we find that <speck> is invariably spelled better than <hem>, that <tame> and <scrape> are spelled significantly differently in H6 and H8, in R9 and R10, and in G6, G8, G9, G10, G11, and G12, and that <spike> and <slime> are spelled significantly differently in H, in R7, and in G5-10, and in G13. With the exception of <hem> and <speck> in H and R, there is a tendency for performance accuracies on identically spelled identical vowels to converge with increase in grade and for performance to be generally better in the *Gymnasium* than in the *Realschule* and in the *Realschule* than in the *Hauptschule*.

Summary
The data provide some support for each hypothesis. The models from Hypothesis 3 fit the data more closely than those derived from Hypotheses 1 and 2. This suggests that the dominant effect is the length of the vowel.

3.   A general model

The measures of frequency, ambiguity and vowel-type were found to be related. Even so, we found that a general model of performance included all three sound characteristics. The results given for each hypothesis separately persisted with minor modifications. The dominant effect is vowel-type. As has already been noted, the impact of vowel-type on performance depended on school and grade. Higher relative frequencies contributed to better performance in the spelling of diphthongs and long vowels. Higher phoneme-grapheme ratios improved performance in the *Realschule* and *Gymnasium*, i.e. the simplest sounds in the sense of having fewer alternative spellings were more likely to have higher scores.

Hypothesis 3'
"The greater the interlinguistic contrasts, the greater the interference." This applies not only to items, but to the fixings of the parameters of orthographic universals.

     In order to appreciate the force of hypothesis 3', it is necessary to consider the relevant proposed orthographic universals. The universals in question are to be found in Justeson (1976), orthographic universals (13) and (14), which, for convenience, we recapitulate here:

J(13) No long vowels are represented distinctly unless some short vowels are.

J(14) No diphthongs are represented distinctly unless some long vowels are.

When digraphs or longer letter sequences are admitted, J(14) is reversed to

J(14a) No long vowels are represented distinctly by letter sequences unless some diphthongs are.

While both German and English observe J(13), English has distinct representation of long vowels (J14a), whereas German by and large does not. Thus, whereas both German and English observe J(13) and J(14a), only English exhibits distinct representation of long vowels, and is thus marked for this feature in relation to German. Thus English exhibits a different markedness hierarchy (complexity) from German and it is to be expected that Germans will find it difficult to acquire the spellings of the English long vowels, which they in fact do. This is support for the Markedness Differential Hypothesis (Eckman 1977).

This general framework enables one to better understand the actual errors made, since it predicts that such errors will be of certain types, interlinguistic and intralinguistic (cf. Luelsdorff 1986, chapters 3 and 4 this volume), including strategy shifts. In respect of the vowel spellings the major error types characteristic of the various grades in the school systems all reflect interlinguistic and intralinguistic transfer triggered by shifts in underlying processing strategies, including processing an unfamiliar word in terms of its proximity to a familiar word, e.g. processing unfamiliar <tame>, <hem>, and <drift> as <time>, <ham>, and <drived!>. The errors, coupled with the error typologies presented in chapters 3 and 4 this volume, speak for themselves. We thus find confirmation for Hypothesis 3' not only in the acquisitional sequence: first short, then long (Figure 1), but also in the predictability of the framework in terms of the actual errors made.

Establishing accuracy orders for groups yields orders of difficulty for the items tested within the group. Using A > B to represent A is more accurate/easier than B, for H5 in Figure 1, we can say that

speck > hem
hem   > thief
thief > creep

This accuracy order is not to be equated with the acquisition order. For any given individual in the group, however, because an individual who writes the vowel of an item in a row of the right-hand column correctly may also write the item in the corresponding row of the left-hand column incorrectly, or both incorrectly, or both correctly, it would be wrong to say that such an item in a row on the left is acquired before the corresponding item in the row on the right.

Moreover, neither accuracy order nor acquisition order (however this latter concept might be defined) say anything about the strategies being used to process the linguistic information under investigation.

One way of shedding light on the processing of linguistic structures is to examine the errors the speaker/hearer/writer/reader makes in their acquisition and production. If such errors are frequent and recurrent, they yield insights into the processing strategies involved. Those error patterns that stay the same through time are indicative of constant processing strategies; those error patterns that change are suggestive of processing strategy shifts and such strategy shifts may result in variable orders of accuracy and acquisition.

On the basis of the above reasoning, we have detailed many of the processing strategies in bilingual orthography acquisition (Luelsdorff 1984a, 1986, chapter 3 this volume, 1987a, chapter 4 this volume). Here it must suffice to exemplify what is meant by spelling processing strategy and processing strategy shift.

The prototypical spelling errors on the long and short vowels in H, R and G are represented in Tables 3, 4, and 5 in Appendix I. The percentages given are the percentages of the most frequent (prototypical) misspelling(s) and the prototypical misspellings themselves are given in angle brackets. For example, the long <a> in <scrape> in H5 in Table 3 was prototypically misspelled <ea> in 20% of the misspellings and prototypically misspelled <ei> in 20% of the misspellings.

The accuracy order on short and long <a> in H5 is <craft> > <damp> > <tame> > <scrape> and in H9 <scrape> > <tame> > <craft> > <damp>. The prototypical error on <craft> is <o> and the prototypical error on <scrape> is <ea>. Germans who write <craft> as <croft> are orthographically processing /ɒ/ as /ɔ/ due to the absence of /ɒ/ in German. /ɔ/ in German is written <o>. Germans who write <scrape> as <skreap> are orthographically processing /e/ as <ea> - surprising insofar as <ea> never spells /e/ in German and only spells /e/ in English in 1% of the cases (cf. Hanna *et al.* 1966). Learning to then spell /e/ as <a...e> amounts to undoing an irregularization and applying the strategy of regularization. The undoing of an irregularization by H9 in words like <scrape> is evidently easier than the perceptual realignment necessitated by words like <craft>, although both display chequered histories.

We thus attempt to explain variable accuracy and acquisition orders by variable orders of processing strategy transitions.

4.   *Prototypical errors*

4.1   *Hauptschule*

The prototypical errors on the long and short vowels in the *Hauptschule* are given in Table 3 (Appendix I).

/ɒ/ in <craft> is most often misspelled <o, ou, oa>. This is due either to the identification of English /ɒ/ with German /ɔ/, the latter of which is uniformly spelled <o>, or the identification of English /ɒ/ with English /ɔ/, which is then spelled either <o> *often*, <ou> *thought*, or <oa> *broad*.

If interlinguistic transfer from German, we are dealing with the transfer of a German PGC. If intralinguistic transfer from English, we are dealing with regularization in the case of <o>, and reregularization in the cases of <ou> *thought* and <oa> *broad*.

The main errors on /ɪ/ in <drift> are <e, ie, iCe>. <e> for <i> exemplifies place of articulation of an English letter name, <ie> for <i> place of articulation of a German or English letter sound, and <iCe> for <i>, the apparent misidentification of unfamiliar <drift> with familiar

\<drive\>. Almost all of the errors on /ɪ/ in \<skid\> appear to be spellings of lax /ɪ/ as though it were tense /i/: \<ea, iCe, ie, e\>. As such they are processed by place of articulation of an English letter(s) sound.

\<hem\> exhibits the single error \<a\>, this apparently due to either the misidentification of unfamiliar \<hem\> with familiar \<ham\> or to hypercorrection by analogy to /mæn/ → /mɛn/, \<a, ea, ee\>, \<ea\>, \<ee\> apparently reflecting the misidentification of unfamiliar \<speck\> (but cf. German *Speck* 'bacon') with familiar \<speak\>.

/æ/ in \<damp\> always has the major misspelling \<e\>. /æ/, absent from German, has in both German and English the nearest neighbor /ɛ/, which, in both languages, is most frequently spelled \<e\>.

In summary, /ɔ/ gets spelled as /o/, /ɪ/ gets spelled as /i/, /æ/ gets spelled as /ɛ/, and /ɛ/ gets spelled as /æ/, with word familiarity being a relevant parameter.

To the extent that the names of the letters used to misspell these vowels do not contain the vowel sounds themselves, these misspellings cannot be said to result from letter-naming or place of articulation of a letter name as processing strategies. Rather the letters used to misspell these short vowels are those letters which are normatively used to spell the target vowel's nearest German or English phonetic neighbors. For his reason, the strategy involved is place of articulation of a letter(s) *sound*, which we have elsewhere termed the "nearest neighbor" (Luelsdorff 1986). Place of Articulation of a Letter Sound must thus be added to the repertoire of processing strategies in bilingual spellers and is an additional constraint on error variables in grammar. Just as native segmental phonological production errors typically involve a difference of one feature specification between attempt and target (Shattuck-Hufnagel 1987), the above bilingual orthographic competence errors exhibit a difference of one feature specification between the vowel spelled in the target and the vowel spelled in the attempt.

Turning to the long vowels, /aj/ in \<spike\> and \<slime\> is most often misspelled \<ai, ei\>. Since /aj/ is spelled \<ei\> in English only 1% of the time and never spelled \<ai\>, and the two most frequent spellings of /aj/ in German are \<ei\> *Seite* and \<ai\> *Saite*, it appears reasonable to assign these two misspellings to the negative transfer of German GPCs.

/e/ in \<tame\> is most frequently misspelled \<iCe, ai\>. Evidently, \<iCe\> is due to the identification of unfamiliar \<tame\> with familiar

<time> and <ai> to the employment of a less frequent PGC (27%) for the more frequent <a...e> (50%), an irregularization. The most common errors on the long vowel in <scrape> are <ea, ei, a>, all attributable to intralinguistic transfer from English /e/: <a> (15%), <ei> (2%) and <ea> (1%) in medial position. Of great interest here is the fact that all such developmental orthographic representations are irregularizations.

/i/ in <creep> and <thief> is most often misspelled <i, ea, i...e>. <i> is the most frequent spelling of /i/ in German, although it occurs in 3% of the cases in English, and <ea> is the most frequent spelling of /i/ in English (32%). <i...e> spells /i/ in English in only 2% of the cases. Since English /i/ is spelled <ee> 29% of the time and <ie> 6% of the time, <ea> for <ee> is a regularization and <i...e> for <ie> is a re-irregularization.

4.2   Realschule

Realschule error prototypes not found in the *Hauptschule* are:

/a/	craft	<a...e>
/aj/	spike	<ee, ai...e>
	slime	<i, ai...e>
/i/	thief	<ee, ea..e>
/æ/	damp	<u>
/ɛ/	speck	<e...e>
/ʌ/	skid	<ee>

In medial position /a/ is spelled <a> in 86% of the cases and <a...e> in 8% of the cases. <a...e> for <a> in <craft> is therefore an irregularization cum complication.

Medial /aj/ is spelled <i...e> (59%) and <i> (26%), and /ae/ in German is spelled <ei, ai, eih>, as in *Seite, Saite,* and *Reihe.* <slim> for <slime> thus appears to be processed by English letter-naming or ir-regularization with simplification and <ai...e> for <i...e> in <slime, spike> processed by both negative transfer of a German PGC and regularization. <speek> for <spike> remains a mystery but is an irregularization if <spike> is misunderstood as <speak>.

/i/ is spelled <ea> (32%), <ee> (29%), <ie> (6%), and <ea...e> (5%). <theef> and <theafe> for <thief> are therefore both reirregularizations.

/æ/ has nearest neighbors in /ɛ/, /a/, and /ʌ/. <dump> for <damp> thus results from Place of Articulation of a Letter Sound as a processing strategy.

/ɛ/ has its major primary correspondence in <e> and a minor secondary correspondence in <e...e>. <specke> for <speck> is therefore an irregularization cum complication.

/ɪ/ has its major primary correspondence in <i> and a minor secondary correspondence in <ee> *been*. <skeed> for <skid> is therefore an irregularization cum complication.

4.3   *Gymnasium*

Prototypical errors exclusive to the *Gymnasium* are:

/a/	craft	<u, aw>
/ɛ/	hem	<i>
	speck	<i>
/ɪ/	skid	<ea...e>
/e/	tame	<ei, ai...e>
	scrape	<ai>
/ay/	spike	<y..e, a...e>
	slime	<y...e>
/i/	thief	<ie...e, ee...e>
/æ/	damp	<a...e>

/ʌ/ is spelled by <u> and /ɔ/ by <aw> in medial position. Since /ʌ/ and /ɔ/ are the nearest neighbors of /a/, we attribute <u, aw> for <a> in <craft> to the processing strategy of Place of Articulation of a Letter Sound.

/ɛ/ and /ɪ/ are most frequently spelled by <e> and <i>, and they are both specified [-Low]. Spelling <speck> as <spick> and <hem> as <him> therefore result from Place of Articulation of a Letter Sound as a processing strategy.

Neither English nor German has a PGC spelling /ɪ/ as <ea...e> in syllable-medial position. Consequently, <skeade> for <skid> is due to neither interlinguistic nor intralinguistic transfer. Rather, it appears to be due to spelling the /ɪ/ in <skid> as though it were the /i/ in words like <ease, please> in which case it would be due to the processing strategy of Place of Articulation of a Letter Sound.

Since English /e/ may be spelled by <ei, ai, ai...e>, as in <vein, pain, praise>, the misspellings <teim, taime> for <tame> and <scraip> for <scrape> may all be treated as irregularizations. The fact that <ei> for <a...e> occurs only in the first year of English, however, suggests that <teim> for <tame> may be rather due to German Letter Naming as a processing strategy.

/aj/ is regularly spelled <i...e>, as in <bike>, and irregularly spelled <y...e>, as in <type>. The writings <spyke, slyme> are therefore irregularizations. For <a...e> in <spike> we have no explanation.

/i/ may be spelled <ie...e> (3%), as in <piece>, or <ee...e> (2%) as in <cheese>, or <ie> (6%), as in <thief>. Spelling <thief> as <thiefe> or even <theefe> are therefore irregularizations of patterns that are already irregular, i.e. reirregularizations.

/æ/ is almost always (98%) spelled <a>, but in one very frequent word <a...e>, <have>. Spelling <damp> as <dampe> is thus an irregularization cum complication.

5. Conclusion

In this chapter, we have established that the school type, the grade, the item, the ranked relative frequency of the item, the ambiguity of the orthographic representation, the perceived relatedness of an unfamiliar word containing an item to a familiar word, and the degree of universality of the orthographic representation all may play a determining role in the acquisition of the short and long vowel spellings of English. Some of these determinants may appear a priori obvious, but others are quite nonintuitive and extremely interesting. These include the last three of the aforementioned.

To say that the ranked relative frequency of an orthographic representation is one of the determinants of its acquisition is to claim that considerations of the relative frequency of the input-intake must be assigned a numerical value. This numerical value may be construed as relative or absolute. We tend towards the relative (i.e., more or less), since no speller/reader of English is in a position to deliver the precise absolute frequencies of the English GPCs.

To say that the degree of ambiguity of an orthographic representation is in fact a determinant of its acquisition is to confirm the Praguian credo (Sgall 1987) to the effect that PGCs may be typologically displayed along an axis of univocality such that the later the PGC on the axis the more it is complex.

To say that the universality of an orthographic representation is a determinant of its acquisition is to say that the less universal an orthographic representation is, the more difficult it will be of access to the language learner. Since no long vowels are represented distinctly unless some short vowels or diphthongs are, the theory of orthographic universals correctly predicts that performance on the spelling of short vowels is on the whole superior to performance on the spelling of long vowels.

Corresponding to our notions of universality (Hypothesis 3) and ambiguity (Hypothesis 2) are the Praguian notions of complexness and univocality (Sgall 1987). It will be shown in the next chapter that the Praguian scales of complexness (universality) and univocality (ambiguity) are powerful predictors of the orders of accuracy and acquisition of the spellings of the entire array of the English inflectional and contracted allomorphs in the case of German learners of English orthography. In this chapter we find further confirmation for the validity and predictive potential of the notions of complexness (universality) and univocality (ambiguity), with the spelling of the long vowels (complexness) as the dominant effect. In addition to the confirmation of these effects, we found further determinants in school type, grade, and the perceived relatedness of dictated unfamiliar words to words, either native or foreign, that were familiar (the word effect). There is thus reason for optimism about the fruitful interaction of studies in orthographic universals (Justeson 1977, Volkov 1981), scales of orthographic complexity (Sgall 1987), and studies in language acquisition with special reference to the orthography, morphology, and phonology interface.

Note

* This work would not have been possible without the dedicated cooperation of several coworkers. For special mention, we single out Cornelia Betz, Urte Friebel, Laurian Gajek, Judith Keller, Alexandra Richter, Evi Scherwitz, and Ulrich Sehm.

** A shorter version of this paper appeared in *IRAL* 2 (1989), 143-156.

APPENDIX I. Tables

Table 1. *Subjects by grade and school system*

Grade	Hauptschule	Realschule	Gymnasium
5	13		57
6	13		30
7	19	28	34
8	13	67	27
9	14	22	
10		45	

Table 2. *Short and Long Vowels*

Short	Long
craft	
drift, skid	spike, slime
hem, speck	creep, thief
damp	tame, scrape

Table 3. *Hauptschule*: Prototypical errors - long and short vowels
Error percentage of most frequent error

ITEM	GRADE	5	6	7	8	9
/a/	CRAFT	10 <o>	0	11 <ou,oa>	38 <o>	20 <o>
/ɛ/	HEM	35 <a>	85 <a>	26 <a>	69 <a>	80 <a>
/i/	DRIFT	10 <e>	8 <ie>	37 <iCCe>	38 <iCe>	13 <iCe>
/e/	TAME	35 <iCe>	23 <ai>	11 <ai,..>	8 <iCe>	7 <ai>
/i/	CREEP	55 <i>	23 <i,e>	32 <ea>	31 <ea>	47 <ea>
/ay/	SPIKE	15 <ei>	8 <ai>	11 <ei>	8 <eiCe>	0
/ay/	SLIME	45 <ei>	32 <ai>	32 <ei>	8 <ei,..>	13 <ei>
/i/	THIEF	75 <i>	46 <i>	37 <iCe>	31 <iCe>	21 <i>
/æ/	DAMP	25 <e>	35 <e>	37 <e>	23 <e>	29 <e>
/ɛ/	SPECK	15 <ea>	15 <a>	21 <ee>	23 <ea>	21 <a>
/i/	SKID	15 <ea>	38 <iCe>	16 <ie>	8 <ea,..>	21 <e>
/e/	SCRAPE	20 <ea,ei>	15 <a>	26 <ea>	38 <ea>	14 <ea>

Table 4. *Realschule*: Prototypical errors - long and short vowels
Error percentage of most frequent error

ITEM	GRADE	7	8	9	10
/a/	CRAFT	21 <aCe>	3 <aCe>	0	0
/ɛ/	HEM	18 <a>	22 <a>	27 <a>	73 <a>
/i/	DRIFT	52 <iCe>	3 <iCe,ie>	0	0
/e/	TAME	14 <iCe>	15 <ai>	36 <ai>	16 <ai>
/i/	CREEP	25 <ea>	18 <i>	9 <i>	25 <ea>
/ay/	SPIKE	7 <ee>	3 <ei>	5 <ai>	2 <aiCe>
/ay/	SLIME	18 <ei>	4 <i>	5 <aiCe>	4 <ai>
/i/	THIEF	32 <ee>	6 <ee>	18 <ee>	7 <eaCe>
/æ/	DAMP	7 <e>	12 <e>	9 <u>	18 <e>
/ɛ/	SPECK	11 <ee>	3 <a>	5 <ee,ea,..>	7 <ea>
/i/	SKID	18 <ie>	7 <ie>	14 <iCe>	4 <ee>
/e/	SCRAPE	11 <A>	16 <a>	0	7 <a>

Table 5. *Gymnasium*: Prototypical errors - long and short vowels
    Error percentage of most frequent error

ITEM		GRADE 5	6	7	8	9
/a/	CRAFT	7 \<aCe\>	23 \<u\>	3 \<o\>	37 \<o\>	3 \<ou\>
/ɛ/	HEM	38 \<a\>	73 \<a\>	29 \<i\>	67 \<a\>	97 \<a\>
/ı/	DRIFT	27 \<iCe\>	33 \<iCe\>	12 \<iCe\>	11 \<e\>	0
/e/	TAME	13 \<ei\>	30 \<ai\>	15 \<aiCe\>	11 \<a\>	20 \<ai\>
/i/	CREEP	19 \<ea\>	40 \<ea\>	35 \<ea\>	26 \<i\>	27 \<ea\>
/ay/	SPIKE	5 \<ea\>	7 \<yCe\>	9 \<aCe\>	0	0
/ay/	SLIME	11 \<ai\>	21 \<y\>	18 \<i\>	7 \<ai\>	7 \<i\>
/i/	THIEF	40 \<i\>	12 \<i,iCe\>	15 \<i\>	4 \<ee,iCe\>	7 \<ee\>
/æ/	DAMP	13 \<aCe\>	7 \<e\>	21 \<u\>	7 \<u\>	3 \<u,aCe\>
/ɛ/	SPECK	18 \<ea\>	27 \<a\>	21 \<i\>	27 \<a\>	10 \<a\>
/ı/	SKID	25 \<e\>	20 \<ie\>	15 \<ie\>	7 \<e\>	3 \<iCe,e,ea\>
/e/	SCRAPE	13 \<ea\>	23 \<ea\>	24 \<a\>	11 \<a\>	7 \<ea\>

Table 5. *Gymnasium* (continued): Prototypical errors - long and short vowels
    Error percentage of most frequent error

ITEM		GRADE 10	11	12	13
/a/	CRAFT	4 \<ou,aCe\>	2 \<aw,oa\>	0	0
/ɛ/	HEM	74 \<a\>	54 \<a\>	27 \<a\>	35 \<a\>
/ı/	DRIFT	0	0	0	0
/e/	TAME	22 \<ai\>	29 \<ai\>	20 \<ai\>	6 \<ai\>
/i/	CREEP	26 \<ea\>	29 \<ea\>	27 \<ea\>	12 \<e\>
/ay/	SPIKE	0	0	0	0
/ay/	SLIME	7 \<ai\>	4 \<ai\>	0	6 \<yCe\>
/i/	THIEF	7 \<ee\>	15 \<ieCe\>	0	12 \<eeCe\>
/æ/	DAMP	7 \<u\>	2 \<e\>	20 \<u\>	6 \<e\>
/ɛ/	SPECK	4 \<a\>	47 \<a\>	0	0
/ı/	SKID	4 \<eaCe\>	13 \<iCe\>	0	0
/e/	SCRAPE	11 \<a\>	6 \<ea\>	7 \<ai\>	6 \<a\>

APPENDIX II

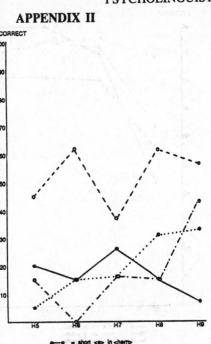

Fig. 1 : Hauptschule : Development of short and long <e>

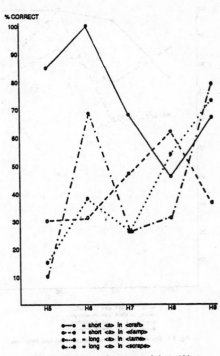

Fig. 2: Hauptschule : Development of short and long <a>

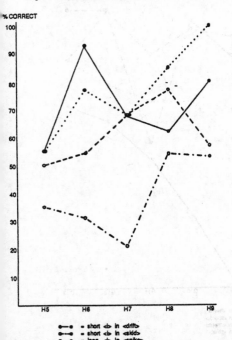

Fig. 3 : Hauptschule : Development of short and long <i>

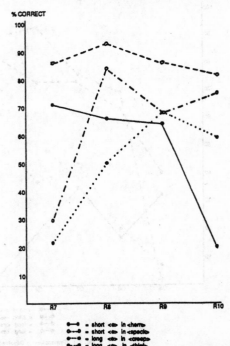

Fig. 4 : Realschule : Development of short and long <a>

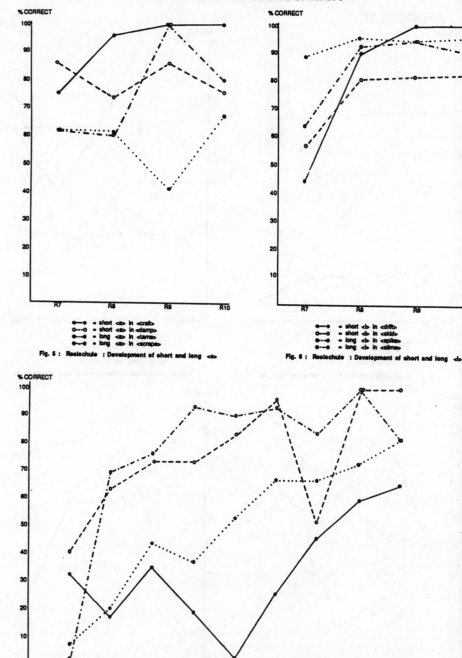

Fig. 5 : Realschule : Development of short and long <a>

Fig. 6 : Realschule : Development of short and long <i>

Fig. 7 : Gymnasium : Development of short and long <e>

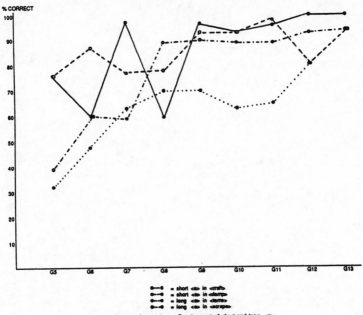

Fig. 8 : Gymnasium : Development of short and long <a>

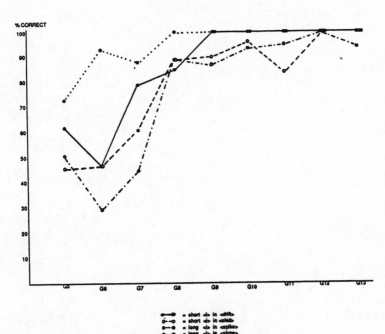

Fig. 9 : Gymnasium : Development of short and long <i>

Developmental Morphographemics

Philip A. Luelsdorff and E. Ann Eyland

0. Introduction

Although morphophonemics has been a subject of linguistic inquiry for almost a century, morphographemics, its orthographic analogue, remains by and large unknown. By "morphographemics" we mean the study of graphemic alternations occasioned by the morphological processes of affixation, in particular, inflection and derivation, for example <thief ~ thieves>, <sincere ~ sincerity>, <cargo ~ cargoes>, and <ready ~ readiness>.

Assuming that inflected and derived forms are literally derived from their respective bases, i.e. the perspective of item-and-process, then the morphographemic alternations (MA) of English may be divided into two fundamental groups. The first group is phonology-bound in the sense that the MA are bound to morphophonemic alternations, as in <thief ~ thieves> and <sincere ~ sincerity>, where the graphemic alternations <v/f> and <Ø/e> are bound to the phonological alternations /v/f/ and /V/V̄/. The second group is phonology-free in the sense that the MA are free from morphophonemic alternations, as in <cargo ~ cargoes> and <ready ~ readiness>, where the graphemic alternations <oe/o> and <i/y> are free from any alternations in phonology.

Depending upon the relations among the graphemes and phonemes in their derived and underived forms, there are morphophonemic and morphographemic substitutions, omissions (deletions), additions (insertions), and displacements (either backward or forward). Examples of phonology-free MA include the substitutions of <i> for <y> in <happy ~ happiness>, the omission of final <e> in <impute ~ imputing>, the addition of stem-final <e> in <cargo ~ cargoes>, and the backward displacement of <r> in <acer ~ acre> to avoid velar softening.

A detailed taxonomy of MA is presented in Luelsdorff (1989a). Here we address the question of the foreign acquisition of English phonology-free MA and what explains it.

In addition to the issue of the typology of these morphographemic processes in terms of additions and deletions and the structural constraints on their combination in nature and number, there is the more difficult and interesting question of the quantity and type of conditions placed on their proper operation, including such subtleties as substituting <i> for <y> at morpheme boundaries, e.g. <heavy ~ heavier, happy ~ happily, rely ~ reliable, beauty ~ beautiful>, unless the suffix is <-ous>, as in <beauty ~ beauteous>, in which case <e> is substituted for <y>, or the stem-final <y> is preceded by a vowel, e.g. <slay ~ slayed, play ~ player>, in which case the <y> is retained, or the suffix is <-ly> and the stem is a monosyllable whose final <y> is preceded by either a digraph or a literal consonant cluster, as in <shy ~ shyly, dry ~ dryly>, as opposed to <day ~ daily, gay ~ gaily>.

Besides the subject of MAs and the conditions on their application, there is the equally important issue of the costs the grammar should attach to both. Within the complexity approach to linguistics (Luelsdorff 1989a), costs should be attached to structures and processes because without such costs it is impossible to know precisely which structures and processes are more difficult, hence harder to acquire and process in production and comprehension. Evidently, greater costs should be attached to morphographemic substitutions than deletions and insertions, because a substitution is a deletion followed by an insertion. Thus, in language acquisition one would expect more errors to be made on alternations of the type <study ~ studies>, where, on one analysis, <i> is substituted for <y> and <e> is inserted than on <rate ~ rating>, where the stem-final <e> is deleted, or <hero ~ heroes>, where a stem-final <e> is inserted. Thus, in addition to posing typological and developmental questions, such as what are the morphographemic alternation types and tokens, and when are they acquired, we may give quantitative formulation to the even more interesting question of why.

1. Purpose

Having established the existence of morphographemics as a legitimate domain of (psycho)linguistic inquiry, including the typology of morphographemic alternations, the structural conditions on their operation, and the desirability of a morphographemic complexity metric, we proceed to ask if some morphographemic alternations are acquired before others and, if so, why. We first place these questions within a language developmental framework and discuss an experiment relevant to the questions raised, then present the results of our own experiment on foreign morphographemic acquisition, and discuss the light this sheds on our understanding of morphographemic acquisition and written language acquisition in general.

In recent years there have been several cognitive developmental proposals on the acquisition of reading and spelling, including Gentry (1982), Marsh, Friedman, Welch & Desberg (1980), Frith (1985, 1986) for L1 English orthography, Günther (1986) for L1 German orthography, and Luelsdorff (1990) for L2 English orthography. The more ambitious of these for L1 English are Marsh & Desberg (1983) and Frith (1985, 1986) in that they, each in their own way, explicitly relate the development of spelling to the development of reading. Moreover, each model is characterized by stages, or phases and steps. Our only purpose here is to try to locate MAs within each of these models, in view of the fact that they are not explicitly mentioned in either.

The reading and spelling model of Marsh & Desberg (1983) contains the stages of Rote Memorization, Combinatorial Rule, and reading and spelling by Analogy. Morphographemic processes are hard to place in this model, because, if productive, they crucially depend upon access to morpheme boundaries and the place of morpheme-boundary acquisition, and its relation to phonology and orthography is not clear. Hence, the Marsh & Desberg model is underspecified for our purposes and we turn to Frith (1985).

Frith (1985) presents a six-step model of skills in reading and writing acquisition, involving related progressions from stages called "logographic", "alphabetic", and "orthographic", whereby the steps in reading and writing are in phase with each other. The alphabetic skills of Stage II refer to knowledge and use of individual phonemes and graphemes and their correspondences, decoding in reading grapheme-by-grapheme, enabling the reader to pronounce (not necessarily correctly) novel and nonsense words. The orthographic skills of Stage III refer to the instant analysis of words into orthographic units without phonological conversion. Such units ideally correspond to morphemes and are internally represented by abstract letter-by-letter strings. The orthographic strategy itself is non-visual and non-phonological. Now, MAs typically implicate the three grammatical components of phonology, orthography, and morphology; in *cargo*, for example, the phoneme /o/ is spelled by the grapheme <o> in the environment of the grammatical category of singular and undergoes the addition of <e> to form the complex grapheme <oe> in the environment of the grammatical category of plural. This intrusive <e> complexifies the task of the speller, but simplifies the task of the reader, who is twice told that the word <cargoes> is in the plural, once by the <s> spelling the plural morpheme ending, and once by the <e> inserted in the plural in the spelling of the stem. This process cannot be simply a question of alphabetic skills, since, in addition to phoneme-to-grapheme correspondences (/o/ to <o>), there are also grapheme-to-grapheme correspondences (<o> to <oe>), and contextual constraints in the form of the singular and plural morphemes. Moreover, since there are written plurals like <buffalos, pianos, photos> which are free of these morphological constraints, the morphographemic alternation <o> ~ <oe> in words of the type <cargo> must be lexicalized, i.e. the plural must be spelled on the lexical route to spelling, rather than by means of subword phonology and morphology-to-orthography. We thus place the acquisition of morphographemics late in Frith's Phase III, *after* the acquisition of advanced orthographic skills in reading, i.e. on Frith's (1985: 311) Step 3b = Orthographic$_2$ in writing.

Having located the acquisition of morphographemics within the advanced orthographic step of writing during the orthographic reading and writing phase, we conclude that the acquisition of the productive command of morphographemics in spelling ought to occur very late, if not last, in productive written-language learning. We turn to a psycholinguistic investigation which sheds further light on the subject.

In an essay on the psychological productivity of written inflectional and derivational morphemes, Sterling (1983: 182-184) found that their productivity was determined by (1) their *frequency* of occurrence, with written inflectional morphemes more frequent, hence productive, than written derivational ones, and (2) their *salience*, where "salience" is defined as the extent to which derivational affixation affects the *phonological* structure of the stem, with salient, neutral suffixes like those in *glad-gladness, morose-morosely, poet-poetess*, and *hope-hopeless* more productive than stemaltering ones like those in *similar-similarity, expand-expansion*. While it seems strange to label neutral suffixes "salient", the author does succeed in identifying both frequency and salience as two of the factors underlying the productivity of written inflectional and derivational morphemes, and this is a landmark in an otherwise *terra incognita*.

Several comments, however, appear to be in order. First, the frequency of a word in a word count (in Sterling's case, Carroll, Davies and Richman's (1971) *Word Frequency Book*) is not necessarily the same as in the (different) mental lexica of the 20 11-year-olds in Sterling's test group. For example, the low productivity of items with stem-altering affixes might be due to unfamiliarity, rather than low salience. Secondly, and just as importantly, the productivity of the same affix with different stems is unfortunately different. Of great interest in this regard are Kettemann's (1988: 330-335) results on American English inflectional and derivational (oral) morphemic productivity and analyzability. In the case of <-ify>, the non-word stems <bine> and <plode> were found to be significantly non-productive, but the non-word stem <sarid> significantly productive. Furthermore, <binify> and <plodify> were found to be significantly non-analyzable, while <saridify> was found to be non-significantly analyzable. Thus, not only should one not induce the universal from the particular, but productivity and analyzability in orthography might very well be different from productivity and analyzability in phonology. In particular, the above results on salience could be due to orthographic factors, rather than phonological, or a combination of orthographic, phonological, and morphological.

Wang & Derwing (1986) have shown that English vowels are related in derivational pairs by the Chomsky-Halle (1968) Vowel Shift Rule only to the extent that they are spelled the same (e.g. <sincere ~ sincerity, divine ~ divinity, sane ~ sanity, verbose ~ verbosity>), but not <profound ~ profundity>. It would seem to follow that preliterate and illiterate English speakers having such vocabulary (if there are any!) should have no Vowel Shift Rule and those literate speaker-writers with such vocabulary should only have a Vowel Shift Rule that is orthographically-based, i.e. from orthography-to-phonology. This, in turn, means that the productivity of the rule(s) depends crucially on the orthography-phonology interface, i.e. that this kind of phonology cannot be productive without rules from orthography-to-phonology, i.e. rules of graphophonology.

The question of the productivity of written inflectional and derivational morphology then becomes a question of the *complexity* of the orthography and orthography-to-phonology of inflected and derived orthographic representations relative to the respective stems. Compare the (hierarchical) orthographic representations in Figure 1:

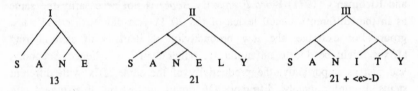

Figure 1. *Orthographic Complexity*

If an arbitrary cost of 1 is attached to each node and edge of each tree and the costs then summed, tree I is cheaper than tree II, and tree II is cheaper than tree III. Tree II is cheaper than tree III because some cost must be added to III as a result of deleting the <e> from I in order to obtain the orthographic representation of the stem in III. On Sterling's concept of salience, II is more salient than III because the suffix <-ly> does not affect the phonological composition of the root, with the result that the suffix and the componential structure of the derivative are highly salient and consequently more productive than <-ity> in III.

On the present, lexical orthographic position, III is orthographically less productive than II, not because it is less salient, but because it is lexically orthographically more complex. In particular, the complexity of the orthographic relation between I and III is greater than that between I and II, i.e. C(I,III) > C(I,II). On the item-and-process view, it would be mistaken to compare the complexity of III with the complexity of II, with the incorrect result that C(III) = C(II), because the complexities in question also partly result from the derivation of different forms

(<sanely>, <sanity>) from the same base (<sane>). Moreover, additional cost must be assigned to III, but not to II, due to the fact that the orthography-to-phonology (graphophonology) of III changes as a result of the suffixation of <-ity>. The fact that the vowel in I is long, while the vowel in III is short, is reflected in the different orthographic constituent structure of the vowels in I and III. Thus, we reject the notion that the productivity of the orthography of inflection and derivation is directly related to lexical frequency and *phonological* salience - this would partly explain *phonological* productivity in inflection and derivation - and advance the view that orthographic productivity in inflection and derivation is directly related to the complexity of the morphographemic interface, such that more complex constructions are less productive than constructions that are less complex. This result is consistent not only with the notion that literate phonology *is* in fact orthography-to-phonology (Wang & Derwing (1986); Derwing & Dow (1987)), but also with the more general position that (psycho)linguistics is *complexity* (psycho)-linguistics, explaining not only the relatively different orthographic productivities of inflectional and derivational morphology, but also other aspects of language structure and processing in acquisition, deterioration, and loss.

Morphographemics is ideal ground to test the productivity of orthography in morphology, because, in the type of morphographemics under discussion, the *phonology* of the stem is constant, while the orthography of the stem varies as a function of the orthography, phonology, morphology and semantics of the ending. In other words, different graphemes of one and the same morphographeme are in complementary distribution in respect of the phonology and morphology of their stem and suffixal environments. For example, <i> is rewritten <y> word-finally (<try>), intervocalically (<player>), and in <C(C)_> stems <lying, dying; shyly, dryly> and after stem-vowels before inflections (<donkeys, monkeys; player; layer; playing, laying>), with exceptions like <said, laid, paid>, and <Galsworthys, Sothebys> (= the respective families) having to be specified as proper nouns to exempt them from the <Ø> to <e> after <i> rule underlying <country ~ countries>. <i> to <y> succeeds before the possessive in <country's>, but fails before the plural and 3sg. in <countries, hurries>. Thus, even from this rough sketch, it is clear that morphographemic rules may be sensitive to stem phonology, various types of affixal morphology, including subcategories of inflection and derivation like possessive vs. 3sg. vs. plural, phonological properties of inflection and derivation, like whether or not the suffix begins with a /C/ or a /V/, and even semantic features like [+ Proper] on nouns. Unless such information is known, English cannot be spelled productively. In learners, including many literate native speller-readers, strategies alternative to rule-formation and application, such as simplification via recourse to mere PGCs and GPCs, or alternative strategies such as rote memorization or non-random guessing reflect *bounded linguistic complexity*.

These considerations suggested a series of hypotheses on the development of morphographemic productivity in learners of English phonology, orthography, and morphology.

On the Familiarity Hypothesis, equal or better performance on unfamiliar words than on familiar would mean that the MA were governed by either rule or analogy. Depending upon the case, the learners in question would be in either Stage II (Rules) or Stage III (Analogy) in Marsh & Desberg's (1983) developmental linguistic model of oral and written language, or in late Phase III of Frith's (1985) developmental model of reading and spelling.

A second issue is the extent to which the productivity of morpho-graphemic alternations correlates with the part of speech of the words in which the alternations occur. If a morphographemic alternation is significantly more productive in, for example, nouns than verbs or in adjectives than adverbs, then membership in part of speech must be given as a condition on the operation of the rule underlying the given alternation. In order to answer this question, we hypothesize that there are no differences in morphographemic productivity across the major lexical classes of nouns, verbs, adjectives, and adverbs. Call this the "Part of Speech Hypothesis".

Previous work (Luelsdorff 1990) indicated a superiority effect for morphographemic productivity in Inflection, as opposed to Derivation, with deletions (e.g. <e>) superior to substitutions (e.g. <y/i>), and substitutions superior to insertions (e.g. <o/oe>). Here, we again ask if morphographemic growth is differentially sensitive to inflection and derivation. If yes, then the notion of morphographemic productivity must be further relativized to the contexts of inflection and derivation. Since inflection and derivation are two of the three branches of morphology, we call the hypothesis that there are no differences in morphographemic productivity in inflection and derivation the "Morphology Hypothesis".

Finally, we inquire into the interesting issue of the relative productivity of three different types of morphographemic alternation, the non-identity substitution <i/y>, the identity substitution <y/y>, and the addition of <e> to <o> to form <oe>. Other things being equal, if <i/y> is more productive than <y/y>, and if <y/y> is more productive than <o/oe>, morphographemic additions would be inherently more complex than morphographemic substitutions, and identical morphographemic substitutions would be inherently more complex than non-identical morphographemic substitutions. The hypothesis that there are no differences we call the "Morphographemic Rule Hypothesis". Here too we shall see that the productivity, hence complexity, of a morphographemic alternation is decisively affected by the complexity of its segmental context.

2.   The Experiment

2.1   The data for this analysis were obtained from an English dictation exercise conducted on October 9, 1986. The dictation, reproduced in Appendix I, consisted of 67 words and was taken by 13 pupils from the ninth grade of the German *Gymnasium*.

2.2   The words were classified by part of speech, morphology and familiarity as follows:

> part of speech   - noun, verb, adjective, adverb;
> morphology   - inflection, derivation;
> familiarity   - familiar, unfamiliar.

2.3   Further classifications were used for the different parts of speech. Nouns were classified by number and the method of constructing the plural if applicable:

> number   - singular, plural

plural   - same (e.g. boy - boys), substitution (baby - babies),
                addition (cargo - cargoes).

Verbs were classified by number and tense:

number   - singular, not applicable;
tense   - present, past, progressive.

Adjectives were classified by degree:

degree   - comparative, superlative.

2.4   The distribution of words by morphology and past of speech is given in Table 1.

Table 1. *Distribution by morphology and part of speech*

		Part of speech			
Morphology	noun	verb	adjective	adverb	all
inflection	24	19	8	0	51
derivation	4	0	6	6	16
all	28	19	14	6	67

Note that all verbs belong to the inflection group whereas all adverbs belong to the derivation group.

The distribution of words by familiarity and part of speech is given in Table 2.

Table 2. *Distribution by familiarity and part of speech*

		Part of speech			
	noun	verb	adjective	adverb	all
familiar	23	18	6	3	50
not familiar	5	1	8	3	17
all	28	19	14	6	67

Familiarity and morphology were not independent factors as can be seen from the following:

	Morphology		
	inflection	derivation	all
familiar	43[38]*	7[12]	50
not familiar	8[13]	9 [4]	17
all	51	16	67

* numbers in brackets are expected numbers based on
independence model. $x^2 = 10,6$ df = 1 p-value = .001

There was a higher proportion of unfamiliar words among the derived words than among the inflected words.

2.5   Further structural zeroes were found. Nouns were classified as singular (4) and the plural nouns were divided into three categories:

plural and singular stems the same   (17)
plural obtained by substitution   (2)
plural obtained by addition   (5)

There were four categories of verbs as follows:

present tense and singular   (2)
present tense only   (4)
past tense   (7)
progressive aspect   (6)

There were three categories of adjectives as follows:

comparative   (5)
superlative   (3)
neither   (6)

There was no sub-division of adverbs.

2.6   The first response variable equals the number out of 13 who spelled a word correctly at the first dictation. The following table gives a summary of the results:

Table 3. *Summary statistics for average number of incorrect spellings by part of speech, morphology, familiarity*

Morphology

Part of speech	Inflection		Derivation		all		
	F*	$\bar{F}$	F	$\bar{F}$	F	$\bar{F}$	all
noun mean	3.8	2.8	2.0	0.0	3.6	2.2	3.3
no.	(20)	(4)	(3)	(1)	(23)	(5)	(28)
verb mean	2.4	12.0	-	-	2.4	12.0	2.9
no.	(18)	(1)			(18)	(1)	(19)
adj. mean	2.6	1.3	1.0	10.8	2.3	7.3	5.1
no.	(5)	(3)	(1)	(5)	(6)	(8)	(14)
adv. mean	-	-	6.0	4.3	6.0	4.3	5.2
no.			(3)	(3)	(3)	(3)	(6)
all mean	3.1	3.4	3.6	7.4	3.1	5.5	
no.	(43)	(8)	(7)	(9)	(50)	(17)	
all	3.1		5.8				3.7
	(51)		(16)				(67)

*F = familiar; $\bar{F}$ = unfamiliar

Statistical analyses using a binomial model (implemented using GLIM) showed the following:

(a)   if we consider the 4 categories of morphology and familiarity, we find that unfamiliar words in the derivation category are more poorly spelled than words in the other 3 categories

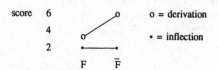

(b)   if we consider the 8 categories of part of speech and familiarity, we find that there are differences between parts of speech

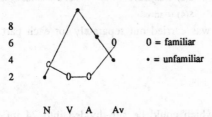

according to the familiarity of the word:

amongfamiliar words, adverbs had the highest error score;

amongunfamiliar words, nouns had the lowest error score, verbs the highest, followed (in descending order) by adjectives and adverbs.

Note that there was only 1 unfamiliar verb.

These results have been deduced from the following model of log $(\pi/\lambda-\pi)$ where π = the probability of spelling a word correctly. It is shown that π is a function of part of speech, morphology and familiarity.

Table 4.   *Model of number of incorrect responses out of 13.*
- binomial model fitted using GLIM 3.77

Parameter	Estimate	s.e.	t-ratio
	- .88	.14	-6.5
M(2)	- .87	.43	-2.0
F(2)	-1.37	.42	-3.3
S(2)	- .61	.22	-2.8
S(3)	- .53	.32	-1.6
S(4)	1.59	.52	3.1
M(2).F(2)	2.97	.58	5.1
F(2).S(2)	5.34	1.13	4.7
F(2).S(3)	1.71	.54	3.2
F(2).S(4)	-2.14	.75	-2.8

Notes

1. M(2) = derivation   S(2) = verb   2. deviance = 280.86   df = 57
   F(2) = unfamiliar   S(3) = adjective   not a well-fitting model
                         S(4) = adverb

Further analysis was carried out separately for each part of speech.

2.7   Nouns

There were 28 nouns which could be sub-divided into 24 inflected nouns
and 4 derived nouns. The inflected nouns were all plural and the derived
nouns singular. The 24 plural nouns were further sub-divided into:
17 in which the stem of the plural was the singular word,
 2 in which the plural was formed from the singular by substitution of
   one letter,
 5 in which an addition was made to the singular noun in forming the
   plural.
Of the 24 plural nouns, 20 were familiar and 4 unfamiliar,
of the 4 singular nouns, 3 were familiar and 1 unfamiliar.
Other classifications were unappropriate.

Summary statistics are set out in Table 5:

Table 5.   *Summary statistics for average number of incorrect spellings
            by morphology (number), plural and familiarity*

		mean	s.d.	n
Plural	noun	3.47	3.94	17
	substitution	2.00	1.41	2
	addition	4.80	3.84	5
Plural	inflection	3.63	3.74	24
	derived	1.5	2.38	4
familiar		3.57	3.70	23
unfamiliar		2.20	3.35	5.
	all	3.32	3.62	28

Analysis using GLIM indicated that the only significant difference was between inflectional and derived words. There was insufficient data to assess whether familiarity and morphemic type interacted since there was only 1 word which was unfamiliar and derived.

2.8   Verbs

There were 19 verbs, all of which were inflected, and 18 of which were familiar. There were 6 present tense verbs, 7 past tense and 6 progressive tense verbs.

Summary statistics are given in Table 6:

Table 6. *Summary statistics of number of incorrect spellings out of 13*

	mean	s.d.	n
Tense present	3.00	2.68	6
past	4.86	3.80	7
progressive	.50	.84	6
All words	2.89	3.23	19

The one unfamiliar word was very different from the other words. It was incorrectly spelled 12 times. The average number of incorrect spellings of the remaining words was 2.39. In fact, the maximum of the remaining words was 7.

The observed difference due to tense was found to be significant. The fitted model indicated that the number of incorrect spellings of progressive tense verbs was significantly smaller than the number of incorrect spellings of present or past tense verbs. This result held even when the outlier was removed.

2.9   Adjectives

There were 14 adjectives. Of these, 8 were inflected and 6 derived. The 8 inflected could be sub-divided into 5 comparative and 3 superlative. Of

the 14 adjectives, 6 were familiar and 8 unfamiliar. Summary statistics
are given in Table 7.

Table 7. *Summary statistics of number of incorrect spellings out of 13*
by morphology, degree and familiarity

		mean	s.d.	n
Degree	comparative	2.4	2.8	5
	superlative	1.7	1.2	3
Inflection				
	comp + sup	2.1	2.2	8
Derived		9.2	4.6	6
Familiar		2.3	2.4	6
Unfamiliar		7.3	5.4	8
All		5.1	4.9	14

Further analysis indicated that the observed differences were significant.
The small numbers meant that interaction effects could not be assessed.
The parameter estimates of the additive model using degree and familiar-
ity are given in Table 8:

Table 8. *Model of log $\pi/(1-\pi)$ in terms of degree and familiarity*

Parameter	Estimate	s.e.	t-ratio
constant	-2.07	.38	5.3
D(2)	-1.42	.68	2.1
D(3)	1.54	.47	3.2
F(2)	1.67	.46	3.6

Notes

1 D(2) = superlative

    D(3) = neither comparative nor superlative

    F(2) = unfamiliar

2 deviance = 52.07   degrees of freedom = 10

This model indicates that comparative words were more likely to be spelled incorrectly than superlative words and that both were less likely to be spelled incorrectly than other words.

Familiar words were more likely to be spelled correctly than unfamiliar words.

2.10   Adverbs

There were 6 adverbs, all of which came from the second morphology category. 3 of the 6 adverbs were familiar and 3 unfamiliar. There was no difference in spelling between familiar and unfamiliar.

3.   Discussion

Morphographemics is concerned with the conditions on the alternations in the graphemic representation of morphemes resulting from affixation (Luelsdorff 1989a). Such alternations are either phonology-bound, in the sense that they are conditioned by morphophonemic alternations, or phonology-free, in the sense that they are devoid qua alternations of phonological motivation. Examples of phonology-bound MA include <sublime ~ sublimity> and <president ~ presidency>, and examples of phonology-free MA include <country ~ countries> and <hero ~ heroes>. In the present study we are mainly concerned with the differential productivity of MA that are phonology-free, asking if the extent of morphographemic productivity is a function of one or several of the following factors: (1) Word Familiarity; (2) Part of Speech; (3) Inflectional or Derivational Morphology; (4) Substitution or Addition.

3.1   The Familiarity Hypothesis

The rank order of accuracy for familiar and unfamiliar words and familiar and unfamiliar inflections and derivations is as follows:

| I | Familiar (3.1) | I | Familiar Inflected (3.1) |
| II | Unfamiliar (5.5) | II | Unfamiliar Inflected (3.4) |

III   Familiar Derived   (3.6)

IV   Unfamiliar Derived   (7.4)

Here, the number in parentheses is the number of subjects out of a total number of 13 who made incorrect responses. It is evident that morphographemic productivity is greater in familiar words than in unfamiliar, and greater in inflected words than in derived. This result could be due to the lower frequency and/or greater complexity of words that are derived. Indeed, inflections with a high frequency and simple morphographemic structure, like <candy ~ candies> and <baby ~ babies>, both with <i/y>, are much less error-prone than derivations with a low frequency and complex morphographemic structure, like <beauty ~ beauteous> and <bounty ~ bounteous>, both with first <i/y>, then <e/i>. Further, among familiar words, simple MA like <play ~ playing>, with the identity alternation <y/y>, exhibit much better performance than complex MA like <say ~ said> and <lay ~ laid>, with the alternations <i/y> and <Ø/e>.

Thus, there is a direct relation between complexity and error-proneness irrespective of familiarity, which establishes complexity as the main determinant of the acquisition of linguistic knowledge.

3.2   The Part of Speech Hypothesis

According to the Part of Speech Hypothesis on MA, there are no significant differences in MA within and among different parts of speech. The parts of speech tested were ADJ, V, N, and ADV. In respect of within-group differences, we find a superiority effect for the MA <oe/o> in the items <goes, does>. For less frequent words, we find a superiority effect in MA of the type <X/Y>, where <X> ≠ <Y>, and <Y> is a simplex grapheme, i.e. consists of one letter over those MA in which Y is a complex grapheme, i.e. consists of two or more letters. Identity MA like <y/y>, <o/o>, and <f/f> are superior to non-identity MA like <oe/o> resulting in graphemes which are complex. In respect of graphemic context, a following <-ing> favors the application of a preceding non-identity mapping <y/ie>, whereas <-ed> strongly disfavors the preceding identity mapping <y/y>. Because <-ed> requires more planning than <-ing>, the complexity of a given MA is partly a function of the complexity of a contextually adjacent phonographemic alternation. Finally, identity mappings are less productive than those which are non-identity, e.g. the productivity of <cliff ~ cliffs> is over three times less than the productivity of <thief ~ thieves>, with the <ff> in <cliff> frequently misspelled <v>. Perhaps this is due to the transfer of training of /v/f/, whence <v/f>, perhaps to the unmarked expectancy of certain alternations in inflection and derivation. In the latter case, morphographemic and, by analogy, morphophonemic alternations are not merely intralexical or lexical, but *interlexical* or analogically interlexical, i.e. lexically paradigmatic, as well as lexically syntagmatic.

In sum, the following determinants of morphographemic productivity appear to obtain:

(1)   more frequent over less frequent;
(2)   simplex over complex;
(3)   frequent over complex;
(4)   non-identical over identical;
(5)   complex over identical;
(6)   simplex context over complex context;
(7)   part of speech more univocal in MA over part of speech less univocal in MA.

Determinants (2,7) support the Complexness and Univocality Scales of Sgall's (1987) theory of orthographic complexity, and determinants (1,2) confirm conclusions reached in Luelsdorff & Eyland's (chapter 7, this volume) study of the psycholinguistic determinants of the foreign acquisition of selected English vowel spellings. Whereas the scales developed there are orthographic, under discussion here are scales that are metaorthographic - a morphographeme is an ordered septuple consisting of base phoneme(s) (Pb), goal phoneme(s) (Pg), base grapheme(s) (Gb), goal grapheme(s) (Gg), base context (Cb), goal context (Cg), and a complexity value (Cv) consisting of the sum of the base complexities, the goal complexities, and the differences between them. If the hypotheses explanatory of orthography and metaorthography are isomorphic, we have all the more reason for thinking that grammar is essentially isotropic, rather than essentially modular.

In respect of between-group differences in morphographemic productivity in different parts of speech, we find

F: ADJ > V > N > ADV

$\overline{F}$:   N > ADV > ADJ > V

These curious effects intensified our search for causes. It turns out that there is a direct relation between the degree of morphographemic productivity in the exponents of a given part of speech and the number of different types of MA that those exponents exhibit (cf. Appendix II). In inflection, for example, ADJs exhibited 2 different types of alternation, Vs 4, Ns 6 and ADJs > Vs > Ns. If we define the complexity in morphographemic univocality of a part of speech as the number of different types of MA it exhibits, *other things being equal*, we may say that morphographemic productivity is a linear function of complexity in morphographemic univocality, i.e. the ratio of part of speech to MA, of the degree of univocality of word class and alternation. This direct relation between productivity and univocality lends additional support to the complexity theoretical framework and demonstrates the deterministic role of morphographemic univocality within word classes in morphographemic theory. If knowledge of this ratio contributes to linguistic productivity, the degree of univocality between word-class and number of MA must be a parameter in morphographemic theory. Under such circumstances, language is not essentially modular, but essentially interactive, with the result that linguistics should focus on this interaction, its functions, and its constraints.

3.3   The Morphology Hypothesis

On the Morphology Hypothesis, morphographemic productivity is the same in inflection and derivation. The results (cf. Appendix II) indicate a superiority effect for morphographemic productivity in inflection for both familiar and unfamiliar words. This result cannot be due to the greater complexity of the MA in derivation, because the complexities of the (tested) MA in derivation are, with one exception, a small proper subset of those of the MA in inflection. Rather, the superiority effect of inflectional morphographemics is due to the fact that the *contexts of alternation* in inflection are typically less complex in inflection than in derivation. Consider an example. As a rule, stem-final <y> changes to <i> before a suffix beginning with a vowel, as in <rely ~ reliable>, and <t> is palatalized before a suffix beginning with <iV>, as in <create ~ creation>. In <beauty ~ beauteous> and <bounty ~ bounteous>, however, <y> alternates with <e>, not <i>, in order to prevent the creation of the same environment in which <t> palatalizes. Since the <e/y> MA is relatively complex, involving transderivational constraints, it is not surprising that its productivity is relatively low. It is so low, in fact, that nobody in the ninth grade spells it correctly. Thus, one of the reasons morphographemic productivity is lower in derivation than in inflection is that MA in derivation are typically subject to greater contextual complexity. A second reason for the morphographemic superiority effect in inflection is that derivational boundaries are more difficult to recognize than inflectional. In our corpus, for example, <i/y> before a suffix beginning with a vowel is spelled correctly before inflectional COMP <-er>, as in <happy ~ happier>, but incorrectly before derivational <-able>, as in <rely ~ reliable>. Since the <y/i> rule is the same before both <-er> and <-able>, the difference in productivity must be due to the greater complexity of the analyzability of <-able>. In sum, among the determinants of the productivity of an MA is contextual complexity, including complexity of contextual analyzability.

3.4   The Morphographemic Rule Hypothesis

Previous work (Luelsdorff 1990) has indicated the following order of acquisition of morphographemic rules:

I   Deletions
II   Substitutions
III   Additions

In the present study (cf. Appendix II), we also find substitutions acquired before additions, with the identity mappings <y/y, o/y, f/f> acquired in between:

I   Deletions
II   Substitutions
      A. Non-identity
      B. Identity
III   Additions

These results are puzzling, because deletions *and* insertions are *logically* less complex than the substitutions they compose (see chapter 2). Thus, the orders of morphographemic productivity cannot be explained solely in terms of the relative complexity of the formal logical relations involved. Rather than view the operations of deletion, substitutions, and addition in isolation, we examined their productivity in their *contexts of occurrence* as well. In isolation, both <i/y> and <y/y> are substitutions, but <i/y> is three times more productive than <y/y>. Here, the difference in the productivity is not explained by the sameness of the operation (substitution). An examination of the relative *complexities of the contexts*, however, reveals that <y/y> is more complex than <i/y>, because it either applies in <v_> (<gay ~ gayer>) or <CC_> (<shy ~ shyer>). Hence, the differential complexity of the contextual constraints on the same formal operation (substitution) accounts for the differential orders of acquisition in the acquisition of morphographemic alternations. Not only is the less complex context <C_+V> (<merry ~ merrier>) the context which is acquired earlier, but also the context to which the learner perforce reverts - the major misspellings of <shyer, dryer> are <shier, drier> - before the requisite complexity evolves, subject to the lawful constraints on complexity growth (cf. chapter 9, this volume).

4.   Conclusion

In the above we have been concerned with the productivity of phonology-free MA in a developmental setting. We hypothesized that morphographemic productivity is influenced by (1) familiarity, (2) part of speech, (3) occurrence in inflected, as opposed to derived words, and (4) MA type as either non-identical substitution, identical substitution, and addition. We find superiority effects for familiarity, for ADJs over Vs, Vs over Ns, and Ns over ADVs, for inflections over derivations, for non-identical substitutions over identical, and substitutions over additions.

Underlying these disparate effects, however, is the all-pervasive factor of relative linguistic complexity. In earlier work (chapter 9, this volume; Luelsdorff & Eyland, chapter 7, this volume), we offered empirical support for Sgall's (1986) theory of orthographic complexity by showing that higher ranking items on his scales of univocality and complexness were in fact acquired later and, in addition, that lower ranked items on a scale of relative lexical frequency are acquired later. This means that the ambiguity, compositional complexness, and relative frequency of a sign decisively determine the order in which that sign is learned. The present study imparts two additional significant dimensions to complexity. Not only does relative morphographemic productivity correlate with different parts of speech, but with the relative number of MAs within each part of speech, i.e. different parts of speech exhibit different degrees of univocality in terms of the number of different types of MA their members exhibit. At one level, this PoS:MA univocality ratio is less general than Sgall's (1987) univocality ratio of phonemes to graphemes. At another level, they are both indices of degrees of violations of biuniqueness, i.e. univocality. The second dimension is that of the relative complexity of context. We find that the same relations are learned earlier or later depending upon the relative complexity of the contexts in which they occur and that different relations in contexts of similar complexity are learned earlier or later depending upon their relative complexity. Evidently, of the two - contextual complexity and relational complexity - it is contextual complexity that is decisive in resolving conflict situations. There is something so inevitable about this that we choose to formulate it in terms of a law, which we call the "Law of Contextual Complexity":

The Law of Contextual Complexity
The complexity of an alternation is always less than the complexity of the context in which the alternation occurs.

We are now in a position to provide an overarching explanation of the linguistic epistemological phenomena presented by Sgall (1987), empirically verified by Luelsdorff & Eyland (chapter 7, this volume), and developed and extended in the above. In Sgall, univocality is a paradigmatic phenomenon, because it deals with relations *in absentia*, and complexness is a syntagmatic phenomenon, because it deals with relations *in presentia*. By regarding the part-of-speech effect as a paradigmatic phenomenon on a par with univocality and the remainder of the effects as syntagmatic phenomena on a par with complexness, we arrive at a general notion of complexity encompassing relations both syntagmatic and paradigmatic.

APPENDIX I. Phonology-free Morphographemic Alternations

ITEM	I II	%E	ITEM	I II	%E
1 tried	(3, 3)	15	17 plays	(5, 5)	42
cried	(1, 0)		lays	(6, 7)	
2 heavier	(0, 0)	12	18 boys	(0, 0)	4
merrier	(3, 0)		toys	(1, 0)	
3 heaviest	(1, 1)	8	19 -donkeys	(2, 3)	8
-merriest	(1, 0)		-monkeys	(0, 1)	
4 happily	(4, 0)	19	20 trying	(0, 6)	0
-merrily	(1, 1)		flying	(0, 0)	
5 -reliable	(12,10)	77	21 shyer	(7, 7)	35
-deniable	(8,10)		dryer/drier	(1, 2)	
6 beautiful	(1, 0)	35	22 -shyly	(8,10)	62
-bountiful	(8, 9)		dryly/drily	(8, 6)	
7 -beauteous	(13,12)	100	23 daily	(6, 6)	39
-bounteous	(13,13)		-gaily	(4, 1)	
8 business	(1, 1)	23	24 Galsworthys	(11,13)	88
noisiness	(5, 5)		Sothbys	(12,13)	
9 tries	(2, 1)	27	25 does	(0, 0)	0
cries	(5, 3)		goes	(0, 1)	
10 babies	(3, 4)	15	26 cargoes	(8, 6)	37
-candies	(1, 3)		heroes	(9, 6)	
11 lying	(0, 0)	4	negroes	(5, 1)	
dying	(1, 4)		potatoes	(0, 0)	
12 played	(2, 3)	54	tomatoes	(2, 1)	
-slayed	(12,12)		27 buffalos	(0, 0)	13
13 player	(0, 0)	0	photos	(1, 2)	
-layer	(0, 1)		pianos	(4, 6)	
14 playing	(0, 0)	8	28 thieves	(3, 1)	15
laying	(2, 0)		wives	(0, 6)	
15 -gayer	(0, 1)	12	wolves	(3, 6)	
-gayest	(3, 3)		leaves	(2, 1)	
16 said	(6, 2)	41	29 chiefs	(8, 6)	39
laid	(7, 8)		cliffs	(0, 0)	
paid	(3, 3)		-proofs	(8, 9)	
			roofs	(4, 2)	

-X = unfamiliar word, I = first run on 10/09/86, II = second run on 12/11/86, and %E = error percentage on I

APPENDIX II. Developmental Morphographemics (N = 13)

F: ADJ > V > N > ADV   F̄: N > ADV > ADJ > V

ADJ	A	I	F/F̄	R	D	F/F̄	ALL
	y/i	-er	12/	2	-able	/77	6
		-est	8/8	1	-ful	8/62	4
	y/e				-ous	/100	
	y/y	-er	35/13	3			13
V	y/i	-ed	15/	4.5			9.5
		-d	41/	7			15
		-es	27/	6			12
	y/y	-ed	15/100	4.5			9.5
		-ing	8/	3			4
		-es	42/	8			16
	ie/y	-ing	4/	2			2
	o/oe	-s	0/	1			1
N	y/i	-es	15/8	3.5	-ness	23/	9.5
	y/y	-s	8/	1	-er	0/0	4
	o/oe	-s	37/	5			14
	o/o	-s	13/	2			7
	f/v	-es	15	3.5			9.5
	f/f	-s	51/62	6			17
ADV	y/i				-ly	39/22	1
	y/y				-ly	62/62	2

X > Y = part of speech X has significantly more total productive morphographemic alternations than part of speech Y; A = Alternation; I = Inflection; D = Derivation; F = Familiar; F̄ = Unfamiliar; X/Y = X alternates with Y; F/F̄ = % incorrect familiar vs. % incorrect unfamiliar; R = within part of speech rank orders correct; ALL = between part of speech rank order correct

Orthographic Complexity and Orthography Acquisition*

Introduction

A frequent finding of first and second language acquisition research is that some linguistic structures are acquired after others. Efforts to explain such differential orders of learning, and the forces that drive them, appeal to notions like perceptual salience, frequency, negative transfer, over-generalization, simplification, regularity, typological markedness, parameter (re)setting, and rule complexity, each with varying degrees of clarity and success (cf. Rutherford 1982 for review).

A virtually uncharted terrain of L2 acquisitional research is developmental orthography. We have some understanding of preliterate spellers' creative spelling (Ferreiro 1983, Read 1986), several stadial theories of the development of English (Ehri 1986, Gentry 1982, Frith 1986) and German (Günther 1986) spelling, and several theories of the processing of English orthography by dyslexic and normal adult readers and spellers (cf. Ellis 1984 for review). What we lack is a theory of second orthography acquisition in reading and spelling by learners literate or quasi-literate in their mother tongue - a theory of developmental biliteracy (Luelsdorff 1986, 1987; Philips 1984). Sorely lacking is a universal theory of orthographic complexity to explain the facts of differential orders of acquisition in spelling and reading in first and second language acquisition, different degrees of processing difficulties in mature readers and spellers, and different kinds of orthography loss in the reading impaired (Coltheart et al. 1980).

Our present purpose is to partially articulate a general theory of orthographic complexity and use it to predict the facts of the acquisition of English orthography by German school children. In particular, we are interested in establishing and explaining differential orders of acquisition of L2-English developmental orthography in the domain of the ortho-graphy of inflection and contraction.

The orthography of inflection and contraction appears to be a promising area of developmental inquiry because the allomorphs of the inflectional morphemes may be spelled quasi taxonomic phonemically, as in the plural and third singular, morphophonemically, as in the regular past and past participle, quasi morphophonemically and morphemically, as in the possessive singular, and purely morphemically, as in the possessive plural. Complicating matters are the contracted forms of third singular and auxiliary and main verb *is* and *has*, which sound like the plural and third singular and possessive singular, but look like only the possessive singular.

There are also several inflection-dependent orthographic phenomena, such as <y> → <ie> in the plural and third singular and the doubling of consonants after stressed, short vowels in the progressive, past, and past participle, and comparative and superlative of the adjective. To the extent that such metaorthographic processes are determined by inflection, they belong to the orthography of inflection.

Our thesis is that the various normative spellings of the inflected and contracted allomorphs of English exhibit various degrees of complexity depending upon the kind and amount of linguistic information needed to relate their sound to their spelling and that this differential complexity determines the order in which the orthography of inflection and contraction is acquired in first and second language acquisition.

In order to test this hypothesis, we adopted and extended a partial theory of orthographic complexity and elicited pupils' written responses to the relevant variables on a sentence dictation test (reproduced in Appendix I). Sentence dictations were essential to the task at hand, since many of the items would have otherwise been morphologically and syntactically ambiguous. The sample tested consisted of intact classes of German pupils in English as a foreign language in grades 6 (N = 32), 7 (N = 26), 8 (N = 18), 9 (N = 14) of the *Gymnasium*. *Gymnasium* pupils have been exposed to the normative spelling of inflection and contraction by their second year of English in grade 6.

Since this is a pilot investigation, we had no way of knowing in advance which order of acquisition to expect in which grades. Consequently, we adopted a design which was both cross-sectional and longitudinal, with the same dictation administered to all the pupils in all the grades on three separate occasions at roughly two-month intervals beginning in September, the start of the school year. The results reported here are restricted to the analysis of the first and third testings in grade 9 (N = 14), where the pupils (average age 15;5) are in their fifth year of English.

Orders of acquisition were determined by applying a modified version of the ordering-theoretic method (Dulay *et al.* 1982: 222-225) according to which a structure A is acquired before a structure B if the percentage of disconfirming cases (where B is right and A is wrong) is "sufficiently small" (5-7%). Furthermore, structures form an unordered pair (are acquired at the same time) if they exhibit a small percentage of disconfirming cases in *both* directions (7% in one direction and not more than 14% in the other).

We adopted the more conservative criterion of grouping if the difference in both directions was 7% or less and the more liberal criterion of otherwise grouping A before B iff the percentage of disconfirming cases was less than that of B before A.

1.   Orthographic complexity

Systemic deviation from grapheme-phoneme biuniqueness is the major source of error in the acquisition of a native or foreign alphabetic script. Therefore, a reasoned typology of such deviations may be used as the basis for a theory of orthographic complexity.

A first step in the direction of such a typology was recently taken by Sgall (1987). According to Sgall's proposal, the deviations from one-to-one correspondence between grapheme and phoneme may be ranked along two scales, a scale of complexness and a scale of univocality.

The scale of complexness is as follows:

i   protographeme - a grapheme no variant of which contains a diacritic sign: Czech <b, f, g, k, l, m, p, r, v>;

ii   complex grapheme with regular subgrapheme (diacritic): Czech <á, é, í, ó, ú; š, ž, č>;

iii   complex grapheme with irregular subgrapheme: Czech <ř>;

iv   protographeme string: Czech <ti>:/t'i/, <di>:/d'i/, <ni>:/n'i/; <ty>:/ti/, <dy>:/di/, <ny>:/ni/;

v   string with some complex elements, but no irregular sub-graphemes: no examples in Czech;

vi   string some of whose elements have an irregular sub-grapheme: Czech <dě>:/d'ɛ/, <tě>:/t'ɛ/, <ně>:/n'ɛ/;

vii   as in (vi), with the irregular subgrapheme corresponding to more than one phoneme in the pronunciation (or with some other difference between the number of phonemes and the number of graphemes): Czech <pě>:/pjɛ/, <město>:/mnjɛsto/.

The logic underlying the scale of complexness appears compelling:

1.   simplex grapheme (protographeme) before complex grapheme;

2.   protographeme string before complex grapheme string;

3.   regular subgrapheme before irregular subgrapheme;

4.   one-to-one before one-to-many;

5.   one-to-one before many-to-one.

The second axis, the scale of univocality, specifies the kinds and degrees of ambiguity of the operations of (oral) reading (pronunciation) and spelling. For spelling, the more complex of the two, the scale of univocality is as follows:

a.   absolute biuniqueness: Czech <b, f, g, ...>;

b.   relative biuniqueness: Czech <a, c, d, e, ...>;

c.   regular deviations: different graphemes are used for a single phoneme with different morphemes, the choice being given by a general rule and corroborated by phonemic alternations in the given morphemic position (with a different phonemic context): Czech <psy>;

d.   as in (c), without the corroborating alternations. No Czech examples;

e.   irregular deviations, the choice being given by a difference between lexical morphemes: Czech <byl>;

f.   irregular deviations, the choice being given by a morpheme whose single graphemic shape is thus ensured: Czech derivational affix <-yne>;

g.   irregular deviations with the choice given idiosyncratically (traditionally, without a functional justification): Czech <jazyk>.

A deviation from biuniqueness is graphemically ambiguous if the relation between grapheme and phoneme is many-to-one, and phonemically ambiguous if the relation between grapheme and phoneme is one-to-many. The above scale of univocality for spelling thus specifies a hierarchy of graphemic ambiguity.

Like the scale of complexness, the scale of univocality has great intuitive appeal. In essence, it states that the degree of complexity of an ambiguous orthographic representation is directly related to the kind and amount of linguistic information needed for its resolution. Such information ranges from context-free phoneme-grapheme correspondences to phoneme-grapheme correspondences whose context is sensitive to phonology, inflectional morphology, derivational morphology, semantics, and lexis.

Sgall's theory of orthographic complexity could be further developed using information derived from studies of orthographic universals (Justeson 1976, Volkov 1982) and profitably used for formulating hypotheses in the areas of developmental and acquired reading disorders, developmental psycholinguistics, and the psychology of reading and spelling. Rather than dwell on such extensions and applications, we turn to orthographic complexity and the orthography of inflection and contraction in an acquisitional setting.

2. Orthographic complexity and orthography of inflection

The theory of linguistic complexity delivers universal categories of linguistic complexity ranked from least to most complex. On the complexity hypothesis on language acquisition, more complex categories are acquired later than those which are less complex. We tested this hypothesis in the area of the orthography of English inflection and contraction. Details of the phonology of English inflection and contraction are given in Luelsdorff (1969, 1983[1987]) and Luelsdorff and Norrick (1983[1987]).

Knowledge of the boundaries and identities of the inflected and contracted morphemes of English is a necessary condition on their correct spelling. Failure to recognize that <whacks> and <tacks> are in the third singular or plural might result in their being spelled <wax> and <tax>. Failure to recognize that <passed> and <packed> are in the preterit or past participle might result in their being spelled <past> and <pact>. Failure to recognize that <boy's> is in the possessive singular might lead to its being spelled as either the plural <boys> or the possessive plural <boys'> or as contracted main verb or auxiliary <is> or <has>, i.e., correctly, but for the wrong reason (Luelsdorff, 1986: 58).

Assuming that the boundaries and identities of the inflected and contracted morphemes are known, the orthography/phonology/morphology interface exhibits the relations displayed in Figure 1.

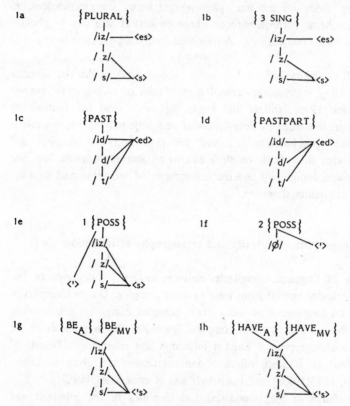

Figure 1: Phonology and orthography of inflection and contraction

The simplest cases are those of the plural, third singular, and the syllabic preterit and past participle. In such instances, either the same letter stands for either of two sounds, or two letters stand for two sounds. This complexity we represent in (1):

(1) a. $\left\{ \begin{array}{c} /s/ \\ /z/ \end{array} \right\} \rightarrow <s>$

b. $/d/ \rightarrow <d>$

c. $/i/ \rightarrow <e>$

(1a-c) rank 1 on the scale of complexness, (1b-c) 1 on the scale of univocality, and (1a) 2 on the scale of univocality, since /s/ and /z/, with major correspondences in <s> in word-final position, are relatively biunique.

Consonant singling and doubling, which are stem-finally implicated by the spelling of the preterit, past participle, and progressive, are more complicated than the plural and third singular, because they are more context sensitive. A stem-final consonant sound is spelled singly if it either follows a tense vowel or occurs in a consonant cluster, as in <dined> and <dented>. In consonant doubling, a single stem-final consonant sound is spelled doubly if it follows a stressed lax vowel and precedes a vowel-spelling, as in <wagged> and <bragged>. Of the two, consonant doubling appears the more complex, since it is sensitive to information in both the preceding and following context for its proper operation and operates on letters, rather than sounds. This relative complexity we represent in (2):

(2) a. $/C/ \rightarrow <C> /X\_\_$
     b. $<C> \rightarrow <CC> /Y\_\_Z$

What is their relative complexity measurement? We propose treating vowel "digraph" + single consonant sequences as strings with the consonant letter a protographeme and the vowel "digraph" a complex grapheme, the latter usually consisting of a protographeme followed by a regular subgrapheme (diacritic), as in <ea, oa; ae, ee, ie, oe, ue; ai, ei, oi, ui; eu, ou>. These complex graphemes have a left-handed head and a right-handed specifier, where the specifier is an instruction to pronounce the head by means of letter naming as a spelling strategy (cf. Luelsdorff 1986). That this singled consonant letter encodes the tenseness of the preceding vowel becomes evident in the orthography of inflection and derivation, where the weight of encoding tenseness is shifted from the vowel complex to the following singled consonant, as in <waged> vs. <wagged>, <biding> vs. <bidding>, and <derisive> vs. <permissive>. Similarly, simplex vowel + doubled consonant sequences are protographeme strings in which the vowel laxness is encoded in the first of the following two consonants before an inflectional suffix beginning with a vowel spelling. On this view, both singled and doubled consonants are constituents of strings with complex elements - singled consonants after doubled vowels and doubled consonants after singled vowels, with doubled consonants more complex than singled because they are complex graphemes with regular subgraphemes (the doubled letter functioning as a diacritic) rather than protographemes. Therefore, on Sgall's scales of complexness and univocality we assign consonant singling and consonant doubling the ranks of 5 and 2, singling with complexity in the vowel, and doubling with complexity in the consonants.

The voiced and voiceless preterit and past participle are sound-letter structures which are both (1) zero-to-one and (2) one-to-one, comprising jointly a relationship which is one-to-many, as in (3):

(3) a. /Ø/ → <e>

     b. $\left\{ \begin{array}{c} /d/ \\ /t/ \end{array} \right\}$ → <d>

In either case, there is one phoneme spelled by two graphemes. Hence, the voiced and voiceless preterit and past participle occupy rank 7 on the scale of complexness and rank 6 on the scale of univocality, since <ed> stands now for /t/, now for /d/, now for /id/, i.e. the relationship is one of irregular deviation, the choice given by a morpheme whose single graphemic shape is thus ensured.

In the voiced and voiceless non-syllabic possessive singular and the non-syllabic contractions, a diacritic <'> is followed by <s> and stands for either /s/ or /z/, i.e. further sound-letter relationships which are one-to-many. These we depict as in (4)

(4) a. /Ø/ → <'>

     b. $\left\{ \begin{array}{c} /s/ \\ /z/ \end{array} \right\}$ → <s>

In each case there is one phoneme spelled by a diacritic and a grapheme. Since <'> has no sound value, it cannot be a subgrapheme. Furthermore, since it stands mainly for either possession or contraction, it cannot be regular. For these reasons, we assign <'s> to rank 8 on the scale of complexity, and, on the scale of univocality, rank 6.

In the possessive plural, the diacritic <'> bears a direct, unmediated relationship to the grammatical category of possession. It differs from the possessive singular in that neither sound nor letter are involved. The possessive plural we represent as in (5):

(5) /∅/ → <'>

Due to the absence of both letter and sound, we assign the possessive plural to rank 9 on the scale of complexity, and, on the scale of univocality, rank 8.

In the syllabic possessive singular and the syllabic contractions of main verb and auxiliary <has> and <is>, syllabic /ɨz/ is uniformly spelled <s'>. This we represent as in (6):

(6) a. /∅/ → <'>

b. /ɨ/ → <∅>

c. /z/ → <s>

In view of the fact that (6) includes (5), which we assigned rank 9 on the scale of complexness, we assign (6) the rank of at least 9 on the scale of complexness and at least 8 on the scale of univocality.

Evidently, the relations among orthography, phonology, morphology and contraction depicted in Figure 1, and the relations among orthography, phonology, and morphology in consonant singling and doubling, may be reduced to the rules presented in (1-6). As it happens, the rules (1-6) may themselves be reduced to three groups: those which are one-to-one (1), those which are one-to-many (2, 3, 4), and those which are none-to-one or one-to-none (5, 6). If it is normal for a sound *signifié* to have a letter *signifiant*, it must be less normal for a sound *signifié* to have several letter *signifiants*, and even less normal for no sound *signifié* to have a letter *signifiant* or a sound *signifié* to have no letter *signifiant*. Accordingly, our hypothesis on the acquisition of the orthography of inflection and contraction is as follows: one-to-one correspondences are acquired before those which are one-to-many, and one-to-many correspondences are acquired before those which are none-to-one or one-to-none.

We indicated above that knowledge of the orthography of inflection necessarily depended upon knowledge of phonology and morphology. Now, since recognition of the morphology depends upon the syntax and the syntax interacts with the semantics, knowledge of the orthography of inflection and contraction depends upon knowledge of syntax and semantics. Since our learners dispose of imperfect knowledge of the syntax and semantics of English, it is to be supposed that this imperfect knowledge will adversely effect their performance on the orthography of inflection and contraction, quite independently of their knowledge of the principles of English orthography themselves. For example, if a possessive is incorrectly categorized as a plural, it will be spelled as a plural, irrespective of whether the speller knows how to spell the possessive. Consequently, some errors cannot be understood without reference to a hierarchy of morphemic complexity.

Brown (1973) provides us with the acquisition order and complexity order of 13 "morphemes" of English. Categories common to both our studies are: (1) plural, (2) past regular, (3) third person regular, (4) contractible copula, and (5) contractible auxiliary. To these we add: (6) contractible main verb *has*, and (7) contractible *has* as an auxiliary. Whatever is known about the possessive (Vachek 1961, Zwicky 1987) is cast within a different framework. Comparison of the scale of grammatical complexity with the scale of orthographic complexity reveals the interesting fact that the two do not coincide. The third singular and the plural, for example, differ in morphemic complexity but are orthographically equally complex, and the syllabic and non-syllabic preterit differ in orthographic complexity but are morphemically equally complex. Were these two scales, the orthographic and the morphological, the same, one might expect the observed acquisition hierarchy to be a function of one or the other. The fact that these parameters are different, however, induces a systemic dynamism or disequilibrium (Vachek 1983), and this dynamism is responsible for the production of classes of errors which cannot be understood on the basis of the scale of orthographic complexity alone.

3. Acquisition of the orthography of inflection and contraction

Applying the above-mentioned methodological procedure to the data of the first dictation, we obtained the results depicted in Table 1. Here, the Roman numerals in the first column represent the acquisitional groups, the Arabic numerals in the second column the number of structures the items in each acquisitional group precede, and the Arabic numerals in the third column the individual structures comprising the acquisitional groups.

Group		Precedes	Structures
I	I	26	3.3, 11.2, 11.3, 11.4, 4.1, 4.2, 4.3, 4.4, 6.1, 6.3, 9.2, 12.2, 6.2
II		20	8.2, 12.1, 5.2, 5.3, 12,3,
III	II	15	3.1, 1.1, 7.2, 9.1, 10.1
IV		11	1.2, 7.1, 11.1, 5.1
V		10	8.1
VI		8	3.2, 10.2
VII	III	3	2.2, 2.1, 7.3, 8.3, 9.3
VIII		0	1.3, 2.3, 10.3

Table 1.   *Acquisition hierarchy at* t_1

In order for the acquisitional groups to not merely be an artifact of the method used for determining them, it appears essential to ask whether the structures within the groups are the products of the *same* set of processing strategies and whether the structures within different groups are the products of a *different* set of processing strategies. Only then can we be relatively sure that our method-derived acquisitional groups correspond to something other than the method.

Acquisitional group I, from this perspective, contains structures which bear a one-to-one relationship between letter and sound - the plural, the syllabic past participle, and the syllabic third singular (but see below).

Groups II, III, IV, V, and VI contain the environmentally conditioned spellings of consonant singling after long vowels, consonant doubling after short vowels, structures with a one-to-many relationship between sound and letter, as in the voiced and voiceless preterit and the voiced past participle, or diacritic and sound, as in the voiced and voiceless non-syllabic possessive singular, and a whole array of non-syllabic contractions (voiceless main verb and auxiliary <is> and <has>). These groups are distinguished from group I by the greater complexity of their sound-letter mapping and the greater complexity of their underlying semantics, syntax, and phonology (cf. Brown 1973: 308-309).

Groups VII and VIII consist of either structures where something, an apostrophe, is used to spell nothing sensible, a zero allomorph, or structures where nothing is used to spell something, namely the vowel in the syllabic possessive singular and the vowels in contracted syllabic main verb and auxiliary <is> and <has>. These last acquired groups thus consist of signs with either a zero *signifiant* or a zero *signifié* and occupy the highest rank on both Sgall's scale of orthographic complexness and Brown's scale of grammatical morphemic complexity.

There is no unambiguous evidence countering the claim that observed order of acquisition does not differ from the order of acquisition predicted by the order of orthographic complexity. Apparent counterexamples include third singular /s/ and /z/ and the syllabic preterit /i/. According to the complexity hypothesis presented above, these three structures are among the simplest, yet the first appears in acquisition group III, the second in acquisition group VI, and the third in acquisition group II. Typical errors include <jumpes, jumped> for <jumps>, <rubbes, robbes> for <rubs>, <wages> for <wags>, and <dentied> for <dented>. If one regards the extraneous vowels as constituents of the endings, i.e. <jump + es, rubb + es, wag + es, dent + ied>, then the observed acquisitional orders contradict the ones predicted. If, however, one treats the extraneous vowels as constituents of the stems, i.e. <jumpe + s, rubbe

+ es, wage + s, denti + ed>, then the acquisition orders observed correspond to the acquisition orders predicted, and there are no counterexamples to the claim that acquisition order = complexity order. In fact, the evidence in support of this hypothesis is so strong that it appears that the complexity order itself may be used to resolve the analytical ambiguity of the errors in question. Moreover, there is independent evidence for the existence of overgeneralizations of long vowel spellings for short in both first (Ehri 1986) and second language acquisition (Luelsdorff 1986).

In sum, the application of a mechanical procedure for partitioning the data into acquisitional groups results in eight major groupings and eight minor groupings of structures in adjacent major groupings. The structures in adjacent major groupings differ from one another by at least two errors, and the structures within major groups and within minor groups differ from one another by at most one. Insistence on unifying principles underlying groupings results in the reduction of the initial eight groups to three. In the first of these, the relationship between letter and sound is one-to-one. In the second, the relationship is either context-sensitive or one-to-many. In the third, either a diacritic stands for no sound or some sound is not represented by a letter. Differences in semiotic principles, rather than rules, thus underlie the differentiation into groups. Inasmuch as the acquisitional groups observed correspond to the acquisitional groups predicted, we conclude that the acquisitional order of the orthography of inflection and contraction supports the theory that complexity explains acquisition.

4.   Acquisitional stages

Ehri (1986: 141) distinguishes three stages in the development of orthographic knowledge of English according to the type of regularity evident in the spellings invented by children in the course of learning to read and spell: (1) the semiphonetic; (2) the phonetic; (3) the morphemic. In the semiphonetic stage children use their knowledge of alphabet letter names to create partial spellings of words, for example, spelling <dress> as <S> or <elevator> as <L>. The phonetic stage emerges when short vowel spellings are learned in the first grade and lasts until spellings break away from a one-to-one relationship between letter and sound. The morphemic stage may begin in the second grade when spellers shift from an exclusive reliance on one-to-one relations to the use of word-based spelling patterns as well. Ehri stresses that phonetic spellings are not abandoned in the morphemic stage, but supplemented by morphemic patterns.

The analysis of the errors in the spellings of the inflections and contractions provides very strong confirmation of a *mixed* stage of phonetic and morphemic spelling in the acquisition of L2-English orthography by German school children. For example, the most frequent error on the syllabic possessive singular and the contractions of syllabic main verb and auxiliary <has> and <is> is the addition of a spurious letter to represent the vowel. Syllabic possessive singular <Rich's> is most frequently misspelled <Richie's> (7x), <Richi's> (2x), <Richy's> (1x), <Richies> (1x), <Rigia's> (1x), and <Bridge's> (1x), where the vowel letter is phonetic and the apostrophe is morphemic. Syllabic auxiliary <has> in <Ross's> is misspelled <Ross is> (8x) and with a syllabic <e> (4x), and <Rich's> is misspelled (Rich is> (5x) and with a syllabic stem vowel (7x). Contracted syllabic main verb <has> is written with an extraneous stem-final vowel in 11/14 cases. Since most of these examples of phonetic spelling - and there are more - also contain the required morphemic <'s>, they persuasively demonstrate the coexistence of phonetic and morphemic spelling.

It would be misguided, however, to construe the morphemic stage as consisting of spelling patterns which are solely word-based, however, because, as repeatedly emphasized above, the very recognition of the inflected and contracted allomorphy presupposes syntactic and semantic categorization above the word. Failure to syntactically categorize or categorize correctly results in errors even if one does know the correct inflected and contracted spellings. Such miscategorizations typically involve spelling the possessive as though it were the plural, main-verb <has>-contractions as though they are the possessive, and auxiliary <has>-contractions as though they were uncontracted auxiliary <is>, i.e. rank-downshifting along the scale of grammatical complexity (see above), without which they cannot be understood. One major example must suffice. Contracted syllabic main verb <has> in <Mitch's> was misspelled <Mitche's> on 8/14 occasions. At first sight, <Mitche's>, with an <e>, for <Mitch's>, appears to be just another example of phonetic spelling, with the vowel letter <e> used to spell the vowel sound /ɪz/. However, <has> as the contracted syllabic auxiliary in <Ross's> was misspelled <Ross is> on 8/14 occasions, not <Rosse's>, as one would expect if auxiliary <has> were being processed like main verb <has>. We suggest that this difference in error types for the same standard language phonetic and orthographic form is correlated with a difference in syntactic processing strategies resulting in a difference in morpheme recognition: <Mitche's> as the *possessive* constituent of the spurious NP [[[Mitche]'s] [photos]] in the dictated sentence *Mitch's photos of America's buffalos* and <Ross is> as the spurious constituent [₇[ₙRoss] [_AUX is]] in the dictated sentence *Ross's often cheated on his hardest tests.* This example at once illustrates that the spellings of the English inflections and contractions are not word-based in their entirety and that the constraints on their misrepresentation can consequently not be fully understood without recourse to a syntactically/semantically based scale of morphemic complexity.

5. Individual variation

The above remarks are generalizations about structures, not the individuals responsible for the production of those structures. Aspects of individual similarities and differences are presented in Table 2. Here, the columns contain the numbers of the structures studied, the rows contain the numbers of the individual subjects, and the cells contain either a 1 or a 0, depending upon whether the subject's performance was normative or non-normative. The Roman numerals I, II, and III stand for the semiotically and psycholinguistically motivated groups, where the underlined structures 3.2, 3.1, and 5.3 in group II, if the above reanalysis is accepted, belong to acquisitional group I.

All subjects performed uniformly correctly on group I, but considerable interindividual variation appears in groups II and III, with some implicational patterning within each of these groups. Within group III, for example, if an individual performs normatively on 2.1, then s/he will perform normatively on 2.2. Within group II, to take another example, if an individual performs normatively on 10.1, then s/he will also perform

Table 2. *Implicational scale at t_1*

Group	Structure	7	2	3	9	11	10	13	1	6	14	5	12	8
III	2.3	o	o	o	o	o	o	o	o	o	o	o	o	o
	10.3	o	o	o	o	o	o	o	o	o	o	o	o	o
	1.3	o	o	o	o	o	o	o	o	o	o	o	o	1
	8.3	o	1	o	o	o	o	o	o	o	o	o	o	1
	2.1	o	1	o	o	o	o	o	1	o	o	o	o	1
	7.3	o	1	1	o	o	o	o	1	o	o	o	o	1
	9.3	1	1	o	o	o	o	o	1	o	o	o	o	1
	2.2	1	o	1	o	1	o	o	o	1	o	o	o	1
II	3.2	1	o	o	1	1	o	o	o	1	o	o	1	1
	10.2	1	o	1	o	o	o	o	o	o	1	o	1	1
	8.1	1	o	1	1	o	o	o	1	1	o	o	1	1
	1.2	1	1	1	1	o	o	1	o	1	o	1	o	1
	7.1	1	1	1	o	1	o	1	1	o	1	o	1	1
	3.1	1	1	o	1	o	1	o	1	o	1	1	o	1
	11.1	1	1	o	1	o	1	1	o	1	o	o	1	1
	5.1	o	o	1	1	o	1	o	1	1	o	1	1	1
	1.1	1	1	1	1	o	1	o	1	o	1	o	1	1
	7.2	1	1	1	1	o	1	1	1	1	o	1	o	1
	9.1	1	1	1	1	o	1	o	1	o	1	o	1	1
	10.1	1	1	1	1	1	o	1	1	o	1	o	1	1
	5.3	1	1	1	1	1	1	o	1	1	o	1	o	1
	12.3	1	1	1	1	1	1	1	1	o	1	o	1	1
	6.2	o	1	1	1	1	1	1	1	1	1	1	o	1
	8.2	1	1	1	1	1	1	1	1	1	1	1	o	1
	12.1	1	1	1	1	1	1	1	1	1	o	1	1	1
	5.2	1	1	1	1	1	1	1	1	o	1	1	1	1
I	3.3	1	1	1	1	1	1	1	1	1	1	1	1	1
	11.2	1	1	1	1	1	1	1	1	1	1	1	1	1
	11.3	1	1	1	1	1	1	1	1	1	1	1	1	1
	11.4	1	1	1	1	1	1	1	1	1	1	1	1	1
	4.1	1	1	1	1	1	1	1	1	1	1	1	1	1
	4.2	1	1	1	1	1	1	1	1	1	1	1	1	1
	4.3	1	1	1	1	1	1	1	1	1	1	1	1	1
	4.4	1	1	1	1	1	1	1	1	1	1	1	1	1
	6.1	1	1	1	1	1	1	1	1	1	1	1	1	1
	6.3	1	1	1	1	1	1	1	1	1	1	1	1	1
	9.2	1	1	1	1	1	1	1	1	1	1	1	1	1
	12.2	1	1	1	1	1	1	1	1	1	1	1	1	1

normatively on 8.2. The most important single generalization, however, is that each individual's performance is better on structures of group I than on structures of group II, and better on structures of group II than on structures of group III, a distribution which follows from the complexity theory of orthography acquisition. Note that this theory constrains the class of individual variants, permitting I > II > III, but prohibiting I > III > II, II > III > I, II > I > III, III > II > I, and III > I > II. Within each acquisitional group, individuals are free to vary outside the confines of the implicational constraints, whatever they may be. Within acquisitional group III, for example, it would be strange to find an individual who could spell the possessive plural after /s/, but not the possessive plural after /z/. Thus viewed, implicational relations follow from orthographic universals and establish and constrain the parameters along which individuals may vary.

6. Developmental orthography

The conclusions drawn thusfar have been based on cross-sectional data elicited from one group of subjects at one point in time. The acquisition orders observed were found to flow from universal scales of orthographic complexity and the errors made from the directed interaction of scales of complexity both orthographic and morphemic. Moreover, individual variation was found to be constrained by the relationship between adjacent complexity groups such that the quality of performance in a more complex group directly predicts the quality of performance in an adjacent group that is less complex. The resultant model of language acquisition is thus constrained by both *adjacency* and *directionality* and, requiring the interaction of different scales of complexity, is *interactive* and modular.

What remains to be shown is the development of the orthography of inflection and contraction and the variation that this development exhibits. To this end, we duplicated the above experiment on the same group of subjects four months later, with the results presented in Table 3.

If it is true that acquisition groups I, II, and III are increasingly more complex, as stipulated by the universal hierarchy of orthographic complexity, and the universal hierarchy of orthographic complexity controls the order of orthography acquisition, as shown above, then (1)

the members of *adjacent* acquisitional groups ought to be acquired before
the members of non-adjacent acquisitional groups, i.e. II to I, and III to
II, rather than III to I; and (2) different acquisitional groups with forgotten members ought to be *adjacent*, and forgetting ought to proceed
from more to less complex. Call (1) the Adjacency and Directionality
Conditions on Acquisition and (2) the Adjacency and Directionality
Conditions on Attrition. Taken together, (1) and (2) constrain linguistic
mental movement up and down the scales of linguistic complexity, hence
language learnability and teachability (cf. Pienemann 1986).

Group		Precedes	Structure
I	I	18	3.3, 11.2, 11.3, 11.4, 4.1, 4.2, 4.3, 6.1, 6.3, 7.2, 8.2, 10.1
			1.1, 5.2, 5.3, 7.1, 9.1, 9.2, 12.2, 4.4
II		12	12.3, 6.2
			11.1, 3.1, 10.2, 12.1
III	II	9	5.1, 7.3, 1.2
IV		7	8.1 8.3
V		5	3.2 2.2
VI		2	10.3, 2.1, 9.3
VII	III	0	2.3, 1.3

Table 3. *Acquisition hierarchy at* t_1

Are the actual observations consistent with these predictions?
Comparison of Tables 1 and 3 reveals the fact that members 2.2, 7.3, 8.3
of acquisition group III in hierarchy I have entered acquisition group II in
hierarchy II and that none have entered acquisition group I. Furthermore,
members 1.1., 5.2, 5.3, 7.1, 7.2, 8.2, 9.1, 10.1 of acquisition group II in
hierarchy I have entered acquisition group I in hierarchy II. Since members of III have entered II and members of II have entered I, while no

members of III have entered I directly, the experimental results are consistent with the Adjacency and Directionality Conditions on Acquisition. Moreover, 1/30 structures, namely the <-ed> in past participle <bragged>, suffers attrition to the extent that it falls to a different acquisitional group. Since this attritional movement is from group I to group II, these experimental results (cf. also below) are consistent with the Adjacency and Directionality Conditions on Attrition.

The Complexity Theory of Orthography Acquisition, including a Hierarchy of Complexity, and Adjacency and Directionality Conditions on Acquisition and Attrition, strongly constrains language learning and language forgetting. If the theory of complexity stipulates that III is more complex than II, and that II is more complex than I, then I is learned before II and II before III. This means that III is more error-prone than II, and that II is more error-prone than I. Furthermore, in acquisition, the members of III will enter II and the members of II will enter I and, in attrition, a lost member of I implies a lost member of II, and a lost member of II implies a lost member of III.

Aspects of the orthographic development of the sample from time t_1 to time t_2 (four months) are given in the transition matrix in Table 4. The numbers of the structures are in the columns, the numbers of the subjects in the rows. 1 in the cells stands for acquired, 0 stands for not acquired, an underlined 1 stands for a structure acquired between t_1 and t_2, and an underlined 0 for a structure forgotten between t_1 and t_2. $0 \rightarrow 1$ and $1 \rightarrow 0$ stand for the numbers of subjects learning and forgetting and the numbers of structures learned and forgotten. The grand totals stand for the total number of changes the subjects and structures underwent.

For any given transition period, the easiest structure is the structure with the most learning and the least forgetting. By the Adjacency and Directionality Conditions on Attrition, a forgotten member of a less complex group implies a forgotten member of a more complex group (directionality) and the two groups must be adjacent. For example, if an individual forgets a structure in group I, then another forgotten structure belongs to group II. Similarly, if an individual forgets a structure in group II, then another forgotten structure will belong to group III. Examples include subjects 14, 10, and 8 in Table 4. Subject 14 forgot the non-syllabic third singular (group I), the non-syllabic auxiliary <is>-contraction (group II) and the possessive singular <'s> (group II). Subject

Item Subject	1			3			11				4				2			5			6			7			8			9			10			12			0→Ī	1→0	Total
	1	2	3	1	2	3	1	2	3	4	1	2	3	4	3	1	2	1	2	3	1	2	3	1	2	3	1	2	3	1	2	3	1	2	3	1	2	3			
1	1	1	0	0	1	1	1	1	1	1	1	1	1	1	0	0	0	1	1	1	1	1	1	1	0	1	0	0	0	0	0	0	1	1	1	4	0	4
2	1	0	0	0	0	1	1	1	1	1	0	0	1	0	1	1	1	1	1	1	1	1	1	1	1	0	1	1	0	1	1	0	1	0	1	4	2	6
3	0	0	1	0	1	1	1	1	1	1	0	0	0	1	0	1	0	1	1	1	1	1	1	1	1	0	0	0	1	0	1	1	0	1	0	5	5	10
4	0	1	0	1	1	1	1	1	1	1	0	1	0	1	1	1	1	1	1	1	0	1	1	0	0	1	0	0	1	0	0	1	1	0	1	3	1	4
5	1	0	1	0	1	1	1	1	1	1	0	1	1	1	1	1	1	1	1	1	1	1	1	1	1	1	0	0	0	1	0	1	1	0	1	4	1	5
6	0	1	1	1	1	1	1	1	1	1	0	0	1	1	0	1	1	1	1	1	1	0	1	1	1	1	0	0	0	0	0	0	0	1	1	4	0	4
7	1	0	1	1	1	0	1	1	1	1	1	0	1	1	0	0	1	1	1	1	0	1	0	1	1	1	0	1	0	0	0	1	0	1	1	8	2	10
8	1	1	1	1	0	1	1	1	1	1	0	0	1	1	0	0	0	1	0	1	1	1	1	1	0	1	1	1	1	1	0	1	0	1	1	2	3	5
9	1	0	1	0	1	0	0	1	1	1	1	0	0	1	0	1	0	1	1	1	0	1	0	1	0	1	0	0	1	0	1	1	1	1	1	5	1	6
10	0	0	0	0	1	1	1	1	0	1	0	0	0	1	0	1	1	0	0	1	1	1	1	1	1	1	0	1	1	0	1	1	1	1	1	5	2	7
11	0	1	1	1	0	1	1	1	1	1	0	1	0	1	1	1	0	1	1	1	0	1	1	1	1	0	0	0	1	0	0	1	1	0	1	6	0	6
12	1	0	0	0	0	1	1	1	1	1	0	0	1	1	0	0	1	1	1	1	1	1	1	1	1	1	0	1	0	0	1	0	0	1	1	1	2	3
13	1	1	0	0	0	1	0	1	1	1	1	0	0	0	1	1	0	1	0	0	1	0	1	1	0	1	0	1	0	1	0	0	1	0	0	5	0	5
14	0	0	0	0	0	1	1	1	1	1	0	0	0	1	1	1	1	0	1	0	0	0	1	0	1	0	0	0	0	0	0	1	0	1	1	0	3	3
0→Ī	3	2	2	2	3	0	2	0	0	0	1	2	0	0	1	1	0	0	0	1	0	0	0	3	1	6	2	0	0	2	0	0	3	1	1			
1→0	1	2	0	1	2	0	1	0	0	0	0	1	0	1	0	1	0	1	0	0	2	0	0	0	0	3	0	1	0	0	0	1	1	0	0			
Total	4	4	1	3	5	0	1	2	0	1	1	2	1	1	0	2	0	4	3	5	6	1	6	2	1	0	3	8	4	4	1	1			

Table 4.   *Transition matrix from t_1 to t_2*

10 forgot the plural with stem change (group I) and the non-syllabic past participle <ed> (group II). Subject 8 forgot the non-syllabic third singular (group I), non-syllabic auxiliary <is>-contraction (group II), and the possessive plural <'> (group III). The fact that there are no subjects who forgot structures in groups I and III, while at the same time not forgetting structures in group II, must mean that language attrition, like language acquisition, is subject to law. This law, we suggest, is the Law of Complexity.

7. Conclusion

A core concern of studies in both first and second language acquisition is the discovery and explanation of differential orders of language learning, including orthography in its use in spelling and reading. In "Psycholinguistic determinants of orthography acquisition" (this volume) we report that input frequency - in the sense of both relative and absolute type frequency - plays a negligible role in determining the order of acquisition of the spellings of the English short and long vowels.

A more promising approach to the explanation of acquisition order is to attempt to significantly correlate orders of acquisition with orders of complexity. In the present paper we present and extend Sgall's (1987) universal scales of orthographic complexness and use them to assign complexity to the orthography of inflection and contraction and the entailed areas of consonant singling and doubling. Since the correct spellings of the inflections and contractions crucially depend upon morpheme recognition, and morpheme recognition in turn depends upon disambiguation by the syntactic and semantic context, the correct spellings of the inflections and contractions also depend upon syntactic and semantic recognition beyond the word.

We hypothesized that the order of orthography acquisition is a function of the order of orthographic complexity and tested this hypothesis for 38 orthographic structures on a sample of 14 fifth-year German learners of English as a foreign language. Disconfirming evidence could only come from simpler structures on the hierarchy of orthographic complexity being acquired after structures that are more complex. The data was found to be consistent with the hypothesis, and apparently disconfirming evidence led to an independently motivated reanalysis.

Moreover, the existence of different types of errors corresponding to morphologically different forms with the same normative surface phonology and orthography suggested the interaction of the scale of orthographic complexity with the scale of morphemic complexity. Other things being equal, misspelled higher ranking morphemes are spelled as morphemes of lower ranks.

The resultant notion of L2-orthography development is not one of stages defined in terms of *rules* appearing in a predictable order (Meisel *et al.* 1981: 110), but of stages defined in terms of successively more complex inclusive *semiotic schemata* defined on relations like one-to-one, one-to-many, none-to-one, one-to-none, and their combinations, upon whose prior, general presence the emergence of particular rules depends.

The complexity theory of orthography acquisition not only explains the order of orthography acquisition, but also constrains the class of possible interpersonal variations, such that the implicational relations among and within the complexity schema provided by the complexity theory must not be violated.

Developmentally, the members of adjacent acquisitional groups are acquired before the members of acquisitional groups that are non-adjacent, and attrition in a less complex acquisitional group implies attrition in an acquisitional group that is adjacent and more complex. These constraints on learning and forgetting were also seen to follow from the theory of orthographic complexity.

The explanatory potential of complexity linguistics invites further exploration and testing in this and other areas of developmental psycho-linguistics, language processing, and language pathology.

* I wish to thank Marta Harasowska, Sigrid Lugmair, Cornelia Scherf, and Beate Waldhauser for insightful discussion of the analysis.

APPENDIX I: Dictation Exercise

Please read each of the following sentences aloud to your pupils twice, stopping each time for a pause at the place marked /. During the second reading have your pupils write the sentences to dictation. Do not explain any unfamiliar words. Tell your pupils to use *contracted forms (Kurzformen) whenever possible*. After the dictation is over, read through the sentences aloud once again. Pupils may make corrections whenever they wish by writing the form they think to be correct over the form they think to be wrong.

1. Rich's father/ teaches swimming/ and horseback riding.
2. Kit's mother/ pushes her/ to try harder.
3. Yesterday/ the Whites' children/ dented their parents' sports car.
4. John's already raked up/ the bigger leaves.
5. Last week/ Jack's brother/ stabbed a bank robber.
6. Susan's three valuable radios.
7. Ross's fattest cat/ rubs its front paws together.
8. Fritz's absolutely reliable.
9. The two boys' uncle/ speaks five languages.
10. Mitch's photos of America's buffalos.
11. Last year/ John's teacher/ cramped all his pupils' progress.
12. Jack's a lot of peaches and potatoes.
13. John's dining on/ fresh oranges.
14. Hank's an expert/ on pianos.
15. The Joneses' Jack's/ humming happier songs/ these days.
16. John's one of/ the country's heroes.
17. Rich's already striped/ his bike white.
18. Mary's often bragged/ about her highest marks.
19. The two judges' horse/ jumps over higher fences.
20. The children's puppy/ wags its tail/ fastest when happiest.
21. Jack's already flopped/ into the biggest bed.
22. Ross's wading/ in the deepest water.
23. Yesterday/ Mary's oldest sister/ trimmed the biggest bushes.
24. Ross's often cheated/ on his hardest tests.

APPENDIX II: Test Words

The numbers in parentheses are the numbers of the sentences (Appendix I) in which the test words occur.

1.1 Possessive singular /s/:<'s>
   Kit's (2), Jack's (5)
1.2 Possessive singular /z/:<'s>
   America's (10), John's (11), country's (16), Mary's (23)
1.3 Possessive singular /iz/:<'s>
   Rich's (1), Ross's (7)
2.1 Possessive plural after /s/:<'>
   Whites' (3), parents' (3)
2.2 Possessive plural after /z/:<'>
   boys' (9), pupils' (11)
2.3 Possessive plural after syllabic /iz/:<'>
   Joneses' (15), judges' (19)
3.1 Third singular /s/:<s>
   speaks (9), jumps (19)
3.2 Third singular /z/:<s>
   rubs (7), wags (20)
3.3 Third singular /iz/:<es>
   teaches (1), pushes (2)
4.1 Plural /s/:<s>
   sports (3), Whites' (3), parents' (3), marks (18), tests (24)
4.2 Plural /z/:<s>
   paws (15), songs (15), days (15), boys' (9), pupils' (11)
4.3 Plural /iz/:<es>
   languages (9), peaches (12), oranges (13), Jones's (15), judges' (19), fences (19), bushes (23)
4.4 Plural with possible stem change
   radios (6), photos (10), buffalo(e)s (10), potatoes (12), pianos (14), heroes (16)
5.1 Preterit /t/:<ed>
   cramped (11)
5.2 Preterit /d/:<ed>
   stabbed (5), trimmed (23)
5.3 Preterit /id/:<ed>
   dented (3)
6.1 Past participle /t/:<ed>
   raked (4), striped (17), flopped (21)
6.2 Past participle /d/:<ed>
   bragged (18)

6.3 Past participle /id/:<ed>
cheated (24)

7.1 <is> contraction: main verb /s/:<'s>
Hank's (14)

7.2 <is> contraction: main verb /z/:<'s>
John's (16)

7.3 <is> contraction: main verb /iz/:<'s>
Fritz's (8)

8.1 <is> contraction: auxiliary /s/:<'s>
Jack's (15)

8.2 <is> contraction: auxiliary /z/:<'s>
John's (13)

8.3 <is> contraction: auxiliary /iz/:<'s>
Ross's (22)

9.1 <has> contraction: main verb /s/:<'s>
Jack's (12)

9.2 <has> contraction: main verb /z/:<'s>
Susan's (6)

9.3 <has> contraction: main verb /iz/:<'s>
Mitch's (10)

10.1 <has> contraction: auxiliary /s/:<'s>
Jack's (21)

10.2 <has> contraction: auxiliary /z/:<'s>
John's (4), Mary's (18)

10.3 <has> contraction: auxiliary /iz/:<'s>
Rich's (17), Ross's (24)

11.1 Consonant doubling: verbs
swimming (1), stabbed (5), humming (15), bragged (18), flopped (21), trimmed (23)

11.2 Consonant doubling: comparative
bigger (4), happier (25)

11.3 Consonant doubling: superlative
fattest (7), biggest (21, 23), happiest (20)

11.4 Consonant doubling: nouns
horseback (1), Jack (5), robber (5), Ross (7), buffalos (10), progress (11), puppy (20)

12.1 Consonant singling: third singular
rubs (7), speaks (9), wags (20)

12.2 Consonant singling: progressive
riding (1), dining (13), wading (22)

12.3 Consonant singling: preterite
raked (4), striped (17), cheated (24)

A Psycholinguistic Model of the Bilingual Speller*

Introduction

Information processing models of skilled monolingual spelling (e.g. Ellis 1984: 73, Goodman and Caramazza 1986: 311) posit two routes to spelling production, one for spellings that are assembled, one for spellings that are addressed. Following Morton (1980), Ellis maintains that the semantic representation of the word being spelled serves as input to a graphemic-word production system where it activates the appropriate unit which releases the correct letter string. Neuropsychological evidence leads Ellis to conclude that the graphemic word-production system stores all familiar spellings, not just those of irregular or unpredictable words, although Günther (1987) warns against drawing inferences from neuropsychological data to normal models of reading. Moreover, the existence of synonyms, heterographic homophones, and homophonous but heterographic allomorphs, such as the /z/ in plural <boys>, possessive singular <boy's>, and possessive plural <boys'>, suggests that the translation from meaning to spelling must also be mediated by syntax, morphology, and sound.

Assembled spellings are thought to involve either analogies or phoneme-grapheme correspondences. Following Campbell (1983), Ellis maintains that skilled spellers use analogies to familiar words when assembling unfamiliar spellings. Campbell dictated words and non-words to normal subjects who tended to spell a non-word like *prein* as <prain> if they had recently spelled the word <brain>, but as <prane> if they had recently spelled the word <crane>. The application of phoneme-grapheme correspondences presupposes the segmentation of the phonemic string into its component syllables and phonemes, and letters must be selected and assembled into candidate spellings. Assembled spellings, like addressed spellings, cannot be effective without prior syntactic, morphological (chapter 9, this volume), and phonological analysis, e.g. distinguishing the contraction <dog's>, from the possessive plural <dogs'>, from the plural <dogs>.

In a recent version of the dual route-to-spelling hypothesis (Goodman and Caramazza 1986: 311), reproduced in Figure 1, familiar words are spelled by accessing the lexicon, novel words by accessing rules for phonological segmentation and phoneme-grapheme correspondences, and, for both oral and written spelling the same lexical (e.g. graphemic output lexicon), and non-lexical (e.g. phoneme-grapheme correspondences) processes are executed, with differentiation of oral and written spelling (e.g. letter name vs. allographic conversion processes) occurring only post-graphemically.

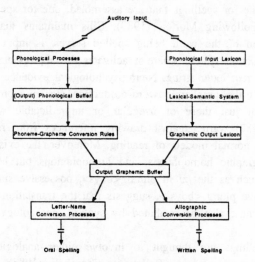

Figure 1.   *The monolingual speller*

The Goodman-Caramazza model of spelling thus consists of lexical, nonlexical, and post-graphemic processing mechanisms. Now, if one imagines this monolingual model of spelling reduplicated for the bilingual, in particular for the German learner of English orthography, as depicted in Figure 2, a number of deficits are predicted which in fact occur.

At the level of Phonological Processes, if the English Auditory Input in spelling to dictation were processed as though it were German,

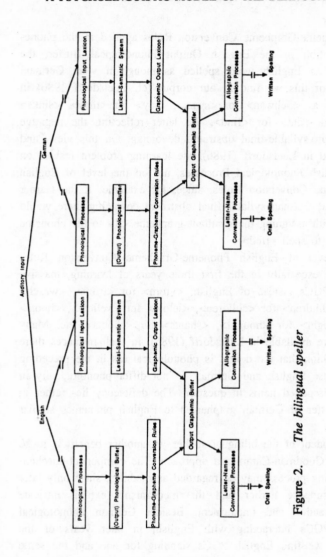

Figure 2. The bilingual speller

and German Phoneme-Grapheme Conversion Rules applied to the phonological representation in the English Output Phonological Buffer, the result would be an English word spelled as though it were German. Ample evidence of this we find in our corpus (cf. Luelsdorff 1986) in misspellings such as <Schwan> for <swan>, <say> for <they>, <sinks> for <thinks>, and <fint> for <find>, the latter reflecting the negative transfer of German syllable-final obstruent devoicing. On this view, and the one developed in Luelsdorff (1986), the learning problem resides on the level of English Phonological Processes, not on the level of English Phoneme-Grapheme Conversion Rules, since, for example, if the learner learned to suspend German syllable-final obstruent devoicing there would be no problem with assigning the resultant grapheme <d> to the phoneme /d/ in his attempt to spell <find>.

On the level of English Phoneme-Grapheme Conversion Rules (PGCs), we find, especially in the first three years of learning, massive use of German PGCs instead of English: <vrom> for <from>, <wasch> for <wash>, <tschildren> for <children>, <jelow> for <yellow>, <boots> for <boats>, <boght> for <bought>, <shauts> for <shouts>, etc. Many more examples are available in Luelsdorff (1986). In such instances there is no reason to think that the deficit is phonological (as in the preceding paragraph), because English and German do not differ phonologically in respect of the misspelled items in question. The deficiency lies rather in the negative transfer of German graphemes to English phonemes similar to German.

For the student of the bilingual speller yet another benefit is to be gained from the Goodman-Caramazza approach. The component mechanisms of the spelling process may be regarded as modules, since only later mechanisms presuppose earlier and the mechanisms exhibit intricate patterns of interaction and impairment. Besides German Phonological Processes and PGCs interacting with English, in later years of the learning process we find English PGCs standing for one and the same phoneme substituted for one another. Listed under the rubric "bilingual intralinguistic orthographic interference", examples include <Camebridge> for <Cambridge>, <jame> for <jam>, <sommer> for <summer>, <pollover> for <pullover>, <braught> for <brought>, <enjoied> for <enjoyed>, <movey> for <movie>, <broaght> for <brought>, <wer> for <wear>, etc., with additional examples to be found in chapter 4, this volume. Just as

Goodman and Caramazza (1986: 322) were able to show that the probability of selecting a particular PGC is determined by the relative frequency of its use in the language, and that there is thus structure internal to the level of PGCs, we found that it is in *individual words* that letter sound correspondences are misspelling-prone (the Word-effect for Spelling Errors) (Luelsdorff 1986; Luelsdorff and Eyland, chapter 7, this volume), that the signifiants of two different signs may be substituted for one another if they have the same signifiés (the Identical Signifié Constraint), and that even *ir*regular spelling patterns may be productive, i.e. used to spell words with regular spelling patterns in the norm. This requires abandoning the Dual Route Hypothesis on Spelling and suggests reexamining the Dual Route Hypothesis on Reading.

It has been repeatedly remarked (Henderson and Beers 1980; Read 1971; Luelsdorff 1984a, 1986, chapter 3 this volume) that beginning monolingual and bilingual spellers employ letter naming as a spelling strategy. In the case of German learners of English, the letter naming may be either German or English. German letter naming includes the articulation of a German letter name, as in <cornfleks> for <cornflakes>, and the place of articulation of a German letter name, as in <Jan> for <John>. English letter naming includes the articulation of an English letter name, as in <Her> for <Here>, the place of articulation of an English letter name, as in <mess> for <miss>, and a sequence of English letter names, as in <could> for <cold>. Now, the Goodman-Caramazza model (cf. Figure 1) does envision a letter name conversion process, but this process is aimed at converting representations in the Output Graphemic Buffer into sequences of letter names, i.e. Oral Spelling. What is needed is a processing mechanism of German Letter Naming and a processing mechanism of English Letter Naming aimed at converting representations in the Output Phonological Buffer into sequences of letters whose names properly contain them, i.e. a set of Phoneme-Grapheme Conversion Rules based on letter naming as a spelling strategy.

Two other, less frequent but nonetheless important categories of error may be accommodated at the level of Phonological Processes in the Goodman-Caramazza model of spelling reduplicated for bilinguals. One is the substitution of the English spelling of an English sound which English sound is the nearest neighbor of the English sound to be spelled, referred to in Luelsdorff (1986: 317) as the *Near Neighbor Constraint*. An example is the substitution of <ace, ea, ai>:/e/, <e>:/ɛ/, and <u>:/ʌ/ for <a>:/æ/, where /æ/ is a phoneme foreign to German. It is suggested that beginning German learners of English classify /æ/ with /e,ɛ,ʌ/ because they are the perceptually most similar sounds to /æ/. This leads to the formulation of an additional constraint on error variables: given any pair of GPCs, where $G_1 = \{L_1, S_1\}$ and $G_2 = \{L_2, S_2\}$, $L_2 \rightarrow L_1$ if S_1 is system-foreign and S_2 is perceptually identified with S_1. Here, we maintain that the near neighbor category of error is located on the level of Phonological Processes because the perceptual identification of S_1 with S_2 is the perceptual identification of sounds.

An example of the second category of error which may be accommodated at the level of Phonological Processes also involves the substitution of the English spelling of an English sound: which English sound is the nearest neighbor of the English sound to be spelled. In the first category, however, the sound to be spelled is absent from the native language, in the second it is present, but with a different distribution. Such a case is the substitution of <a,ah>:/a/ and <ou>:/ɔ/ for <u,o>:/ʌ/, where /ʌ/ does not occur in stressed position in German. It is suggested that beginning learners of English classify stressed English /ʌ́/ with stressed English /á/ and /ɔ/ because /á/ and /ɔ/ are the nearest neighbors to /ʌ/ in the perception of such learners. Such examples lead to the framing of a further constraint on error variables: given any two GPCs, where $G_1 = \{L_1, S_1\}$ and $G_2 = \{L_2, S_2\}$, $L_2 \rightarrow L_1$, if S_1 is common to but differently distributed in the target and native language, and S_2 is perceptually identified with S_1. This constraint on substitution error variables we call the *Close Relative Constraint*.

Both the Near Neighbor Constraint and the Close Relative Constraint fairly severely constrain the interaction of bilingual orthographies in the case of phonological heteromorphism in the languages involved. Since almost all of the near-neighbor type substitutions we have encountered (cf. Luelsdorff and Eyland, chapter 7 this volume, for further exemplification) entail precisely such phonological heteromorphism, it is tempting to claim that the phonological heteromorphism is the cause of the near-neighbor type misspellings. Consider, however, one of several exceptions. The phonemic inventories of both English and German contain /i/ and /ɪ/. In a word dictation to pupils in a German *Hauptschule*, the main errors on /ɪ/ in <drift> are <e, ie, iCe>. <e> for <i> exemplifies place of articulation of an English letter name, <ie> for <i> place of articulation of a German or English letter sound, and <iCe> for <i> apparently the misidentification of unfamiliar <drift> with familiar <drive>. Almost all of the errors on /ɪ/ in <skid> appear to be spellings of lax /ɪ/ as though it were tense /i/: <ea, iCe, ie, e>. As such they are processed by place of articulation of an English letter(s) sound. The presence of /i, ɪ/ in both English and German and the misspelling of the /ɪ/ in <drift> and <skid> as though the /ɪ/ were /i/ demonstrates that there are near-neighbor misspellings which are not based on phonological heteromorphism, but on place of articulation of an English letter *sound* (*not* name!). With this in hand, we formulate the Adjacency Constraint on error variables: given any pair of GPCs, where $G_1 = <L_1, S_1>$ and $G_2 = <L_2, S_2>$, L_2 DD> L_1 if S_1 and S_2 are phonologically adjacent. Since both the Near Neighbor Constraint and the Close Relative Constraint are special cases of the Adjacency Constraint, it appears that the former two may be replaced by the latter. Deeper research in this area, however, may reveal that errors reflecting the Near Neighbor Constraint are more frequent, in which case the constraint should be retained.

There is a further class of spelling errors (cf. Luelsdorff and Eyland, chapter 7 this volume, for some discussion) which cannot be accommodated in terms of the framework of inter- and intralinguistic transfer of PGCs developed above. These include attempts <ham, time, drived [sic]> for targets <hem, tame, drift>. Two features seem to characterise such misspellings: (1) they cannot be derived from transfer, either interlinguistic or intralinguistic; (2) unfamiliar targets are being spelled in terms of familiar attempts. The phenomenon is reminiscent of the beginning reading strategy (cf. Marsh *et al.* 1980: 342) of using syntactic and semantic context along with partial graphemic cues as the basis for the substitution of a known word for an unknown word, the child often relying on the first letter or the first and last letter to determine the substitution. Since the words in our examples were unfamiliar and occurred in word dictations, neither semantic nor syntactic contexts were available to the speller as aids to spelling. Rather the similarity in phonological shape between the unfamiliar word and the familiar word led to the unfamiliar word's being substituted for and spelled like the familiar. This suggests that if a similarity condition is met by representations in the Phonological Processes of the nonlexical route, on the one hand, and representations in the Phonological Input Lexicon of the lexical route, on the other, the resultant spelling will be derived via the Graphemic Output Lexicon. This process, which might be called "Familiarization", occurs within the English portion of the psycholinguistic model of the bilingual speller and is analogous to the processing of false friends, discussed below, in which the similarity of English Phonological Processes to representations in the German Phonological Input Lexicon leads to such representations being processed in the German Graphemic Output Lexicon and transferred to the Graphemic Output Lexicon of English.

Goodman and Caramazza (1986: 310) maintain that disruption to the Output Graphemic Buffer results in impaired performance on both oral and written spelling of words and non-words in the form of letter substitutions, deletions, transpositions, and additions. While letter additions and deletions abound (Luelsdorff 1986, chapter 5), and they are context sensitive, it is often difficult to tell if the context is purely literal, purely phonological, or a combination of both literal and phonological. What is clear is that the rank orders of the contexts (defined literally) for both addition and omission frequencies are very similar, as shown in Figure 3, indicating that whatever probability statements attach in the *performance* grammar to addition also attach to deletion. Below, we conclude that there is also no significant difference between misspellings of addition and deletion in the developing *competence* grammars of false friends.

	Vowel additions	Vowel omissions
	C_C	C_≠
	C_≠	C_C
	C_V	V_C
Frequency	V_C	C_V
	V_≠	V_≠
	≠_C	≠_C
	V_V	V_V
	≠_V	≠_V

Figure 3. *Ranked contexts by frequency of vowel additions and omissions*

It is also clear that many errors of letter addition and letter omission are products of the orthography/phonology interface. In terms of vowel letters added (Luelsdorff 1986: 136) 67% consist in the addition of <e>, almost 50% in C__≠ position, and almost 50% in C__V. Closer inspection of the <e>-addition errors in C__≠ reveals that they are *not* attributable to regularization to primary vowel-patterns in <-VCe≠>, involving as it does augmentation by <-e>, as, for example, <righte> for <right> might suggest, but to the *phonetic* spelling of (1) English allophonic aspiration of word-final voiceless non-continuant obstruents, as in the attempts <pute, leate, lefte> for the targets <put, late, left>, (2) the *phonetic* spelling of carefully articulated or spelled nasals and semivowels, as in attempts <ice-creame, theye> for targets <ice-cream, they>, and (3) overgeneralizations of secondary vowel-patterns to primary, as in <newyspeaper, leate> for <newspaper, late>. Since category (3) entails a secondary vowel-pattern representation of a single vowel sound (diphthong), this error type is perhaps better regarded as instantiating a substitution rather than an addition. There is thus little doubt that some errors of letter addition are phonetically motivated and that the context of such errors is phonetic or phonological, rather than graphemic. Consequently, the input to the error mechanism of addition cannot be the Output Phonological Buffer, as Goodman and Caramazza propose, but the Output Phonological Buffer containing phonetic and phonological representations. In terms of vowel letters omitted, 83% consist in the omission of <e>, 46% in C__≠ position, and 43% in C__V, rendering <e> that vowel which is most favored under both misaddition and misomission and C__≠ the most favored environment for that vowel. Closer inspection of the omissions of <e> in C__≠ reveals that the majority of these omissions can be explained in terms of English and German letter naming as a spelling strategy, for example, <Her> for <Here> (English letter naming) and <Hir> for <Here> (German letter naming) and the negative transfer of German GPCs, as in <Preis> for <prize> and <prais> for <prize>. Here, the engagement of one or another processing strategy, English or German letter naming, or German PGCs, triggers the error mechanism of substitution which, in turn, triggers the error mechanism of omission.

Like additions and omissions, letter substitutions cannot be stated in terms of letters alone (Luelsdorff 1986, chapters 3 and 8), but rather in terms of a letter *signifiant* X being substitutable for a letter *signifiant* Y if X and Y have the same or similar *signifiés*. For example, if <u> spells /U/ in the norm, as in <pullover, full, beautiful>, it may be misspelled <o, ou, oo>, as in <pollover, foul, biutefool>, whereas if <u> spells /ʌ/ in the norm, as in <must, summer>, it may be misspelled <a, o>, as in

<mast, sommer>. That is, the substitutability of a letter X for a letter Y depends upon the relationship between the phonological value of X and the phonological value of Y. Since substitutability depends upon phonology, errors of substitution cannot be generated from letter strings alone, i.e. they cannot be generated from the Output Graphemic Buffer. Rather they originate from processing strategies engaged on the non-lexical route at the level of phoneme-grapheme correspondences (PGCs).

Errors also originate on the lexical route to spelling which cannot be understood as the result of the operation of Error Mechanisms on graphemic representations in the Output Graphemic Buffer. Such is the case with errors in heterographic homophones. Spelling <one> as <won>, <whether> as <weather>, or <which> as <witch> does not mean that one has substituted elements of the graphemic shape of the latter for those of the former, but substituted the meaning of the former for the meaning of the latter, i.e. they are errors which must be defined as relations between attempts and targets and their respective Phonological and Lexico-Semantic representations, i.e. information not available in the Output Graphemic Buffer.

We have seen a variety of examples of errors originating on the nonlexical and lexical routes to spelling. Some have involved errors in phonological processes, others phoneme-grapheme correspondences, others semantics. The general conclusion is that errors in spelling cannot be defined in terms of (pairs of) strings of graphemes, i.e. in terms of the Output Graphemic Buffer. Two solutions suggest themselves: (1) error mechanisms (properly constrained) be permitted to apply on each of the levels of processing along the nonlexical, lexical, and postlexical routes - the local solution - or (2) error mechanisms (properly constrained) be permitted to apply only to the Output Graphemic Buffer (OGB), where the representation in the OGB be permitted to either inherit or access all representations on the other levels of their derivational histories - the global solution. In either case, the conception of the OGB as a repository of strings of graphemes must be abandoned.

Locating errors of substitution, addition, omission, and transposition (= displacement) at the level of the Output Graphemic Buffer, in accordance with the global solution above, is appealing to the extent that such errors are errors of performance. This amounts to the claim that processing strategies along the nonlexical and lexical route to spelling are the effective causes of the deviant spelling attempts which exhibit simple and complex relations of S, O, A, and T to their normative targets derived via the lexical route on the level of the Output Graphemic Buffer. Once the discrepancy between the erroneous attempt and the subjectively correct norm has been identified in terms of erroneous S, O, A, and D, the speller-monitor may engage the converse of these error mechanisms (see chapter 2) to effect the required corrections, i.e. error correction follows error identification in terms of error mechanisms and their converse.

Most spelling errors made by beginning German spellers of English, however, are errors of competence, rather than errors of performance (cf. Luelsdorff 1986: 231). The error statistics indicate that many errors are made in the categories S, O, and A, but few corrected. Taking the fact of an error's having been monitored as an index of its status as a performance error, most of the beginners' errors made are errors of competence. How do these fit into the psycholinguistic model of the bilingual speller? The essential fact about such errors is that the individual norm is at variance with the community norm. In terms of the psychogenesis of competence errors, either the individual has been exposed to the community norm, but forgotten all or part of it, or there has been no such exposure and the individual has had to grapple with the spelling either by means of the non-lexical route or analogy. Exposure to the community norm followed by competence errors manifested in uncorrectable performance errors is a familiar learning situation. The short- or long-term memory loss operates on the normative input to produce the non-normative intake and output in terms of the familiar elements and relations of transfer discussed above. In such situations where the input $\neq$ intake, we believe the discrepancy to be *mediated* by the mechanisms of S, O, A, D, triggered by the familiar processing strategies discussed above and in chapter 3, this volume. In the case of performance errors, we assume S, O, A, D, to be defined on the level of the Output Graphemic Buffer, since mistaken attempts are being compared with known targets. In the case of competence errors after prior norm-exposure, however, we must specify a normative orthographic (and possibly phonological and lexico-semantic) input, but with an intake *mediated* by processing strategies as in Figure 4.

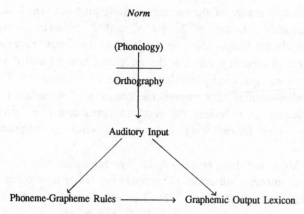

Figure 4.   *Preprocessing structure*

Figure 4 shows that exposure to the (pronunciation and) spelling of a particular word may lead to that word's being misspelled via the non-lexical (PGC) route in which case the spelling is stored as a competence error in the speller's Graphemic Output Lexicon. The spelled word is processed by strategies which trigger processing mechanisms such as S, O, A, and D.

Thus, the psycholinguistic difference between performance error and competence error is reflected by a formal difference in processing structure. Performance errors (or slips-of-the-pen) are defined in the Graphemic Output Buffer by relations between the norm and norm deviation(s) such as S, O, A, and D. Competence errors after prior norm exposure are defined on the relation between the (non-normative) repre-sentation in the Graphemic Output Lexicon and the original, but partially forgotten, normative orthographic exposure.

In our discussion of the psycholinguistic model of the bilingual speller above we have been basically concerned with phoneme-grapheme relations *within* the word, i.e. with orthographic processes within the word without regard for conditioning factors which are lexical, with *sublexical* orthography. There are, however, interlinguistic orthographic processes which are lexical. Such processes we subsume under the rubric *lexical orthography* because the speller must dispose of word-level knowledge for the processes in question to operate. In previous work (Luelsdorff 1986, and chapter 3 this volume) we divided the data under examination into instances of Cognatization and Decognatization, with each being either Partial or Total, and both falling under the heading of Interlinguistic Transfer. Given two differently spelled cognate words, if the attempt to spell the target resembles the native language spelling more closely than the foreign, then the spelling is an instance of Cognatization, Partial if the L2-L1 resemblance is partial (e.g. <preis> for <prize>), Total if the L2-L1 resemblance is total (e.g. <mußt> for <must>). In Decognatization the resemblance between the L2-L1 norms decreases in the attempt, as in <Bäter> as an attempt to spell <better>, where <Bäter> bears less of a resemblance than German <besser> to English <better>. While Cognatization, especially Partial Cognatization, is frequent enough, Total Cognatization and Decognatization are rare.

In the present paper we establish the existence of a lexical route to spelling in German learners of English, in particular that English false friends are spelled under the lexical influence of their German congeners and that this lexical interference is greater in some types of pairs of false friends than in others. This supports a new class of interlinguistic grapheme-grapheme correspondences based on interlinguistic interlexical identification. The psycholinguistic spelling models of English and German must therefore be permitted to interact at the lexical level of the Output Graphemic Buffer in the case of lexical items exhibiting a high degree of phonological similarity.

1.   The experiment

False friends are sets of lexical items, drawn from two or more languages, which are similar in sound, spelling, morphology and meaning. For example, the German adjective <allein> and the English adjective <alone> both sound alike and mean "alone", but German <allein> is spelled with two <ll>s and no final <e>, while English <alone> is spelled with one <l> and a final <e>. It was reasoned that if such false friends exhibited a higher incidence of spelling errors than non-false friend controls, then the relative learning complexity of the target language false friends would be due to their similarity with their native language congeners, and the English spellings in question would be accessed via their German congeners. If the incidence of error on different types of false friends significantly differs, then different classes of false friends must be assigned different transfer probabilities. Finally, if the error incidence indicates that some operations, such as addition, needed to generate English false friends from German were more error-prone than others, such as deletion, then it would be necessary to assign such operations a higher rank in the hierarchy of interlinguistic grapheme-grapheme relations.

For example, assume that English medial doubled consonants are significantly more frequently singled in false friends like <gallery> (cf. German <Galerie>) than in non-false friends and that this false friend error-proneness was due to target language-native language similarity. Next assume that English medial doubled consonants (<gallery>) are significantly more frequently singled than word-final doubled consonants like <grass> (cf. German false friend <Gras>). If this were representative, we would conclude that one type of false friend containing <-CC->, as in <gallery>, was inherently orthographically more complex than another type of false friend containing <-CC≠>, as in <grass>, i.e. that the learning of medial orthographic geminates occurred at a later developmental stage than the learning of final orthographic geminates. Finally, assume that the incidence of error on medial consonant gemination in false friends like <gallery> is higher than on medial consonant singling in false friends like <alone> (cf. German <allein>). If this were representative, we would conclude that the operation of letter addition required to convert the single <l> in German <Galerie> to the double <ll> in English <gallery> is inherently more difficult than the operation of letter deletion required to convert the double <ll> in German <allein> to the single <l> in English <alone>. Such results would follow from a theory of complexity in which it was stipulated that (1) false friends are more complex than non-false friends, (2) medial geminate consonant spellings are more complex than final geminate consonants, (3) letter additions are more complex than letter omissions, and (4) familiar words are less error-prone than unfamiliar.

Accordingly, we tested the following four hypotheses:

Hypothesis 1: false friends = non-false friends
Hypothesis 2: type 1 = type 2 = type 3
Hypothesis 3: additions = deletions
Hypothesis 4: familiar = unfamiliar

A word dictation consisting of 74 items (cf. Appendix I) was presented by the regular classroom teacher to an intact class of 23 pupils in grade 9 of the German *Gymnasium*. The items on the test were all real English words, randomized according to a table of random numbers. Unfamiliar real words are marked with an asterisk. The words were divided into six test groups (Appendix II) and six corresponding control groups (Appendix III). The test groups were labelled A, A', B, B', C, and C'. Belonging to test group A were those English false friends which end in a final <-e≠>, corresponding to German false friends without a final <-e≠>. Examples include English <culture>, corresponding to German <Kultur>, and English <medicine>, corresponding to German <Medizin>. In test group A' were words with no final <-e≠> in English, corresponding to false friends with a final <-e≠> in German. For example, English <address> corresponding to German <Adresse>. In test group B were words with a final <-CC≠> in English, corresponding to German false friends with a final <-C≠>. Examples include English <grass> corresponding to German <Gras> and English <staff> corresponding to German <Stab>. Belonging to group B' were English words ending in a final <-C≠>, corresponding to German false friends ending in a final <-CC≠>. Examples include English <violet>, corresponding to German <Violett>, and English <rebel> corresponding to German <Rebell>. Group C includes English words in medial <-CC->, corresponding to German words in medial <-C->. Examples are English <gallery>, corresponding to German <Galerie>, and English <cannon>, corresponding to German <Kanone>. Finally, group C' consisted of English words in medial <-C->, corresponding to German words in medial <-CC->. Examples here include English <weapon>, corresponding to German <Waffen>, and English <career> corresponding to German <Karriere>. The entire corpus of test words is presented in Appendix II and the entire corpus of control words is presented in Appendix III.

It will be noted that A, B, and C differ from A', B', and C' in one essential respect. The items in the former group, from the point of view of German, all contain letter *additions*. The items in the latter group, from the point of view of German, all contain letter *deletions*. If it can be shown that there is interlexical transfer from German to English - i.e. either that a German lexical item is being inserted into the English lexicon or that a German lexical item in the German lexicon is being accessed while English is being spelled - then it would follow that the English items in A, B, and C are being spelled, when spelled correctly, by means of an orthographic rule of addition, while the English words in A', B', and C', when spelled correctly, are being spelled by means of an orthographic rule of deletion. Looking at the English items independently of German, it is not obvious that either addition or deletion should be involved. English <genitive>, for example, appears to have a final <-e≠> which is either lexical (not rule governed) or spelled by means of a general rule attaching <-e≠> to words otherwise ending in <v> or <u>, i.e. not one which results from its addition in relation to its absence from German. To take another example, <method> appears to simply end in a <d>, rather than in an <Ø> resulting from the deletion of <-e≠> from German.

Some words belonged to more than one of the groups A, B, C, A', B', C'. For example, <alone> belongs to group A as it ends in a final <-e≠> whereas the corresponding German word <allein> does not. As well, <alone> belongs to group C' because it has a single medial <l> whereas the German word <allein> has a double medial <l>. The basis of the experiment, then, were not single words but rather orthographic features. The number of correct spellings per feature was obtained. For the word <alone>, all 23 participants used a final <-e≠>, whereas 4 of the participants used <ll> instead of <l>. Hence as a member of group A, the number of correct spellings was 23 whereas as a member of group C', the number of correct spellings was 19. In all the number of orthographic features was 112.

2.   The results

The four hypotheses were assessed together by modelling the proportion of correct spellings in terms of nearness to German, orthographic type and word familiarity. These are defined as follows:

Nearness to German	test: a similar German word exists
	control: a similar German word does not exist
Type	-e≠ present in one of the words
	-CC≠ in the English-German word-pair
	-CC-
Operation	addition: in English-German word-pairs, English has extra letter
	deletion: in English-German word-pairs, German has extra letter
Familiarity	English word to be spelled is familiar or unfamiliar

Analysis of variance techniques were used with response variable being arcsin {p, where p is the proportion of correct spellings.

The first hypothesis is supported (F 3.5, df 3&35, p-value .02). Words which had a German neighbor (test word) were less likely to be spelled correctly than words without a German neighbor (control words). This is made clear when we compare test with control words for the two sets of words, familiar and unfamiliar, separately (Table 1).

Table 1.

	Nearness to German	size	mean	s.d.
familiar	test	25	16.2	5.7
	control	17	19.2	4.3
unfamiliar	test	13	12.0	4.5
	control	57	14.8	7.5

The second hypothesis that error-proneness is related to ortho-graphic type is supported (F = 6.0, df 2&35, p-value .006). In this analysis, only words with a German neighbor were used i.e. test words. Words with <-e≠> were less error-prone than words with <-C≠> which were less error-prone than words with <-C->. The result persisted even when allowance was made for the disparity in the number of familiar and unfamiliar words between the two groups (F 4.9, df 2&34, p-value .01).

The third hypothesis that orthographic operation is associated with correct spelling is not supported. Again, this hypothesis was assessed using only the test words. Adjustment was made for both word familiarity and orthographic type (F .61, df 3&31, p-value .61).

The fourth hypothesis that familiar words are more likely to be spelled correctly than unfamiliar words is strongly supported as can be seen from the table of means given under the first hypothesis.

3.   Discussion

Comparison of the test and control scores indicates that spelling perform-ance is poorer on each of the six categories of false friends than on the matched, non-false friend controls, despite the fact that almost all of the controls were unfamiliar words. The sole exception is English final <-CC≠>. The control items in question are (56) <embarrass> and (57) <success>, a familiar word, was correctly spelled on 19/23 occasions. It is thus possible that if the control corpus had been larger and/or consisted only of familiar words, the performance would have been better on <-CC≠> controls than on the corresponding false friend test words.

This false friend inferiority effect requires an explanation. We sub-mit that the *lexical phonological similarity* between the auditory L2 intake and the stored L1 false friend pronunciation is the responsible common denominator, since it is this *lexical phonological similarity* which distin-guishes the false friends in the test group from the non-false friends in the controls.

This interlinguistic theory of lexical transfer of false friends re-ceives strong support from a consideration of test groups A', B', C, and C'. In test group A' are English items without a final <-e≠> (<cannonØ>) corresponding to German items with a final <-e≠> (<Kanone>). There is nothing in the *phonological* structure of the English items which would motivate a final <-e≠>. Consequently, we attribute the frequent English misspelling in final <-e≠> to the association of the English auditory inputs with their German false friend lexical counter-parts. The fact that this interlinguistic interlexical association applies to both familiar (<address, control>) and unfamiliar (<cannon, medal>) lexi-cal items with roughly equal frequency indicates that interlinguistic inter-lexical transfer of orthography is, at this level of learning, quite indiffer-ent to familiarity. The errors in group B', C, C' could be due to the negative transfer of German consonant singling and doubling (but cf. Luelsdorff & Eyland, chapter 7 this volume), but this hypothesis would leave unexplained why the percentages of error on the test words are so much higher than on the controls. This test-control error differential leads us to conclude that false friends are subject to interlinguistic interlexical transfer, rather than the transfer of native language PGCs, in this case German consonant singling and doubling.

The explanation of the type results poses a formidable problem to the theory of orthographic universals (Justeson 1976, Volkov 1982). According to Ferguson (1984), implicational universals contain an antecedent term which is more complex, more difficult to learn, and, consequently, more error-prone. In the context of the data above, one relevant universal is Volkov (23), according to which

"If there is a complex unilateral syntagm, then there is a simple unilateral syntagm."

On Volkov (23): orthographic strings containing geminate consonants (complex), which determine the shortness of the pronunciation of the preceding vowel (unilateral syntagm), are more complex and hence should be learned later than single orthographic consonants (simple), which determine the length of the preceding vowel (unilateral syntagm). In point of fact, however, whereas English medial <-CC->s are performed on worse than English medial <-C->s, English final <-CC≠>s are performed on better than English final <-C≠>s, the latter in contradiction to the prediction made by the orthographic universal Volkov (23). Nor does it remedy the situation to view this result solely in terms of German, for while the corresponding German false friends in final <-C≠>s are indeed performed on better than those in final <-CC≠>s, German false friends in medial <-C->s are performed on worse than German false friends in medial <-CC->s, the latter also on contradiction to the prediction of orthographic universal Volkov (23). Thus, neither the English nor the German false friends can be said to support the theory of orthographic universals on this point.

Moreover, the data contradict the predictions of universal orthography on a second point. According to Volkov (19):

"If there is a progressive syntagm, there is also a regressive syntagm (a regressive syntagm may be found without a progressive, but not vice-versa)."

Accordingly, progressive syntagms should be more complex, more error-prone, and harder to learn than regressive.

Now, most of the data in (A), with a final <-e≠> in English, but no final <-e≠> in German related false friends, results from the addition of <-e≠> to otherwise final <-u≠, -v≠>, i.e. the addition of graphotactic <e>, as pointed out by Venezky (1970). If this is so, then there is a syntagmatic relation between the <u, v> and the following <e> such that the presence of <e> is progressively determined by the preceding <u, v>. According to Volkov (23), this progressive relation should be more complex, harder to learn, and more error-prone than either consonant singling (B', C') or consonant doubling (B, C), but, contrary to the predictions of Volkov (23), the very opposite is true: final <-e≠> is learned first, then consonant singling and doubling in final position, then consonant singling and doubling in medial position. Evidently, the theory of orthographic universals is in need of emendation or revision so that its predictions correspond to the facts. Several aspects seem worth considering. One is that there are cognates in German and English with final <-e≠> in German (<Adresse, Kanone, Kontrolle, Medaille>, etc.), with no final <-e≠> or schwa-like sound in English (<address, cannon, control, medal>, etc.). These words appear simple because of the nature of English and the English-German relation. Other items have no <-e≠> in German (<allein, Literatur, Genitiv>, etc.), but have English cognates with silent final <-e≠> (<alone, literature, genitive>, etc.). These items seem easy to learn because the final <-e≠>, although silent, is regular in the sense that it appears either after otherwise final <u, v>, after cognates of German words ending in <-ur, -in>, or in major secondary spellings <-ore, -one>. Taken together, it is these relations between English and German which are easier to learn than those found in cognate consonant doubling and singling. In respect of consonant doubling and singling in final and medial positions, the data suggest that final position is a simpler position than medial position, especially for consonant doubling. If these various syntagmatic and positional effects are repeatedly upheld, then it appears that they ought to have a place in orthographic universals if the theory of orthographic universals is to explain the facts of orthography acquisition.

Assuming that the interlinguistic interlexical transfer hypothesis is correct, we further conclude that the English items in Groups A, B, and C are interlexically orthographically processed by *orthographic additions*, while the English items in groups A', B', and C' are interlexically orthographically processed by *orthographic deletions*. In the former case (A, B, C), this implies that the final <-e≠> in words of the type <genitive, passive> is neither learned by rote nor as a result of the rule that words otherwise ending in <u, v> take a final graphotactic <-e≠>, but rather by learning that certain German words like <Genitiv, Magazin> have cognate English words in <-e≠>. With the acquisition of fluent English spelling, however, it is likely that this German orthographic base is abandoned in favour of one that is strictly English. Conversely, in the case of groups A', B', and C' the implication is that the spellings of the English items are learned via deletions from the spellings of the German cognates, rather than independently. Thus, English <address> is learned via deletion of the <-e≠> from German <Adresse>, English <violet> via the deletion of the <t≠> from German <Violett>, and English <alone> via the deletion of the <-l-> from German (allein>.

Our previous taxonomy of processing strategies in the incipient bilingual speller (chapters 3 and 4, this volume) envisages processing strategies that are interlinguistic and intralinguistic. The interlinguistic processing strategies are sublexical and lexical. The sublexical strategies are German letter naming (Luelsdorff 1984a) and the employment of German PGCs. In the information processing model of the bilingual speller, German letter naming and German PGCs must be taken to interact with English letter naming and English PGCs. The lexical processing strategies, in addition to the spelling of items which cannot be sublexically derived, have been termed partial and total cognatization (Luelsdorff 1986). In this chapter, we have shown that a subclass of cognates termed "false friends" is significantly more error-prone in the spelling of the German learner of English than otherwise matched items that are not false friends. This led us to conclude that the English auditory input is associated with the German Input Lexicon where the items in question are associated with German orthographic representations, either resulting in an English/German cognate spelled as though it were German (total cognatization), or spelled part German, part English (partial cognatization), or spelled in English as a result of derivation via addition and deletion from German, i.e. correctly, but for the wrong reasons.

4.   Conclusion

The above considerations lead us to the psycholinguistic model of the bilingual speller presented in Figure 5.

This bilingual model is similar to monolingual models in that it incorporates nonlexical, lexical, and postlexical processing *routes*. The nonlexical route is for spelling unfamiliar words, the lexical route for spelling familiar words; and the postlexical route for oral or written spelling. Moreover, the bilingual model incorporates the processing *levels* of each of the three routes of the monolingual model.

First, it was found that the monolingual model had to be enriched by a level of Morphological Processes (MP) along the nonlexical route and Morphological Structure (MS) along the lexical route, because there are words in English which cannot be correctly spelled without reference to their morphological structure. Second, we found that the monolingual model had to be enriched by levels an relations permitting the production, detection, and correction of orthographic errors of performance and competence. Processing strategies are responsible for the production of such errors along both the nonlexical and lexical routes to spelling, and errors are recognised as such in the Graphemic Output Buffer (GOB) by means of defining the relations of S, O, A, and D there between attempts and targets. In order for this comparison to be effective, it is essential for the graphemic representations in the GOB to be able to access the various types of linguistic information contained on all the levels of the routes from which they are derived, a view which we have referred to as the "global position". Once the relation(s) have been defined and the error(s) thereby detected, the speller is free to engage the converse of the relations in question in order to effect error correction. On a correct error perception, error correction reverses the error relations defined on the pair (attempt, target), yielding an attempt which is the same as the target, i.e. A = T. Such an attempt, edited to conform to a target, is then free to either undergo Letter-Name Conversion (LNC) in Oral Spelling (OS) or Allographic Conversion Processes (ACP) in Written Spelling (WS).

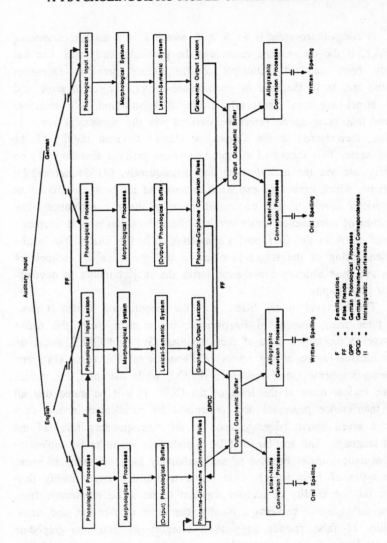

Figure 5. *The beginning bilingual speller*

A competence error is an A ≠ T, where T is a normative spelling to which, if the competence error is to be psychologically real, one has already been exposed. Attempts to (re)produce previous exposures (targets) are, as in the case of performance errors, subject to error, and these errors are most frequently errors of substitution. We therefore suggest that competence errors be derived via the *non*lexical route to spelling, then stored in the Graphemic Output Lexicon (GOL) of the lexical route. This theory of competence errors predicts that they (1) do not originate via the lexical route and consequently, (2) do not exhibit any errors which cannot be explained in terms of the processes found on the various levels of the nonlexical route or their combination. The correction of competence errors involves the recognition of a discrepancy between an A in the GOL and a normative T in the intake. The nature and sequencing of the stages involved in the correction of competence errors and their ultimate explanation forms the subject matter of developmental orthography.

The bilingual model differs from the monolingual in that it specifies three main sources of interference, hence error, from the native language to the target. Two of these sources, GPP and GPCE, occur on the nonlexical route at the levels of Phonological Processes (PP) and Phoneme-Grapheme Correspondences (PGCs), while the third, FF, occurs via the lexical route at the level of the OGB. It will be noted that all three interference processes are constrained by parallelism in that they relate a given native language level to the corresponding level of the target language. The spelling of false friends was found to be subject to interlinguistic transfer because of their relatively high incidence of error. Some types of false friends were found to transfer more readily than others, but the facility of transfer was not found to be predictable from known orthographic universals. Finally, the error distribution and transferability of false friends suggests a category of grapheme-grapheme correspondences from the native language to the target in which additions appear more complex and subject to later learning than deletions.

The information-processing model of the bilingual speller has, we believe, far-reaching implications for the understanding of the L2 speech and spelling errors of the bilingual aphasic and dysgraphic. Such investigations have often focused on establishing taxonomies of speech and spelling errors in terms of more-or-less defined categories such as syntagmatic error, paradigmatic error, and errors of anticipation, duplication, metathesis, addition, omission, and substitution, and the quantities of each in normals and the speech impaired. The research objective has been to ascertain whether the differences between normals and non-normals are quantitative or qualitative, and to what extent. Söderpalm Talo (1980), for example, arrives at several quantitative (but not qualitative) differences made by normals and aphasics; the former commit more syntagmatic (over 80%) errors than paradigmatic and phonemic metatheses are common, whereas the latter make more paradigmatic (over 60%) errors than syntagmatic, and phonemic metatheses are rare, indicating a weakened capacity for accurate speech planning and a generalised weakened awareness of errors, i.e., primarily a sequencing difficulty in normals as opposed to primarily a selection difficulty in aphasics.

In the information-processing approach to spelling and reading, however, a distinction is drawn between error mechanisms, such as addition, omission, displacement, and substitution, on the one hand, and on the other, processing strategies, such as German/English Letter Naming, German/English PGCs, Cognatization, and Familiarization, which are held to be their cause; i.e. the errors are defined by the model in terms of the causal processing strategies delivered by the model, not in terms of the error mechanisms which, on this view, appear epiphenomenal. In addition to being causal, the advocated approach differentiates the same error mechanism in terms of different processing strategies. Thus, while attempts <bost, her, hir> for targets <pot, here, here> are all substitutions, <bost> for <post> derives from Phonological Processing, <her> for <here> from English Letter Naming, and <hir> for <here> from German Letter Naming.

In the final analysis, it is of little interest to know that various speech productions are instantiations of error mechanisms, because such derivative facts follow from error causation in the form of processing strategies and the constraints thereon.

It follows from the above that any differences between normal and dysgraphic bilingual spellers be stated in terms of the differences between the normal and the dysgraphic bilingual spelling models. The model given in Figure 4 was developed for normal bilingual spellers at the age of 12-14 with German as their native language and 2-4 years of English. The comparison of this model with that of a matched sample of German dysgraphics might reveal differences along several routes and levels, including relative excessive transfer of German Phonological Processes, German Phoneme-Grapheme Correspondences, German and English Letter Naming, relatively underdeveloped Intralinguistic Interference vis-à-vis Interlinguistic Interference, excessive Familiarization and overdeployment of the processing strategy of False Friends. In short, if the level of explanatory adequacy in the study of the monolingual and bilingual processing of written language is to be achieved, we submit that a causally-orientated, processing strategic model be adopted. We hope to have shown in the above that this target is at least worth the attempt.

APPENDIX I.   False friends: Words to dictation

Please read each of the following words to your pupils *three* times. On the first reading, ask your pupils to *listen* carefully to the pronunciation of the word. On the second reading, ask your pupils to *write* the word to dictation. After the dictation is over, read the words a third time, asking your pupils to *correct* any misspellings by writing the spelling they think to be correct over the spelling they think to be wrong. Thank you.

* 1.	to assure	26.	to arrive	*51.	to assemble
* 2.	gallery	*27.	to assign	*52.	account
* 3.	accustomed to	*28.	coffin	*53.	attitude
4.	alone	29.	passive	54.	immediately
5.	literature	30.	telegram	*55.	gramophone
* 6.	violet	*31.	to surrender	*56.	to embarrass
* 7.	committee	*32.	scissors	57.	success
* 8.	aggression	*33.	to appeal	58.	buses
9.	opportunity	34.	weapon	59.	model
*10.	to surround	*35.	to attract	*60.	opponent
*11.	to approve	36.	control	*61.	culture
*12.	to attempt	37.	enemy	*62.	apparent
*13.	rebel	38.	medicine	*63.	abbreviation
14.	to apply	*39.	medal	*64.	staff
15.	address	*40.	banquet	65.	interest
16.	accident	*41.	exaggerate	66.	shadow
*17.	to announce	*42.	career	*67.	to annoy
*18.	to appoint	*43.	to attend	68.	metal
*19.	to accompany	*44.	attention	69.	glass
20.	to appear	45.	according to	70.	method
*21.	to assume	*46.	to attach	71.	before
*22.	cannon	*47.	to approach	72.	superlative
23.	genitive	48.	platform	73.	active
24.	magazine	49.	grass	*74.	to accuse
25.	adjective	*50.	accent		

*   Starred items were unfamiliar to the pupils

214   DEVELOPMENTAL ORTHOGRAPHY

APPENDIX II.   False friends: Test words

A. English final -e≠
German no final -e≠

4.	alone	alleinØ
5.	literature	LiteraturØ
23.	genitive	GenitivØ
24.	magazine	MagazinØ
25.	adjective	AdjectivØ
29.	passive	PassivØ
38.	medicine	MedizinØ
*55.	gramophone	GrammophonØ
*61.	culture	KulturØ
71.	before	vorherØ
72.	superlative	superlativØ
73.	active	aktivØ

A'. English no final -e≠
German final -e≠

15.	addressØ	Adresse
*22.	cannonØ	Kanone
36.	controlØ	Kontrolle
*39.	medalØ	Medaille
65.	interestØ	Interesse
70.	methodØ	Methode

B. English final -CC≠
German final -C≠

49.	grass	Gras
*64.	staff	Stab
69.	glass	Glas

B'. English final -C≠
German final -CC≠

* 6	violet	Violett
*13	rebel	rebell
30.	appeal	Appell
*40.	banquet	Bankett
59.	model	Modell
68.	metal	Metall

C. English medial -CC-
German medial -C-

* 2.	gallery	Galerie
* 7.	committee	Komitee
15.	address	Adresse
*22.	cannon	Kanone

C'. English medial -C-
German medial -CC-

4.	alone	allein
34.	weapon	Waffen
36.	control	Kontrolle
*42.	career	Karriere
55.	gramophone	Grammophon
58.	buses	Busse
65.	interest	Interesse

*   Starred items were unfamiliar to the pupils

APPENDIX III.   False friends: Control Words

A.   English final -e≠

* 1.	assure	*21.	assume	*51.	assemble
*11.	approve	26.	arrive	*53.	attitude
*17.	announce	*41.	exaggerate	*74.	accuse

A'.   English no final -e≠

*10.	surroundØ	*28.	coffinØ	48.	platformØ
*12.	attemptØ	*31.	surrenderØ	*52.	accountØ
16.	accidentØ	*35.	attractØ	*56.	embarassØ
*18.	appointØ	*43.	attendØ	57.	successØ
20.	appearØ	*44.	attentionØ	*60.	opponentØ
*27.	assignØ	*46.	attachØ	*62.	apparentØ
*47.	approachØ				

B.   English final -CC≠

*56.	embarrass	57.	success

B'.   English final -C≠

20.	appear	27.	assign	*28.	coffin	*31.	surrender

C.   English medial -CC-

* 1.	assure	*18.	appoint	*35.	attract	*53.	attitude
* 3.	accustomed	*19.	accompany	*41.	exaggerate	54.	immediately
9.	opportunity	20.	appear	*43.	attend	*56.	embarrass
*10.	surround	*21.	assume	*44.	attention	57.	success
*11.	approve	26.	arrive	45.	according	*60.	opponent
*12.	attempt	*27.	assign	*46.	attach	*62.	apparent
14.	apply	*28.	coffin	*47.	approach	*63.	abbreviation
16.	accident	*31.	surrender	*51.	assemble	*67.	annoy
*17.	announce	*32.	scissors	*52.	account	*74.	accuse

C'.   English medial -C-

* 1.	assure	26.	arrive	37.	enemy
66.	shadow	*74.	accuse		

Starred items were unfamiliar to the pupils

APPENDIX IV.   The Results

Summary statistics for each of the 6 word categories

Category	Test words			Control words		
	mean	s.d.	n.	mean	s.d.	n.
A	17.7	4.5	12	20.1	4.0	9
A'	17.3	5.2	6	20.3	4.9	19
B	16.3	3.2	3	8.5	5.0	2
B'	12.4	4.9	7	23.0	0.0	4
C	7.3	2.3	3	11.1	6.3	35
C'	12.6	6.4	7	21.4	2.5	5

Developmental Orthography

Introduction

Studies in native developmental orthography (e.g. Eichler 1976, Frith 1986, Gentry 1982) address the structure and growth of the cognitive processing strategies underlying the spelling of normals and dyslexics on the basis of the analysis and description of orthographic errors. Such first language inquiries are of immense value to the researcher in second language acquisition, because much of their methodology is transferable to second orthography acquisition, and their results serve to answer questions about first and second orthography acquisition differences.

1.   L1-English orthography

Let us consider two models of L1-English developmental orthography which differ in interesting and instructive ways. Gentry (1982) presents a five-stage model of development in learning to spell:

1.	Precommunicative	(4),
2.	Semiphonetic	(5;1),
3.	Phonetic	(5;1-6;1),
4.	Transitional	(6;1),
5.	Correct	(6-11 or 12).

Each stage is characterized by features or strategies which are either unique to that stage or continuous across several stages and hence a matter of degree.

In the Precommunicative Stage spellers exhibit some knowledge of the alphabet, but no knowledge of letter-sound correspondences. In addition, the speller may or may not know the principle of left-to-right directionality for English spelling.

In the Semiphonetic Stage the child first begins to conceptualize the alphabetic principle. Spellers learn that letters have sounds which may be used to represent the sounds in words and where possible the speller represents words, sounds or syllables with letters that match their letter names and begins to grasp left-to-right sequentiality.

In the Phonetic Stage the child represents all of the surface-sound features of a word and such phonetic details as tense and lax vowels, preconsonantal nasals, syllabic sonorants, -ed endings, retroflex vowels, affricates and intervocalic flaps.

In the Transitional Stage vowels appear in every syllable, nasals are represented before consonants, vowel and consonant letters are used instead of a letter name strategy, vowels are represented before syllabic r, vowel digraphs appear, and the use of final silent -e replaces letter naming for tense vowels. Above all, the speller relies less on phonology and more on morphology and visual strategies in spelling.

In the Correct Stage the speller's knowledge of the rules of English orthography is established, including knowledge of word structure, the ability to distinguish homonyms, increasing command of silent consonants and consonant doubling, visual identification of misspelled words as a correction strategy, irregular spellings and the spelling of Latinate vocabulary.

Gentry (1982: 198) emphasizes that the transition from one spelling stage to another is gradual rather than abrupt and that exemplars from different stages may coexist in one and the same writing sample as the speller moves from one stage to the next. The development is continuous, proceeding from simple to more complex and from concrete to more abstract.

In the space of very few pages Gentry manages to present a rich picture of the growth of monolingual spelling in terms of fairly clearly defined stages, suggest forces driving development such as complexity and abstraction, and offer motivated guidelines to teachers for helping children acquire foundations for spelling competency. Nevertheless, despite the fact that the subject of developmental orthography is within the domain of developmental psycholinguistics, Gentry's discussion is not cast within the framework of a psycholinguistic model of the monolingual speller, no attempt is made to define what is meant by "developmental stage", or to elucidate the potentially explanatory notions of complexity and abstractness as principles driving first orthography acquisition.

As distinct from Gentry's five-stage model of spelling, Frith (1986) develops a six-*step* model of both reading and spelling, consisting of three processing *strategies* common to both reading and spelling and three discrete, rather than continuous *phases*, as in Figure 1.

Step	Reading				Writing
1a	logographic	L1			(symbolic)
1b	logographic	L2		→ L2	logographic
2a	logographic	L3		A1	alphabetic
2b	alphabetic	A2 ←		A2	alphabetic
3a	orthographic	01		A3	alphabetic
3b	orthographic	02		→ 02	orthographic

Figure 1. *The six-step model of reading and spelling development*

Each phase, represented by the three input-output mechanisms in the center of the figure, is characterized by one or two processing strategies which are held to apply in the acquisition of both reading and writing. The logographemic strategy characterizes the first phase in the beginning of reading. It applies to the recognition of known words and sentences to the extent that their visual details are salient. Phonological recoding follows visual recognition, and the most common mistakes are either no response or guessing. The alphabetic strategy characterizes the second phase and entails phonological recoding as a precondition on semantic access and with it the observance of sequentiality. The orthographic strategy marks the third phase and entails the automatic analysis of words into orthographic units corresponding to morphemes and frequent letter sequences and semantic access without phonological recoding. The strategy is called "orthographic" because the internal representation of the letter sequences is subject to graphotactic regularity.

For Frith (1986: 225) reading and writing are processes with contrasting aims. The logographemic strategy is well-suited for reading, the alphabetic for writing. The orthographic, permitting rapid word recognition in reading and accurate writing, appears well-suited for both.

In Figure 1 the logographemic strategy is first used for reading at step L1. Once engrams have been formed for the recognition of familiar words, they are used in graphic production at step L2, forming a system of reading-input and writing-output. The alphabetic strategy is first used for writing, because the writing-system is the more frequent (A1), and a certain level must be attained before the alphabetic strategy can be engaged in reading (A2). The orthographic strategy is first used in reading at step O1. Word recognition is far in advance of word production, with the most frequent spelling errors due to use of the alphabetic spelling strategy. The orthographic strategy must have reached a certain level (O2) before it can be used to serve its second function, writing.

Frith regards her model as dynamic because of the polarity between reading and writing it introduces and at best a sketch of a theory of reading and writing. Of primary importance to her is the nature of the transition from one phase to another, including questions such as why one phase relieves another, do earlier phases persevere or disappear, and what in general are the causes of learning and development. She suggests that established strategies are amalgamated with new ones, rather than new learned in addition to old, because the former hypothesis permits the child to build the new on the old, rather than start anew, and the acquisition of a new strategy does not guarantee its use. In the above case of reading and writing, the alphabetic strategy is seen to transform *(umgestalten)* the logographemic strategy by the introduction of the principle of sequentiality, a transformation which is necessary to arrive at the orthographic strategy via a strategic dialectic of thesis (logographemic), antithesis (alphabetic), and synthesis (orthographic). The orthographic strategy is thus viewed as a synthesis of immediate word recognition and sequential processing with subsequent phonological representations. In general, old strategies are not abandoned, but latently carried on in the new.

K.B. Günther (1986: 361) presents a model of the development of written language similar to Frith's (1986: 225). This model, reproduced in Figure 2, contains both the modalities of reading (reception) and spelling (production) as vehicles of acquisition strategies; five two-step phases from the preliteral-symbolic beginnings through to integrative-automated competence; in each of these phases a new strategy is introduced and alternately applied between the two modalities, imparting a new level

(Niveau) to the acquisition process, whereby an earlier strategy in one modality is preserved in the other modality until the next phase has been reached.

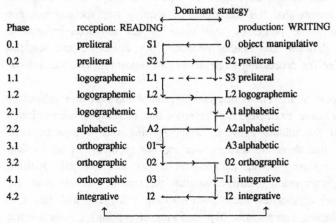

Figure 2.   *Written-language acquisition as a multi-phasic, strategy-determined developmental process*

Günther's model differs from Frith's in that it introduces two new phases, the preliteral-symbolic (phase 0) and the integrative-automated (phase 4). The preliteral-symbolic phase is considered a precondition on learning reading and writing. Through the detachment of pictorial representations from the intended objects and through the reduction of three dimensional objects to two dimensional spaces, the contemplation of pictures implies a greater degree of abstraction than sensorimotor perception, while remaining preliteral because it is representational. The integrative-automated phase does not contain a new strategy, but refers to written language use in the competent reader and writer in an autonomous, structurally and functionally specific system of language representation.

Frith and Günther concur in the views that the development of reading and spelling go hand in hand, that the process is best understood in terms of phases, that phases are best understood in terms of the emergence and exchange of acquisitional strategies, that the strategies are the same for reading and writing, and that later stages emerge through synthesis with earlier ones (Günther 1986: 366). The transitions between phases are held to be fluent *(fließend)* and characterized by overlappings and displacements *(Verschiebungen)*.

Eichler (1986: 234-245) offers a sweeping critique of the Frithian three-phase model of the acquisition of written language in reading and spelling. He argues that the modalities of reading and spelling are not subject to the same processes, that some of the advanced processing strategies are deficient and neither necessary nor sufficient, and that the directionality of the processing strategies is not sequential, but hierarchical and parallel.

In support of the claim that reading and writing are not subject to the same processing strategies, Eichler notes that there have been cultures (antiquity and the middle ages) in which writing was a separate craft from reading, that there are readers who are not spellers, but no spellers who are not readers (barring pathological cases), that normally spelling instruction follows reading instruction, that the reading process soon (in the first grade) dissociates itself from spelling strategies, and that differently developing components (the motorics of writing) greatly overlie writing, giving rise to other strategies. The issue, however, is whether or not reading and writing (spelling) are subject to the same strategic development. In order to address this issue, strategies must be defined and experiments designed to test if the defined strategies are capable of explaining the errors in reading and writing. It is our persuasion that strategies can be defined, but not in such a way that they would be as applicable to reading as to spelling; consequently, reading and spelling cannot be governed by the same processes. There may be a spelling strategy according to which the sound /X/ is written as the letter <Y> if the name of <Y>, /Z/, contains /X/, and there may be a reading strategy according to which the letter <Y> is to be pronounced /X/ if the name of <Y> is /Z/ and /X/ = /Z/, and there may be spellers who apply both strategies alternately in spelling and reading, but this would not mean that this type of spelling and reading was governed by the same processes, because the processes are in fact different.

Eichler's second objection to the Frithian model relates to the processing strategies themselves. He sees no need for Frith's first, logographemic (Eichler's "logographic") strategy, finding only an alphabetic beginning to early writing (= spelling), which maintains itself as a "component" in self-correction and overlay by orthographic strategies.

Second, an "expansion" is called for in Frith's notion of orthographic strategy, which Eichler thinks is mistakenly restricted to the "formal" side of language such as letter combinations, word formation, the recognition of word stems, endings, etc. This then leads to the suggestion (in reliance on Goodman) that reading is a strategy for testing hypotheses about semantic and structural expectations.

Finally, Eichler claims that the directionality of the processing strategies is not sequential, but hierarchic and parallel. Opposed to Frith's position that earlier strategies fuse to produce later strategies, in particular the logographemic fuses with the alphabetic to produce the orthographic, is Eichler's view that recourse may be had to earlier strategies, and strategies may be parallelly engaged, but acquisitional stages build upon each other in sequence. In neither case is it clear what drives the process of the acquisition of orthography in its two main uses in reading and spelling as a means to writing in either first or second orthography development.

It is clear from the above survey of approaches to developmental orthography that the focus is on the *what* of what is being acquired and not the *why*, on theories of developing orthographic competence and not theories of learnability (cf. Rutherford 1987 for critical discussion). The concern of the former is which grammatical structures are acquired in what order, while the concern of the latter is the principles explaining such sequences. It is theories of learnability that are needed to explain language development. Several such theories have been advanced in recent years in the form of principles and models, hypotheses and approaches, including the *Subset Principle* (Berwick and Weinberg 1984), the *Uniqueness Principle* (Pinker 1984, 1986), and *Preemption Theory* (Rutherford 1987). On the Subset Principle narrower grammars are learned before wider ones, where the narrower is a "subset" of the wider. On the Uniqueness Principle different forms imply different meanings, thus one of a pair of synonymous forms "preempts" the other. Rutherford (1987: 21) asks if preemption differs in L1 and L2 and if SLA research has anything to contribute to learnability theory in general.

2.   Learnability: Subsets vs. complexity

Wexler and Manzini (1987: 44) formulate the Subset Principle as follows. Different values of the same parameter yield different languages, whereby one language is "smaller than" or contained in the other. "... the learning strategy specified by the Subset Principle is that the learner select the value which yields (the smaller or contained language) first." If this value is the correct choice, the learner will stay with the value; if it is the wrong choice, there will be positive evidence from the containing language which the learner will eventually hear.

> "The Subset Principle specifies that when positive evidence which shows that L(i) is the wrong language is encountered, the learner will switch to the parameter value which yields language. In short, the Subset Principle is a method for specifying a markedness hierarchy when alternative values yield languages which are in a subset relation."

The Subset Principle leaves open such questions as what a parameter is, how many values a parameter can take, why different languages associated with different fixings of the same parameter must be in the relationship of subset to superset (as opposed to complementarity, intersection, disjunction, etc.), and why it should be a principle, as opposed to a hypothesis.

In the following we try to show that there are acquisitional sequences in which terms learned earlier are not a subset of terms learned later but are lower ranked on either or both of two scales of complexity, namely, a scale of complexness and a scale of univocality (Sgall 1987). Evidently, complexness and univocality may each be viewed as parameters, each having a number of values whose action and interaction have consequences for orthography acquisition. It remains to be seen if such scales have a set-theoretic interpretation, but the onus of proof lies with the proponents of the Subset Principle.

According to Sgall's (1987) proposal, the deviations from a one-to-one correspondence between grapheme and phoneme may be ranked along two scales, a scale of complexness and a scale of univocality. For Czech examples, the reader is referred to Sgall (1987).

The scale of complexness is as follows:

(C1) protographeme - a grapheme no variant of which contains a diacritic sign;

(C2) complex grapheme with a regular subgrapheme (diacritic);

(C3) complex grapheme with an irregular subgrapheme;

(C4) protographeme string;

(C5) string with some complex elements, but no irregular subgraphemes;

(C6) string some of whose elements have an irregular subgrapheme;

(C7) as in (C6), with the irregular subgrapheme corresponding to more than one phoneme in the pronunciation (or with some other difference between the number of phonemes and the number of graphemes.

The logic underlying the scale of complexness appears compelling:

1. simplex grapheme (protographeme) before complex grapheme;

2. protographeme string before complex grapheme string;

3. regular subgrapheme before irregular subgrapheme;

4. one-to-one before one-to-many;

5. one-to-one before many-to-one.

The first axis or parameter, the scale of complexness, concerns different types of phoneme-grapheme relationships in terms of number and types of representing graphemes, their regularity, and the kinds of influences they exert on the realizations of neighboring graphemes. The second axis or parameter, the scale of univocality, specifies the kinds and degrees of ambiguity in the operations of (oral) reading and spelling. For spelling, the more complex of the two, the scale of univocality is as follows:

(U1) absolute biuniqueness;

(U2) relative biuniqueness;

(U3) regular deviations, with different graphemes used with a single phoneme with different morphemes, the choice being given by a general rule and corroborated by phonemic alternations in the given morphemic position (with a different phonemic context);

(U4) as in (U3), without the corroborating alternations;

(U5) irregular deviations, the choice being given by a difference between lexical morphemes;

(U6) irregular deviations, the choice being given by a morpheme whose single graphemic shape is thus ensured;

(U7) irregular deviations with the choice given idiosyncratically (traditionally, without a functional justification).

In essence, the scale of univocality states that the degree of complexity of an ambiguous orthographic representation is directly related to the kind and amount of linguistic information needed for the resolution of its ambiguity. Such information ranges from PGCs that are context-free to those context-sensitive to phonology, inflectional morphology, derivational morphology, semantics, and lexis.

The 7 values of each of the parameters of complexness and univocality can be plotted against each other, yielding a two dimensional matrix with 49 cells. As Sgall (1987: 19) points out, such a matrix can aid the classification of orthographic rules to the extent that they specify the operations of spelling and pronunciation for the given orthographic system. Especially noteworthy is the claim that the different degrees of the scale of univocality correspond to different degrees of easiness of the orthography and of its appropriateness for writing and reading. The complexity theory of orthography is thus linked to the complexity theory of learnability in reading and spelling.

3.   Bilingual developmental orthography

3.1   *Transfer: Interlinguistic and intralinguistic*

In this section we will test the Subset and Complexity Principles of learnability theory on a large body of SLA developmental orthographic data elicited from German school children in the acquisition of English orthography (cf. references in the bibliography). The various types of evidence include German letter naming, English letter naming, German PGCs, English PGCs, Simplification, Complication, Regularization, Irregularization, consonant doubling, the spelling of the regular preterit, the spelling of some short and long vowels, and 38 different types of phonological-morphological-orthographic relations in the orthography of English inflection and contraction. In each case, it will be seen that the Subset Principle of learnability theory fails to predict the acquisitional sequences observed, whereas various settings of the parameters of univocality and complexness succeed. Complexity thus appears to be the more promising approach to the explanation of language learning sequences.

Transfer

I   Intralinguistic
     A.   English Letter Naming
         1.   Articulation of English Letter Name:
             A: \<Her\> :: T: \<Here\>
         2.   Place of Articulation of an English Letter Name:
             A: \<mess\> :: T: \<miss\>
         3.   Sequence of English Letter Names:
             A: \<could\> :: T: \<cold\>
     B.   English Letter Sounding
             A: \<skeade\> :: T: \<skid\>
     C.   English PGCs
         1.   Regularization:
             A: \<pritty\> :: T: \<pretty\>
         2.   Irregularization:
             A: \<leate\> :: T: \<late\>
         3.   Simplification:
             A: \<juse\> :: T: \<juice\>
         4.   Complication:
             A: \<cload\> :: T: \<clothes\>
     D.   Familiarization
             A: \<time\> :: T: \<tame\>

II   Interlinguistic
     A.   German Letter Naming
         1.   Articulation of German Letter Name:
             A: \<cornfleks\> :: T: \<cornflakes\>
         2.   Place of Articulation of German Letter Name:
             A: \<Jan\> :: T: \<John\>
     B.   German PGCs
             A: \<steschen\> :: T: \<station\>
     C.   Cognatization
         1.   Partial:
             A: \<preis\> :: T: \<prize\>
         2.   Total:
             A: \<mußt\> :: T: \<must\>
     D.   Decognatization
             A: \<Bäter\> :: T: \<better\>

Table 1.   Intra- and interlinguistic orthographic transfer

In Table 1 we present the types of processing strategies in bi-lingual spellers (cf. Luelsdorff 1986 and chapter 3, this volume, for detailed discussion). These strategies run *parallel* throughout grades 6-9 (ages 11-14) of the German *Hauptschule* and *Gymnasium* and grades 7-9 (ages 12-14) of the German *Realschule*, in the sense that evidence of their application may be found in some spellings throughout these grades, but the *extent* to which they are applied varies with age, school system, and increased exposure to written English. Whereas the frequency of implementation of the processing strategies of German and English letter naming decreases, the frequency of implementation increases in the case of English PGCs and decreases in the case of PGCs that are German (cf. Luelsdorff 1986: 320).

More precisely, the strategies adopted earliest and phased out soonest are the various forms of Letter Naming as a spelling strategy. The language yielded by the Letter Naming strategy is indeed a subset of the language yielded by the application of PGCs, but this is not the reason why the spellings under Letter Naming are the spellings to be learned first. Rather, letter-named spellings are learned before non-letter-named spellings because the former are rule governed and the latter must be learned more or less by rote. The simple regularity involved is spelling a sound with a letter whose name (either properly or improperly) includes the sound. A more complicated form involves spelling a sound with a letter whose name is a sound adjacent to the sound to be spelled, such as spelling target: <miss> with attempt: <mess>. In such cases, the relationship between sound and letter is motivated by the letter name, and the letter name is used as a device to aid in processing the orthographic information. Aids are present in some other cases, such as Place of Articulation of a Letter Sound, as in target: <hem> spelled attempt: <ham>, but in the majority of other instances the relation between phoneme and grapheme is arbitrary and must be memorized if it is to be mastered. Most of the normatively correct spellings, on the other hand, even in the case of the rule-governed spellings of the short and long vowels in monosyllables, must be learned by heart, i.e. without recourse to the various forms of letter naming as a spelling strategy. In short, the spelling learner has selected the parameter value which yields the smallest or contained language first not because it is a subset of a superset, but because it is easier to process.

Of the processing strategies of German Letter Naming and English Letter Naming, it is German Letter Naming which is the first to be phased out. Hence, German Letter Naming should yield a subset of

English Letter Naming. Instead it would appear that they intersect, since there are letter-named spellings which are unique to German <a, e, i>, and letter-named spellings which are unique to English <a, e, i>, and letter-named spellings which are common to both German and English <o, u>. Since Letter Naming in English and German does not yield languages which are subsets of one another, i.e. either English a subset of German or German a subset of English, but German Letter Naming is added and dropped before English, the Subset Principle forces a subset-superset relation which is empirically unmotivated.

On the complexity theoretic interpretation of the phonology-orthography interface, not only are letter-named segments rule-governed, but absolutely biunique on the scale of univocality and protographemes on the scale of complexness. As such, they are the maximally simple orthographic representations, with the remaining phoneme-grapheme correspondences obtained by more complex settings of the values of these parameters.

Of the processing strategies of German PGCs and English PGCs, it is German PGCs which are the first to be phased out. Hence, German PGCs should be a subset of English PGCs. As in the cases of German and English Letter Naming, however, the languages defined by the respective fixations of the values of the parameters for German and English do not form a relation of subset-superset, but intersection. Thus, there are PGCs belonging only to German, such as /ö/:<ö>, /ɛ:/:<ä>, and /ü/:<ü>, and PGCs belonging only to English, such as /g/:<gh>, /Ø/:<gh>, /oy/:<oy>, and PGCs belonging to both German and English, such as /f/:<f>, /p/:<p>, and /a/:<a>. Rather than the notion of subset, what explains the fact that German is gradually being phased out is the undoing, given increasing exposure to English, of the overgeneralization which we have referred to elsewhere as the *Identical Signifié Constraint* (Luelsdorff 1987a) according to which any letter (German or English) may be used to spell a segment providing that letter stands for that segment. This overgeneralization, in time, is dissolved into constituent generalizations which are lexically (not only segmentally) constrained, a universal quantification turned into something much more particular, a simple statement becoming much more complex. Cast in the terms of the theory of complexity, a one-many relationship, one which is relatively biunique, becomes lexicalized along the scale of univocality, the setting which is in fact the most complex. This is not a question of sets and subsets, but of successive layering of increasingly more complex information, akin to Zobl's (1983) notion of markedness.

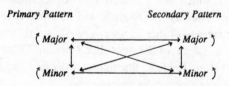

Error Type		Attempt	Target
1.	Primary Regularization	<Camebridge>	<Cambridge>
2.	Primary Reregularization	<jame>	<jam>
3.	Primary Irregularization	<sommer>	<summer>
4.	Primary Re-irregularization	<pollover>	<pullover>
5.	Secondary Regularization	<braught>	<brought>
6.	Secondary Reregularization	<enjoied>	<enjoyed>
7.	Secondary Irregularization	<movey>	<movie>
8.	Secondary Re-irregularization	<broaght>	<brought>
9.	Regularization cum Simplification	<wer>	<wear>
10.	Reregularization cum Simplification	<movi>	<movie>
11.	Irregularization cum Simplification	<pice>	<piece>
12.	Re-irregularization cum Simplification	<laghe>	<laugh>
13.	Regularization cum Complication	<Caimbridge>	<Cambridge>
14.	Reregularization cum Complication	<geit>	<gate>
15.	Irregularization cum Complication	<coulled>	<called>
16.	Re-irregularization cum Complication	<wear>	<were>

Table 2.   Intralinguistic substitution - error types

At this juncture, we are basically left with a large class of errors subsumable under the rubric "Intralinguistic Interference". Elsewhere (chapter 4, this volume) we presented a taxonomy of such errors of the bilingual speller, which we reproduce here in Table 2. Each item in this taxonomy belongs to the language defined by one value on each of two parameters in the Attempt in relation to the language defined by one value on each of the same two parameters in the Target (norm). The parameters are Regularity, with the values Regular (most frequent) and

Irregular, and Complexity, with the values Simple (one letter) and Complex (two or more letters), the former corresponding to positions 1 and 2 on Sgall's (1987) scale of univocality, the latter to positions 1 and 2 on Sgall's scale of complexness. Here, the intention is to provide a framework for the categorization of intralingual spelling errors made after some exposure to the standard orthographic norm. For example, if a speller spells <late> as <leat> after exposure to <late>, where <aCe> is Regular, <ea> Irregular, and both <aCe> and <ea> Complex (Secondary), we describe the substitution as a Secondary Irregularization. This framework provides a finely graded taxonomy of intralinguistic errors of the substitution type and is exhaustive in the sense that it categorizes all the substitution errors in evidence. Furthermore, it is motivated in the sense that its terms are based on known prior exposure to the norm. Difficulty would arise, however, if it were shown that there are discrepancies between the ranked relative frequencies in the spellers' total written output and those in the norm. In the above example, if <ea> were the Regular spelling of the vowel in words such as <late>, then attempt:<leat> for target:<late> would, psycholinguistically speaking, be a Regularization and not an Irregularization.

By far the most frequent errors of intralinguistic interference are errors of the Regularization type. Assuming that there is a parameter of univocality with the value Regular which is specified either + for Regular or - for Irregular, the Subset Condition (cf. Wexler and Manzini 1987) requires either that the regular language be contained in the irregular or the irregular language in the regular. But + and - partition a set into two *disjoint* subsets, not into sets contained one in the other. Evidently, the Subset Condition is too strong. On the other hand, Complexity Theory predicts that there will be more errors of Regularization than Irregularization, because regular correspondences occupy a lower place on the scale of univocality than correspondences that are irregular.

3.2 Graphemic and phonemic ambiguity

Systemic deviation from phoneme-grapheme biuniqueness, i.e. degree of univocality (Sgall 1987), is a major cause of error in the acquisition of a native or foreign alphabetic script. Such deviation is graphemically ambiguous if the relation between grapheme and phoneme is many-to-one and phonetically ambiguous if the relationship between grapheme and phoneme is one-to-many. Previous research (Luelsdorff 1987a) has shown that the acquisitional order of the resolution of phonemic ambiguity in morphemic spelling is predictable on the basis of the degree of complexity of the relation between orthography and phonology in the case of German learners of English. Further study (Luelsdorff and Eyland, chapter 7, this volume) showed that the acquisitional order of the resolution of graphemic ambiguity follows the same pattern for the same population. Although German and English have quite similar rules of consonant doubling and singling, German pupils acquire English consonant doubling later than English consonant singling and later before some suffixes (the regular past) than before others (the present progressive). If these differential acquisitional orders (singling vs. doubling, past vs. progressive) were due to transfer from German to English, the differences observed ought not to be significant because the relevant rules in the two languages are so similar. Rather, the cause resides in the fact that consonant doubling is more complex on the scale of complexness (Sgall 1987) than consonant singling and more complex in the environment of some suffixes (the preterit) than in the environment of others (the progressive). Note that the Subset Principle cannot be properly invoked to explain these differences for neither is consonant singling a subset of consonant doubling, nor is consonant doubling in the environment of the progressive a subset of consonant doubling in the environment of the past. Although the single letter <C> appears to be a subset of the doubled letters <CC>, the environment of the rule of consonant singling is not a subset of the environment of the rule of consonant doubling, because the former operates after long vowels and the latter operates after short vowels. Moreover, consonant doubling before the progressive is not a subset of consonant doubling before the preterit, because neither the phonology, nor the orthography, nor the morphology of the progressive is a subset of the phonology, orthography, and morphology of the preterit. Rather, the preterit has a more *complex* phonology, orthography, and morphology than the progressive, and it is this complexity which makes the orthography of preceding consonant doubling more complex, a kind of complexity by contagion. It is hard to determine the positions of orthographic consonant singling and consonant doubling within the Frithian and

Güntherian frameworks, but since they require segmental phonological, suprasegmental phonological, orthographic and morphological information for their proper operation they would seem to straddle strategies both alphabetic and orthographic. The fact that doubling is acquired later than singling is then due to its requiring more complex information, reflected in traditional accounts (cf. Reid and Hresko 1981: 268) in which rules are given for doubling but not singling. Here, correct consonant doubling requires the ability to simultaneously distinguish (1) simple vowel letters from digraphs, (2) stressed from unstressed vowels, (3) single consonant letters from consonant-letter clusters, and (4) stems from suffixes. Even if the rule(s) involved could be cast in strictly phonological and morphological terms (instead of partially orthographic), the rule(s) would still reference terms that are (1) phonological (both segmental and suprasegmental), and (2) morphological (morpheme boundaries), meaning that the speller must simultaneously access both phonology and morphology, i.e. Frith's alphabetic and orthographic strategies.

We then looked into the order of acquisition of the spelling of the regular past tense allomorphs (Luelsdorff 1987a), fairly consistently finding better performance on /ɪd/:<ed> than on /d/:<ed> and on /d/:<ed> than on /t/:<ed>. Initially, in order to explain this distribution we advanced the Abstraction Hypothesis according to which orthographic representations which are less abstract are acquired earlier than those which are more abstract, where abstractness is measured in terms of the number of rules relating the orthographic representations to the phonetic. Just as the Abstractness Hypothesis on morphemic spelling predicts the order of acquisition of the <ed> spellings of the regular past tense allomorphs - first /ɪd/, second /d/, third /t/ - it naturally also predicts the relative frequencies with which these allomorphs will be *mis*spelled - first /t/, second /d/, third /ɪd/. Moreover, the Abstractness Hypothesis on morphemic spelling, augmented by a theory of phonetic spelling and a theory of transfer, also predicts the actual major misspelling types of the regular allomorphs of the past tense morpheme themselves: <t> for /t/, <d/t> for /d/, and <id/it> for /ɪd/. These results are equally explicable within the Complexity Theory of Sgall (1987), which contains two scales, a scale of complexness and a scale of univocality. Both /d/:<ed> and /t/:<ed> are more complex than /ɪd/:<ed>, since they each use two letters for one sound, and /d/:<ed> is more univocal than /t/:<ed>, since /d/:<d>

is relatively more biunique than /t/:<d>. It is hard to see, however, how these results fall out of the Subset Principle. The Subset Principle would require /ɪd/:<ed> to be a subset of /d/:<ed> and /d/:<ed> to be a subset of /t/:<ed>. Generatively, /d/ might be derived from /ɪd/ and /t/ might be derived from /d/. /d/ might be construed as a subset of /ɪd/, in which case the Subset Principle makes the wrong prediction because /ɪd/ should be a subset of /d/, or /t/ might be construed as a subset of /d/, if features specified minus are construed as subsets of features specified plus (cf. Rutherford 1987), in which case the Subset Principle also makes the wrong prediction, since /d/ should be a subset of /t/. Consequently, the Subset Principle must be rejected and Complexity Theory accepted. As in the case of consonant doubling, so too in the case of morphemic spelling, the processing strategies involved are partly alphabetic, partly orthographic, in the terminology of Frith and Günther. But alphabetic together with orthographic processing strategies alone are insufficient to discriminate among the three structures involved to the extent that they are differentially acquired. A more differentiated conception is required, and we suggest that that conception is the scales of complexity and univocality as articulated in Sgall (1987) and developed in chapter 9, this volume.

3.3   Short and long vowels

In a study of the psycholinguistic determinants of orthography acquisition (Luelsdorff and Eyland, chapter 7, this volume), we tested four hypotheses explaining the differential acquisition of the short and long English vowel graphemes <a, e, i>.

On the first hypothesis, performance improves with phoneme-grapheme frequency. Here, four measures of phoneme-grapheme frequency were used:

1. the absolute frequency of phoneme-grapheme occurrence;
2. the rank within each grade of the absolute frequency of phoneme-grapheme occurrence;
3. the relative frequency of phoneme-grapheme occurrence;
4. the rank within each grade of the relative frequency of phoneme-grapheme occurrence.

From the statistical analysis, we found that the best specification of phoneme-grapheme frequency was the ranked relative frequency, since this specification produced models which more closely represented the data than other models. In general, we found support for the hypothesis that as ranked relative frequency increases so does performance (the higher the rank, the higher the relative frequency of phoneme-grapheme occurrence). We conclude from this that each phoneme, together with the totality of its associated graphemes, is a psycholinguistic module, with that phoneme-grapheme correspondence being used productively in the spelling of unfamiliar real words which exhibits the highest ranked relative frequency. Put differently, regularly spelled vowels in unfamiliar real words will be spelled correctly in a statistically significant number of cases because in such cases foreign spellers (possibly native?) engage those vowel spellings for the given vowels which are the ranked relatively most frequent. Note that while the phoneme-grapheme correspondence with the highest ranked frequency is a subset of the entire set of phoneme-grapheme correspondences for that phoneme, it is not learned and used because it is a subset, in accordance with the putative Subset Principle, but because it is the highest ranked phoneme-grapheme occurrence. This is true of foreign learners and native dysgraphics (cf. Goodman and Caramazza 1986: 317) as well. We thus reject the Subset Principle and accept the Principle of Ranked Relative Frequency of the scale of univocality.

On the second hypothesis, performance decreases with grapheme ambiguity, i.e. the more alternative ways there are of spelling a particular phoneme, the poorer performance is expected to be. This result does not appear to hold in three of the thirteen grades surveyed, viz. years 6 and 9 of the *Hauptschule* and year 8 of the *Gymnasium*, but it does hold in a sufficiently large number of cases for the hypothesis to have significant support. The Subset Principle cannot explain this intuitively pleasing and experimentally supported result, because phoneme-grapheme correspondences which are less ambiguous (hence, on the above, learned earlier) are not a subset of phoneme-grapheme correspondences which are more ambiguous (hence, on the above, learned later). Even if less ambiguous PGCs were a subset of more ambiguous PGCs, their performance differential would not be explained by their subsetness, but by the fact that they are less ambiguous. Nor does the Uniqueness Principle explain these results. On the Uniqueness Principle different forms imply different meanings, one of a pair of synonymous forms thus "preempting" the other. Different letters standing for the same sound have the same meaning, i.e. the sound they stand for. They may preempt each other, and they are very typically synonymous, but they do not preempt each other *because* they are synonymous - synonymy is a condition on preemption - but because they have a higher ranked relative frequency and are less ambiguous.

On the third hypothesis, the acquisition of the spelling of short vowels precedes that of diphthongs and long vowels. This hypothesis has some merit, because, for each of the thirteen classes tested, performance on long vowels is poorer than on short vowels and diphthongs. In one grade in one school system performance on diphthongs is better than on short vowels, otherwise there is little difference between short and diphthongal vowels although short vowels have the edge. On the strictly literal level, it may seem plausible to treat the letter <V> as a subset of <VV> and <V...V>, although it may be hard to find a phonologist or phonetician who would treat short vowels as subsets of diphthongs and long vowels. But orthography does not deal with letters, but with the relationships of alphabets and syllabaries to grammar (including phonology). On this view, PGCs for short vowels are no more of a subset of PGCs for diphthongs and long vowels than PGCs for long vowels and diphthongs are a subset of PGCs for short vowels. Rather, the reasons why short vowel spellings are acquired before those of long vowels are to be found in universal grammar (cf. Justeson 1977), the markedness differential hypothesis (Eckman 1977), and the scales of complexity (and univocality) (Sgall 1987). According to UG, no long vowels are represented distinctly unless short vowels are; consequently, in English, long vowel spellings are learned later than short vowel spellings. According to the Markedness Differential Hypothesis, English long vowel spellings are harder for German learners to learn than English short vowel spellings. And, according to the Praguian scale of complexness, a double vowel spelling is harder to learn than a single, because it either consists of a protographeme string or a protographeme string with one vowel letter functioning as a diacritic. All this has less to do with subsets and more to do with frequency, complexness, and univocality, i.e. with the Praguian concept.

On the fourth hypothesis, the same vowels with the same spellings in different words are misspelled in different ways. Here we find that items in pairs like <speck, hem>, <tame, scrape>, and <spike, slime> are spelled significantly differently in various grades. This is not because the more correctly spelled terms are subsets of the less correctly spelled terms, whatever that might mean, but either because the more correctly spelled term is associated with a known word with the vowel in question (e.g. <speck> associated with German <Speck>) or because the more correctly spelled term is paired with a less correctly spelled term which is associated with a known word with the wrong spelling (e.g. <tame> wrongly associated with <time>). Here, the cause of correct performance is the correct analogizing of the unfamiliar with the familiar and the cause of the incorrect performance the incorrect analogizing of the unfamiliar with the familiar. In time, performance accuracies on identically spelled identical vowels converge, reflecting cessation of the above type of analogizing and increased reliance on productive PGCs.

The above considerations have led to the conclusion that ranked relative frequency, degree of complexness, and degree of univocality, together with other factors, such as age and school system, are among the parameters which constitute the psycholinguistic determinants of orthography acquisition. Since the fixings of the parameters learned first are not a subset of the fixings of the parameters learned later, the Subset Principle runs afoul of explaining acquisitional sequences. Furthermore, the alphabetic strategy in Frith's and Günther's models of reading and spelling must accordingly be subdivided into strategies of frequency, strategies of complexness, and strategies of univocality which are independent in principle, but dependent (interactive) in practice, since spelling performance depends not only on the fixings of one, but the fixings of all, with the fixing of the complexity parameter most dominant. Moreover, beginning bilingual spellers are sensitive to a familiarity parameter, whereby the spelling of an unfamiliar word is to some extent a function of the spelling of a phonologically similar familiar word. Further parameters may yet be uncovered, but it is certain that the notion of alphabetic strategy is a complex one which must be further analyzed into its underlying, interacting constituent parts.

3.4   Orthography of inflection and contraction

A core concern of native and foreign language acquisition studies is the discovery and explanation of differential orders of language learning, including orthography in its uses in spelling and reading. In Luelsdorff and Eyland (chapter 7, this volume) we report that input frequency - in the sense of both absolute and relative type frequency - plays a minor role in determining the order of acquisition of the spellings of the English short and long vowels.

A more promising approach to the explanation of acquisition order is to attempt to significantly correlate orders of acquisition with orders of complexity. In chapter 9, this volume, we present and extend Sgall's (1987) universal scales of orthographic complexity and use them to assign complexity to the orthography of inflection and contraction and the related areas of consonant singling and doubling. We hypothesized that the order of orthography acquisition is a function of the order of orthographic complexity and tested this hypothesis on 38 orthographic structures in a sample of 14 fifth-year German learners of English as a foreign language. Disconfirming evidence could only come from simpler structures on the hierarchy of orthographic complexity being acquired after structures which are more complex. The data was found to be consistent with the hypothesis.

The existence of different types of errors corresponding to morphologically different forms with the same normative surface phonology and orthography suggested the interaction of the scale of orthographic complexity with the scale of morphemic complexity (Brown 1973): other things being equal, misspelled higher ranking morphemes are spelled as morphemes of lower ranks.

The emerged notion of L2-orthography development is not one of stages defined in terms of *rules* appearing in a predictable order, but of stages defined in terms of successively more complex *semiotic schemata*, defined on relations like one-to-one, then one-to-many, then none-to-one and one-to-none, and their combinations, upon whose prior, general presence the emergence of particular rules depends.

The complexity theory of orthography acquisition not only explains the order of orthography acquisition, but also constrains the class of possible interpersonal variations by prohibiting the violation of the implicational relations among and within the complexity schema provided by complexity theory.

Developmentally, the members of adjacent acquisitional groups amalgamate before the members of acquisitional groups that are non-adjacent, and attrition (loss) in a less complex acquisitional group implies attrition in an acquisitional group that is adjacent and more complex. These constraints on learning and forgetting were also seen to follow from the theory of orthographic complexity.

Inflection/contraction Acquisition Group I contains structures which bear a one-to-one relationship between letter and sound - the plural, the syllabic past participle, and the syllabic third singular. Acquisition Group II contain the environmentally conditioned spellings of consonant singling after long vowels, consonant doubling after short vowels, structures with a one-to-many relationship between sound and letter, as in the voiced and voiceless preterit and the voiced past participle, or between diacritic and sound, as in the voiced and voiceless non-syllabic possessive singular, and a whole array of non-syllabic contractions (voiceless main verb and auxiliary <is> and <has>). This Group is distinguished from Group I by the greater complexity of its sound-letter mapping and the greater complexity of its underlying semantics, syntax, and phonology (Brown 1973: 308-309). Group III consists of either structures where something, an apostrophe, is used to spell nothing sensible, a zero allomorph, or structures where nothing is used to spell something, namely the vowel in the syllabic possessive singular and the vowels in contracted syllabic main verb and auxiliary <is> and <has>. This last acquired group thus consists of signs with either a zero signifiant or a zero signifié and occupy the highest rank on both Sgall's scale of orthographic complexness and Brown's scale of grammatical morphemic complexity.

On the Subset Principle it would be necessary for relations which are one-to-one to be a subset of relations which are one-to-many and for relations which are one-to-many to be a subset of relations which are either none-to-one or one-to-none. While it may be possible to treat one-to-one relations as a subset of relations which are one-to-many - i.e. to consider one a subset of many - it is hardly possible to regard relations which are one-to-one or one-to-many as subsets of relations which are none-to-one or one-to-none. Introducing the notion that the null set is a subset of every set renders the set-theoretic interpretation of learnability theory even worse, for then relations that are none-to-one and one-to-none would have to be acquired first, instead of last. On the other hand, there is no unambiguous evidence countering the claim that observed order of acquisition does not differ from the order of acquisition predicted by the order of orthographic complexity.

3.5   Vowel spelling vs. consonant doubling vs. morphemic spelling

It is most instructive to compare the growth rates of several different processing strategies inferred for the same samples with an eye to discovering significant differences. Since the Subset Principle predicts differential learning effects for different settings of only the *same* parameter, evidence of differential learning effects across different parameters would argue against the Subset Principle of learnability theory. We draw such evidence from a comparison of performance on the long and short vowels (Luelsdorff and Eyland, chapter 7, this volume), consonant doubling (Luelsdorff and Eyland, chapter 5, this volume), and the morphemic spelling of the regular preterit. In all but 2 of the 12 test words for the vowels, performance is well above 80%, and, in most cases, above 90% in grade 9 of the *Gymnasium*. In the same grade and school system, performance on consonant doubling is 82%, and performance on voiceless stems <ed> a mere 53%. Evidently, the performance hierarchy is short and long vowel spellings > consonant doubling > voiceless stems: <ed>. This result cannot be explained by the Subset Principle, because neither are short and long vowel spellings a subset of doubled consonant spellings, nor are doubled consonant spellings a subset of the <ed> spelling of the preterit after voiceless stems. On the theory of complexity, however, short vowels occupy setting (C1) on the scale of complexness because they are protographemes, long vowels occupy position (C2-3) because they are complex graphemes, consonant doublings occupy (C5) because they are strings with some complex elements (<CC>s saying the preceding vowel is short) with no irregular subgraphemes, and <ed> after voiceless stems occupies position (U6) because it is an irregular deviation with the choice given by a morpheme whose single graphemic shape is thus ensured. In other words, the observed order of accuracy follows from respectively higher settings of various values of the orthographic parameters of complexness and univocality and not from the Subset Principle, which is another reason for accepting the former and rejecting the latter.

3.6 Developmental morphographemics

Above and elsewhere we have had occasion to observe that apparently one and the same process of orthography is differentially sensitive to what appears to be one and the same environment. Thus, there are learning spellers who correctly double the consonant in words such as <bragging>, but fail to do so in words such as <bragged>. Since the words involved were unfamiliar real words, we concluded that consonant doubling is learned in some environments before others, the domain of application of the rule, as it were, expanding. We pursued this phenomenon in work in progress, focusing on the issue of <e>-elision or retention in stem-final position before (1) inflectional suffixes such as <-ed, -er, -est, -ing> and (2) derivational suffixes such as <-al, -able, -ous, -ful, -less, -ly, -ment, -ness, -some, -th>. We find significant interaction between <e>-elision and affix type - either inflectional or derivational - such that <e>-elision or retention is learned later before derivational endings than before inflectional. On the Subset Principle this result can only be explained by maintaining that inflectional endings are a subset of derivational. Since Sgall's theory of orthographic complexity does not make provision for "morphographemic" alternations of the type <e>-elision (<true ~ truth>), substitutions <y> → <i> (<country ~ countries>), <i> → <y> (<lie → lying>), additions (<peace, piece>), and displacements ("transpositions" (<acre>), all of which relate letters to nothing, letters to letters, rather than sound to letters, or nothing to letters, we suggest that they rank highest in complexity accordingly as they affect complexness or univocality. The above results may alternatively be due to the overgeneralization of the prevocalic environment in which <e>-elision applies in inflection to erroneously include the preconsonantal environment of much derivation, in which case the explanation would not be related to suffix type, but quite high error rates on vowel-initial suffixes such as <-al, -able> argue against this.

In a related study in preparation we tested performance on the morphographemics of pluralization in such plurals as <boy ~ boys>, <donkey ~ donkeys>, <buffalo ~ buffalos>, <cargo ~ cargoes>, <thief ~ thieves>, <chief ~ chiefs>, and <Galsworthy ~ Galsworthys>, predicting the greater the rule competition, the poorer the performance. The Theory of Competition (Bates and MacWhinney 1987) accounts for the observed poorer performance on <donkeys> than <boys>, since <-ey> competes with <-ie> in <donkeys> but not in <boys>, for the poorer performance on <cargoes> than <buffalos>, since <cargoes> but not <buffalos> requires the addition of an <e>, but not for the poorer performance on <chiefs> than <thieves> or the poorer performance on <Galsworthys> than <thieves>. <chiefs> is frequently misspelled with <v>, indicating the overgeneralization of the morphophonemic alternation in words of the type <thief ~ thieves>, and <Galsworthy> is frequently misspelled with <ie>, indicating an overgeneralization of the morphographemic alternation in pairs like <country ~ countries>. To say that there is paradigm competition is another way of saying that different systemically motivated signifiers compete for the same signifieds, and this we have found to be the major generalization holding of interlinguistic and intralinguistic transfer. The next question is which factors determine the outcome of such competition and we have attempted to partly answer this question with ranked relative input frequency, degree of ambiguity, the universal markedness hierarchy in a contrastive setting, and the word familiarity effect (Luelsdorff and Eyland, chapter 7, this volume). In the above cases of the morphographemics of pluralization the relevant data is missing, but the fact that (counterintuitively) <chiefs> is acquired after <thieves> might be due to prior, excessive exposure to <thief ~ thieves> which would then be transferred to <chief>, i.e. to cases where the irregularity in the standard becomes the regularity in the language of the learner, to cases of irregularization.

In a final study of the morphographemics of <y> → <i> in inflection and derivation before inflectional suffixes <-ing, -er (comp), -est, -es (3sg), -es (pl), -ed> and derivational suffixes <-er, -ness, -ful, -ly, -able> we found over twice as many errors made before derivation than before inflection, and, within inflection, 2/3 more errors made before <-es (3sg), -es (pl), -ed> than before <-ing, -er (comp), -est>. This latter result cannot be due to the presence of the suffix-initial vowel letter, because there is a suffix-initial vowel letter in all the cases. Rather, it is due to the relatively greater complexity of the phonology/orthography/morphology interface in the 3sg, plural, and regular preterit. Since the interface of the progressive, comparative, and superlative is not a subset of the interface of the 3sg, plural, and regular preterit, it is hard to imagine how the Subset Principle could explain the observed orders of acquisition.

Comparison of the results of our studies of <e>-deletion, <e>-addition, and <y> → <i> substitution yields the conclusions that both <e>-deletion and <y> → <i> substitution are acquired in inflection before derivation and that <e>-deletion is acquired before <y> → <i> substitution. <e>-addition in nouns (<cargo> ~ cargoes>) is acquired last. This result squares with a conclusion of our study of addition and deletion in the acquisition of false friends (Luelsdorff and Eyland, chapter 10, this volume), namely that letter additions are acquired later than letter deletions. We thus have empirical support for the following Hierarchy of Morphographemic Acquisition in an acquisitional setting: first inflection, then derivation; first deletion, then substitution, then addition. Cast in terms of implicational relations, if a bilingual speller's performance on the morphographemics of morphology is x, then his performance on the morphographemics of inflection will be $x+y$, and his performance on the morphographemics of derivation will be x-z. If his performance before invariant inflectional morphemes is x, then his performance before variant inflectional morphemes is x-y. If his performance on deletion is x, then his performance on substitution will be x-y, and his performance on addition will be x-y-z.

The above Hierarchy of Morphographemic Acquisition, which was empirically induced, may be used to supplement Sgall's (1987) scale of univocality. Note that this scale already assigns a lower rank to inflection than derivation, inflections occupying rank U3, derivations occupying rank U6. Because additions are more complex than substitutions, and substitutions are more complex than deletions in inflection *and* derivation, morphographemic additions, substitutions, and deletions are evidently different values of an *independent* parameter. This parameter we call "morphographemic". Other things being equal, the fixing of a higher value on the morphographemic parameter results in a construction which is more complex and hence more difficult to learn. Asking why a higher ranked value is more complex and difficult to learn than a lower ranked value is, in this (pervasive) case tantamount to asking why a nothing-to-one relation is more complex than a something$_1$-to-something$_2$, and why a something$_1$-to-something$_2$ relation is more complex than a relation which is one-to-nothing. This amounts to asking why is there an S-to-S condition, where S2 is first $\emptyset$, then non-$\emptyset$, then S1 $\emptyset$, i.e. (S1, $\emptyset$), (S1, S2), ($\emptyset$, S2). We suggest that the answer does not lie in the S-to-S condition itself - after all, the number of elements and types of elements in each relation are the same or similar - but in the quantity (number of) conditions on the S-to-S condition, i.e. on the degree of metaconditionality. Thus, <e> is deleted before inflectional endings with initial vowels (e.g. <arrive ~ arrived>) unless preceded by another <e> (e.g. <flee ~ fleeing>), the metaconditions being the following vowel and the preceding <e>. <i> is substituted for <y> before inflectional endings with initial vowels (e.g. <heavy ~ heavier>) unless it is preceded by a vowel (e.g. <gay ~ gayer, gay ~ gayest>), before the preterit spelled <d> (e.g. <say ~ said, lay ~ laid>), unless it is the 3sg or plural and a consonant is preceding, in which case <ie> is written (e.g. <baby ~ babies, try ~ tries>), or unless it ends a family name after a consonant (e.g. <Galsworthy ~ Galsworthys, Sothby ~ Sothbys>), in which case the <y> is retained, etc. Obviously, the metaconditions on the morphographemic condition of substitution are far more numerous, hence complex, than those on deletion. Finally, our test case for <e>-addition amounts to having to learn a list of plurals which take <e> (<cargoes, heroes, negroes, potatoes, tomatoes>) and a list of those which do not (<buffalos, photos, pianos>), lists being more complicated than rules.

It is instructive to compare the results of the acquisitional staging on (1) the orthography of inflection and contraction (chapter 9, this volume) and (2) the morphographemics of inflection and derivation (Luelsdorff, in progress). This we do in Table 3, where the first column contains structure labels, the third % correct, and the fourth the rank order of the structures acquired, averaged over two samples of 9th graders (N = 13, N = 23) who were in their 5th year of English in the *Gymnasium*.

The defining characteristics in the orthography of inflection and contraction are sound-letter relations which are 1:1, 1:n+1, and either 1:$\emptyset$ or $\emptyset$:1, and the defining characteristics in morphographemics are letter-letter relations which are either 1:$\emptyset$, 1:1 or 1:2, or $\emptyset$:1, in that acquisitional order. What is of interest is that the absolute order of the several structures in each of the major groupings changes into a relative order when both of the major groupings are simultaneously considered, suggesting such strong interaction of the two groupings that it appears misguided to regard them as in principle separate. Rather than modular (inflection and contraction vs. morphographemics), rather than interactive modular (modules with constraints on their interaction), the essence of the second orthography acquisition process appears to be *interactive*. If the orthography is modular and the acquisition of the orthography interactive, it is clear that there is a dissociation between grammar and acquisition along deeper lines than simply differentiating between theories of grammar and theories of learnability. In the present case, the complexity theory of orthography, coupled with the complexity theory of learnability, predict with great accuracy the structural order within each of the modules, but fail to predict why relations of deletion and substitution are learned before relations that are one-to-many, or why relations of addition in inflection, and deletion and substitution in derivation are learned before relations that are one-to-none or none-to-one.

Table 3.   *(Phono)morphographemic acquisition*

		Example	% Correct	Rank
I.	*Phonomorphographemics*			
	A. one-to-one	\<boys\>	100	1
	B. one-to-many	\<pickₑd\>	74	4
	C. one-to-none	\<church'Øs\>	14	8
	none-to-one	\<boys'_\>		
II.	*Morphographemics*			
	A. Inflection			
	1. Deletion	\<largØest\>	94	2
	2. Substitution	\<trįes\>	77	3
	3. Addition	\<cargoₑs\>	63	6
	B. Derivation			
	1. Deletion	\<truØly\>	67	5
	2. Substitution	\<prestigious\>	56	7

4.   Conclusion

Comparing the results of selected developmental investigations of English as a first and second orthography, we are in essential agreement with Gentry (1982) when he maintains that the transition from one developmental stage to another is gradual, rather than abrupt and that development is continuous, proceeding from simple to more complex and from concrete to more abstract. Our contribution has been to frame this discussion within a psycholinguistic model of the bilingual speller (Luelsdorff and Eyland, chapter 10, this volume), to impart precision to the notion "developmental stage" (Luelsdorff 1987a, 1987b), and to elucidate and exemplify the explanatory value of the notion of complexity for a wide range of phenomena in second orthography acquisition.

We are also in agreement with Frith (1986) when she stresses that the acquisition of spelling is governed by psycholinguistic processing strategies. Since our informants were 10-15 years of age, we must leave open the question of the existence of the logographemic strategy for bilingual spellers. Our contribution has been to analyze the alphabetic and orthographic strategies into several subtypes and rank these subtypes along developmental lines. The result is a finely graded sequence and hierarchy of phoneme-grapheme, phoneme-grapheme-morpheme, and phoneme-grapheme-grapheme-morpheme relations proceeding from less to more complex.

In respect of the directionality of processing strategies, we find no contradiction between Frith's (1986) claim that it is sequential and Eichler's (1986) claim that it is hierarchical and parallel. On the contrary, we observe some strategies acquired later than others (sequential), some strategies contained in others (hierarchical), and some strategies engaged at the same stage as others (parallel). What we do not find is more complex strategies engaged before strategies which are less complex, where complexity is defined by the scales of complexness, univocality, and graphogphonemics.

As an explanatory theory of orthographic learnability we advanced the (extended) Theory of Complexity. Contrasting the complexity theoretic with the subset theoretic approaches to learnability, only Complexity Theory attains explanatory adequacy by predicting the observed orders of orthography acquisition, confirming our belief that the structure and development of orthography are enlightening subjects of linguistic inquiry.

Author Index

Subject Index

References

Aho, A.V. and J.D. Ullman. 1972. *The theory of parsing, translation, and compiling.* Vol. I. *Parsing.* New Jersey: Prentice-Hall.

Augst, Gerhard (ed.). 1986. *New trends in graphemics and orthography.* Berlin: Walter de Gruyter.

Baker, Wm.J. and Bruce L. Derwing. 1982. "Response coincidence analysis as evidence for language acquisition strategies." *Applied psycholinguistics* 3, 193-221.

Bates, Elizabeth and Brian MacWhinney. 1987. "A functionalist approach to the acquisition of grammar". In: René Dirven and Vilém Fried (eds.), 209-264.

Batóg, T. and M. Steffan-Batogowa. 1980. "A distance function in phonetics." *Lingua posnaniensis* 23, 47-58.

Beers, J.W. 1980. "Developmental strategies of spelling competence in primary school children." In: E.H. Henderson and J.W. Beers (eds.), 36-45.

Berwick, Robert C. and Amy S. Weinberg. 1984. *The grammatical basis of linguistic performance: Language use and acquisition.* Cambridge: The MIT Press.

Bierwisch, M. 1972. "Schriftstruktur und Phonologie." *Probleme und Ergebnisse der Psychologie* 43.

Booij, Geert E. 1984. "Principles and parameters in prosodic phonology." *Linguistics* 22, 249-280.

Brown, Roger. 1973. *A first language. The early stages.* Cambridge, Mass.: Harvard University Press.

Campbell, R. 1983. "Writing nonwords to dictation." *Brain and language*, 19, 153-178.

Chomsky, Noam. 1957. *Syntactic structures.* The Hague: Mouton.

Chomsky, Noam and Morris Halle. 1965. "Some controversial issues in phonological theory." *Journal of linguistics* I/2, 97-138.

Chomsky, Noam and Morris Halle. 1968. *The sound pattern of English.* New York: Harper and Row.

Coltheart, Max. 1984. "Writing systems and reading disorders." In: L. Henderson (ed.), 67-80.

Coltheart, Max, Karalyn E. Patterson and John C. Marshall (eds.). 1980. *Deep dyslexia.* London: Routledge and Keagan Paul.

Cook, L. 1981. "Misspelling analysis in dyslexia: observation of developmental strategy shifts." *Bulletin of the Orton Society* 31, 123-134.

Cutler, Anne. 1980. "La leçon des lapsus." *La recherche* 11, 686-692.

Cutler, Anne. 1981. "The reliability of speech error data." In: Cutler, A. (ed.), 561-579.

Cutler, Anne (ed.). 1981. *Slips of the tongue and language production.* *Linguistics* 190 (7/8). Berlin: Mouton.

de Beaugrande, Robert. 1987. "Determinacy distributions in complex systems: Science, linguistics, language, life." *Zeitschrift für Sprachwissenschaft und Kommunikationsforschung* 40 (2), 147-190.

Derwing, Bruce L. and Maureen L. Dow. 1987. "Orthography as a variable in psycholinguistic experiments." In: Philip A. Luelsdorff (ed.), *Orthography and phonology*. Amsterdam: John Benjamins, 171-186.

Deyes, A.F. 1972a. "Learning from dictation." *ELT* 23, 226-231.

Deyes, A.F. 1972b. "Learning from dictation." *ELT* 26, 149-154.

Dirven, René and Vilém Fried (eds.). 1987. *Functionalism in linguistics*. LLSEE 20. Amsterdam: John Benjamins.

Dulay, Heidi, Marina Burt and Stephen Krashen. 1982. *Language two*. New York: Oxford University Press.

Eckman, Fred R. 1977. "Markedness and the contrastive analysis hypothesis." *Language learning* 27 (2), 315-330.

Ehri, Linnea C. 1986. "Sources of difficulty in learning to spell and read." In: M.L. Wolraich and D.K. Routh (eds.), *Advances in developmental and behavioral pediatrics*, Vol. 7. Greenwich, Connecticut: JAI Press, 121-195.

Eichler, Wolfgang. 1978. *Rechtschreibung und Rechtschreibunterricht. Ein Handbuch für den Deutschlehrer*. Königstein/Taunus: Scriptor.

Eichler, Wolfgang. 1986. "Zu Uta Frith' Dreiphasenmodell des Lesen (und Schreiben) Lernens. Oder: Lassen sich verschiedene Modelle des Schrifterwerbs aufeinander beziehen und weiterentwickeln?" In: Gerhard Augst (ed.), 234-247.

Eisenberg, Peter. 1983. "Writing system and morphology: Some orthographic regularities of German." In: Florian Coulmas and Konrad Ehlich (eds.), *Writing in focus*. Berlin: Mouton, 63-82.

Ellis, Andrew W. 1984. *Reading, writing, and dyslexia: a cognitive analysis*. London: Lawrence Erlbaum.

Ferguson, Charles A. 1984. "Repertoire universals, markedness, and second language acquisition." In: William E. Rutherford (ed.), *Language universals and second language acquisition*. Amsterdam: John Benjamins, 247-258.

Ferreiro, Emilia. 1983. "The development of literacy: A complex psychological problem." In: Florian Coulmas and Konrad Ehlich (eds.), *Writing in focus*. Berlin: Mouton, 277-290.

Friedrichs, H. 1970. *English*. Ausgabe H, vol. I. Berlin: R. Oldenbourg Verlag.

Friedrichs, H. 1971. *English*. Ausgabe H, vol. II. Berlin: R. Oldenbourg Verlag.

Frith, Uta. 1985. "Beneath the surface of developmental dyslexia." In: Karalyn E. Patterson, John C. Marshall and Max Coltheart (eds.), *Surface dyslexia: Neuropsychological and cognitive studies of phonological reading*. London: Lawrence Erlbaum, 301-330.

Frith, Uta. 1986. "Psychologische Aspekte des orthographischen Wissens: Entwicklung und Entwicklungsstörung." In: Gerhard Augst (ed.), 218-233.

Fromkin, Victoria (ed.). 1973. *Speech errors as linguistic evidence*. The Hague: Mouton.

Fromkin, Victoria (ed.). 1980. *Errors in linguistic performance. Slips of the tongue, ear, pen, and hand*. The Hague: Mouton.

Gentry, J. Richard. 1982. "An analysis of developmental spelling in GNYS AT WRK." *The reading teacher* 36 (2), 192-199.

Gentry, J. Richard and E.H. Henderson. 1980. "Three steps in teaching beginning readers to spell." In: E.H. Henderson and J.W. Beers (eds.), 112-119.

Goodman, Roberta Ann and Alfonso Caramazza. 1986. "Phonologically plausible errors: Implications for a model of the phoneme-grapheme conversion mechanism in the spelling process." In: Gerhard Augst (ed.), 300-325.

Günther, H. 1987. "Phonological recoding in the reading process." In: Philip A. Luelsdorff (ed.), *Orthography and phonology*. Amsterdam: John Benjamins, 151-170.

Günther, Klaus B. 1986. "Entwicklungs- und sprachpsychologische Begründung der Notwendigkeit spezifischer Methoden für den Erwerb der Schriftsprache bei sprachenwicklungsgestörten, lernbehinderten und hörgeschädigten Kindern." In: Gerhard Augst (ed.), 354-382.

Hanna, P.R., J.S. Hanna, R.E. Hodges and E.H. Rudorf. 1966. *Phoneme-grapheme correspondences as cues to spelling improvement*. Washington, D.C.: U.S. Department of Health, Education and Welfare.

Henderson, E.H. and J.W. Beers (eds.). 1980. *Developmental and cognitive aspects of learning to spell: A reflection of word knowledge*. Newark, Delaware: International Reading Association.

Henderson, L. 1984. *Orthographies and reading: Perspectives from cognitive psychology, neuropsychology, and linguistics*. London: Lawrence Erlbaum.

Hudson, Richard A. 1987. "Zwicky on heads." *Linguistics* 23, 109-132.

Justeson, John S. 1976. "Universals of language and universals of writing." In: Alphonse Juilland et al. (eds.), *Linguistic studies offered to Joseph Greenberg*. Vol. I: General linguistics. Studia linguistica et philologica 4. Saratoga, CA: ANMA LIBRI, 57-94.

Kelley, J.L. 1955. *General typology*. New York.

Kettemann, Bernhard. 1988. *Die Phonologie morphologischer Prozesse im amerikanischen English*. Tübingen: Günter Narr.

Larsen-Freeman, Diane. 1976. "An explanation for the morpheme accuracy order of learners of English as a second language." *Language learning* 26 (1), 125-135.

Learning English, Ausgabe A, Teil 1. Grammatisches Beiheft. Stuttgart: Ernst Klett, 1972.

Learning English HS2. Stuttgart: Ernst Klett, 1975.

Luelsdorff, Philip A. 1969. "On the phonology of English inflection." *Glossa* 3, 39-48.

Luelsdorff, Philip A. 1975. *A segmental phonology of Black English*. The Hague: Mouton.

Luelsdorff, Philip A. 1982. "Differential linguistics: a program for research." *Folia phoniatrica* 34, 173-181.

Luelsdorff, Philip A. 1984a. "Letter naming as a spelling strategy." In: R.N. Malatesha and H.A. Whitaker (eds.), 159-166.

Luelsdorff, Philip A. 1984b. "Derivational errors: Mechanisms and processes." Unpublished ms, Universität Regensburg.

Luelsdorff, Philip A. 1985. Orthographic representation. Unpublished ms, Universität Regensburg.

Luelsdorff, Philip A. 1986. *Constraints on error variables in grammar: Bilingual misspelling orthographies*. Amsterdam: John Benjamins.

Luelsdorff, Philip A. 1987. "The abstractness hypothesis and morphemic spelling." *Second language research* 3 (1), 76-87.

Luelsdorff, Philip A. 1983[1987]. "On contraction in English." *Orbis* 32 (1/2), 171-183.

Luelsdorff, Philip A. 1989a. "Morphographemic alternations." Submitted.

Luelsdorff, Philip A. 1989b. "Parametric orthography and orthographic complexity." *Theoretical linguistics*, vol. 15, no. 1/2, 113-132.

Luelsdorff, Philip A. "Developmental morphographemics II." Submitted.

Luelsdorff, Philip A. and E. Ann Eyland. 1989. "Psycholinguistic determinants of orthography acquisition." *IRAL* XXVII/2, 145-158.

Luelsdorff, Philip A. and Neal R. Norrick. 1983[1987]. "On *have*-contraction". *Orbis* 32 (1/2), 184-193.

Luszczewska-Romahnowa, S. 1961. "Classification as a kind of distance function." *Studia logica* 12, 41-81. (Reprinted in: *Twenty-five years of logical methodology in Poland*, edited by M. Przelecki, R. Wojcicki. Warszawa, Dordrecht, 1977.)

Malatesha, R.N. and H.A. Whitaker (eds.). 1984. *Dyslexia: A global issue.* NATO Advanced Science Institute Series D: Behavioral and Social Sciences No. 18. The Hague: Martinus Nijhoff.

Marsh, George, Morton Friedman, Veronica Welch, and Peter Desberg. 1980. "The development of strategies in spelling." In: Uta Frith (ed.), *Cognitive processes in spelling.* London: Academic Press, 339-354.

Marsh, George and Peter Desberg. 1983. "The development of strategies in the acquisition of symbolic skills." In: Don Rogers and John A. Sloboda (eds.), *The acquisition of symbolic skills.* New York: Plenum, 149-154.

Meisel, Jürgen M., Harald Clahsen and Manfred Pienemann. 1981. "On determining developmental stages in natural second language acquisition." *Studies in second language acquisition*, 3 (2), 109-135.

Mel'čuk, Igor A. and Nikolaj V. Percov. 1987. *Surface syntax of English: A formal model within the meaning - text framework.* Amsterdam: John Benjamins.

Mentrup, W. 1981. *Die Regeln der deutschen Rechtschreibung.* Second, revised edition. Mannheim: Dudenverlag.

Menzel, Wolfgang. 1985. "Rechtschreibfehler - Rechtschreibübungen." *Praxis Deutsch* 69, 9-12.

Menzel, Wolfgang (ed.). 1985. *Praxis Deutsch* (Supplement) 69.

Modern English Seven. 1976. München: R. Oldenbourg Verlag.

Morton, J. 1980. "The logogen model and orthographic structure." In: Uta Frith (ed.), *Cognitive processes in spelling.* New York: Academic Press.

Nelson, Hazel E. 1980. "Analysis of spelling errors in normal and dyslexic children." In: Uta Frith (ed.), *Cognitive processes in spelling.* New York: Academic Press, 475-494.

Ortmann, Wolf Dieter. 1976a. *Beispielwörter für deutsche Rechtschreibungen.* München: Goethe Institut.

Ortmann, Wolf Dieter. 1976b. *Beispielwörter für deutsche Leseübungen.* München: Goethe Institut.

Philips, Donald J. 1984. "A prototypical procedure used for designing specific teaching alphabets to enable L2-learners to read English more effectively." *Australian journal of applied linguistics,* 179-192.

Pienemann, Manfred. 1986. "Is language teachable? Psycholinguistic experiments and hypotheses." *Australian working papers in language development* 1 (3), 41.

Pinker, Stephen. 1984. *Language learnability and language development.* Cambridge, Mass.: Harvard University Press.

Pinker, Stephen. 1986. "Productivity and conservatism in language acquisition." In: W. Demopoulos and A. Marras (eds.), *Language learning and concept acquisition.* Norwood, N.J.: Ablex.

Prideaux, G.D. 1987. "Processing strategies: A psycholinguistic neo-functionalism?" In: René Dirven and Vilém Fried (eds.), 297-310.

Read, Charles. 1971. "Preschool children's knowledge of English phonology." *Harvard educational review* 41, 1-34.

Read, Charles. 1986. *Children's creative spelling.* London: Routledge and Kegan Paul.

Reid, D. Kim and Wayne P. Hresko. 1981. *A cognitive approach to learning disabilities.* New York: McGraw-Hill.

Rutherford, William E. 1982. "Markedness in second language acquisition." *Language learning,* 32 (1), 85-108.

Rutherford, William E. 1987. "Learnability, SLA, and explicit metalinguistic knowledge." Unpublished ms. University of Southern California.

Schmidt, H. and G. Volk. 1976. *ABC der deutschen Rechtschreibung und Zeichensetzung: Ein Regel- und Übungsbuch.* Leipzig: VEB Bibliographisches Institut.

Schreiber, P. and C. Read. 1980. "Children's use of phonetic cues in spelling, parsing, and - maybe - reading." *Bulletin of the Orton Society* 30, 209-224.

Selkirk, Elizabeth O. 1982. *The syntax of words.* Cambridge, Mass.: MIT Press.

Selkirk, Elizabeth O. 1984. *Phonology and syntax: The relation between sound and structure.* Cambridge, Mass.: MIT Press

Sgall, Petr. 1987. "Towards a theory of phonemic orthography." In: Philip A. Luelsdorff (ed.), *Orthography and phonology.* Amsterdam: John Benjamins, 1-30.

Shattuck-Hufnagel, Stefanie. 1986. "The representation of phonological information during speech production planning: evidence from vowel errors in spontaneous speech." *Phonology yearbook* 3, 117-149.

Söderpalm Talo, Ewa. 1980. "Slips of the tongue in normal and pathological speech." In: Victoria A. Fromkin (ed.), *Errors in linguistic performance: Slips of the tongue, ear, pen, and hand*. New York: Academic Press, 81-86.

Sommerfeldt, K.-E., G. Starke, D. Nerius, *et al.* 1981. *Einführung in die Grammatik und Orthographie der deutschen Gegenwartssprache*. Leipzig: VEB Bibliographisches Institut.

Staczek, John J. and Frances M. Aid. 1981. "Hortographía himortal: Spelling problems among bilingual students." In: Guadelupe Valdes, Anthony G. Lozano, and Rodolfo Garcia-Moya (eds.), *Teaching Spanish to the Hispanic bilingual*. New York: Teachers College, 146-156.

Sterling, C.M. 1983. "The psychological productivity of inflectional and derivational morphemes." In: Don Rogers and John A. Sloboda (eds.), *The acquisition of symbolic skills*. New York: Plenum, 179-186.

Toman, Jindřich. 1984. *Wortsyntax: Eine Diskussion ausgewählter Probleme deutscher Wortbildung* (Linguistische Arbeiten 137). Tübingen: Max Niemeyer Verlag.

Vachek, Josef. 1961. "Some less familiar aspects of the analytical trend of English". *Brno studies in English* 3, 9-71.

Vachek, Josef. 1983. "Remarks on the dynamism of the system of language." In: Josef Vachek (ed.), *Praguiana: Some basic and less known aspects of the Prague Linguistic School*. Amsterdam: John Benjamins, 241-254.

Vachek, Josef. Forthcoming. "Some remarks on revaluations of redundant graphemes." In: Philip A. Luelsdorff (ed.), *Praguiana* II. Amsterdam: John Benjamins.

Venezky, Richard L. 1970. *The structure of English orthography*. Janua Linguarum, Series Minor No. 82. The Hague: Mouton.

Volkov, Aleksandr A. 1982. *Grammatologija: Semiotika pis'mennoj reči*. [Grammatology: The semiotics of written speech]. Moscow: Izdatel'stvo moskovskogo universiteta.

Wang, H. Samuel and Bruce L. Derwing. 1986. "More on English vowel shift: The back vowel question." *Phonology yearbook* 3, 99-116.

Wełna, J. 1982. *English spelling and pronunciation*. Warsaw: Państwowe Wydawnictwo Naukowe.

Wexler, Kenneth and M. Rita Manzini. 1987. "Parameters and learnability in binding theory." In: Thomas Roeper and Edwin Williams (eds.), *Parameter setting*, 41-76. Dordrecht: D. Reidel.

Zobl, Helmut. 1983. "Markedness and the projection problem," *Language learning*, 33 (3), 293-313.

Zwicky, Arnold M. 1985. "Heads," *Linguistics* 21, 1-30.

Zwicky, Arnold M. 1986. "The general case: Basic form vs. default form," *Berkeley Linguistics Society* 12, 305-314.

Zwicky, Arnold M. 1987. "Suppressing the Zs," *Journal of linguistics* 23, 133-148.